VIA FERRATAS OF THE ITALIAN DOLOMITES

VOLUME 1: NORTH, CENTRAL AND EAST

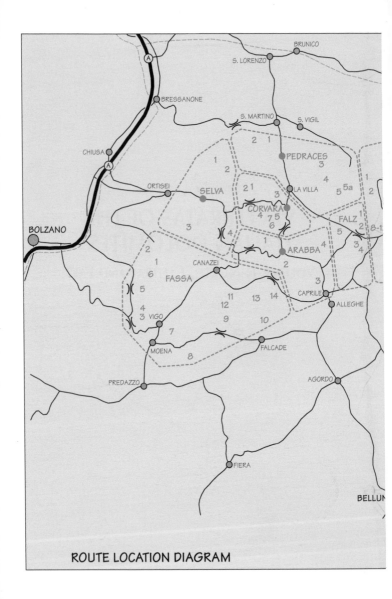

ROUTE LOCATION DIAGRAM

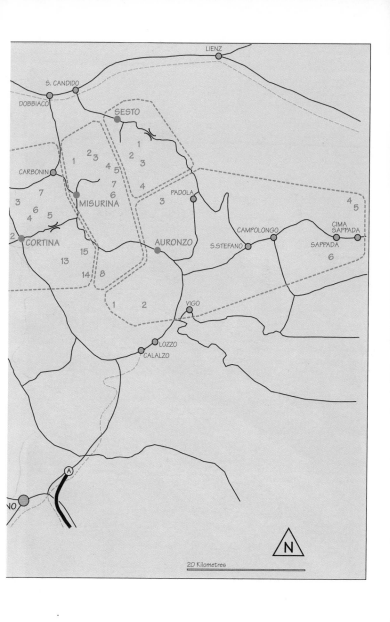

The final steep wall on VF Cesare Piazzetta (Arabba Route 1)

VIA FERRATAS OF THE ITALIAN DOLOMITES

VOLUME 1: NORTH, CENTRAL AND EAST

by

John Smith and Graham Fletcher

CICERONE

2 POLICE SQUARE, MILNTHORPE, CUMBRIA, LA7 7PY
www.cicerone.co.uk

© John Smith and Graham Fletcher 2002
ISBN 1 85284 362 4
Revised and reprinted 2004
Photographs: © John Smith and Graham Fletcher, unless otherwise indicated

A catalogue record for this book is available from the British Library.

DEDICATION

We dedicate this guidebook to Meg and Marion, with whom we have enjoyed many brilliant via ferrata climbing days, and who have both helped with, and endured, the less active pastime of putting this book together!

SPECIAL THANKS

We want to give special thanks to Tom, Dee and Phil particularly, but also to Sarah, Antonia and everyone who has been connected with Collett's Mountain Holidays in Arabba and Pedraces. They have made this book possible by providing the springboard, in Arabba, which started our love affair with the Dolomites and via ferratas in particular. Many, many thanks to everyone.

DISCLAIMER

Most routes in this guide will be found on Tabacco or Kompass maps of the respective areas, with either walking or mechanical access as explained in the guidebook. However, inclusion of a route in the guidebook does not automatically give right of access or freedom to climb.

Climbing via ferratas involves many dangers. There is no substitute for mountain experience and sound judgement; this book is not a substitute for either.

The guidebook writers, publishers and distributors do not accept any liability for injury or damage caused to, or by, climbers, third parties, or property arising from the guidebook's use.

The decision to climb a via ferrata is entirely yours and you do so at your own risk.

Front cover: Descending to the wind gap at the end of the first climbing section of the Via delle Trincee (photo: Collett's Mountain Holidays)

CONTENTS

ROUTE LISTING

KEY TO DIAGRAMS

)(	Significant ridge, with col/forcella
▲	Summit
	Lake
	Glacier
—Ⓐ—	Autostrada, with access point
— SS 48 —	Principal road, with reference number
——	Minor road
----------	Road not useable by general traffic
■——■	Cable cars & other lifts
----------	Railway line
----------	Footpath
— — —	Via ferrata/Sentiero
PEDRA 1	Route reference number
■	Rifugio/hotel with overnight accommodation
⊠	Bivouac
□	Cafe/Rifugio without overnight accommodation

ABOUT THE AUTHORS

John Smith has been walking and climbing mountains around the world for about 30 years, but until 1998 had never been to the Dolomites. On his first visit, with Marion, Dave and Deborah, he fell in love with the mountains, culture and via ferratas. In ticking off routes with a growing passion, he recognised the need for an up-to-date English-language guidebook; this first volume is the result of many enjoyable days in the Dolomites.

When *Graham Fletcher* started climbing, you had to file the threads out of nuts to make running belays and Bonington was clean-shaven. However, the demands of an academic life and, later, a busy professional career, took care of the next 30 years. After rediscovering his sense of priorities, he took early retirement and took up where he left off. He's still trying to figure out how Friends work.

PREFACE

We both went to the Dolomites for the first time in 1998, just as the popularity of via ferratas was growing. We realised very quickly that the previous English-language guidebook to via ferratas in the Dolomites (*Via Ferrata: Scrambles in the Dolomites*, Cicerone Press) was becoming out of date; after initially making notes for our own use we decided to take this a step further and write a new guidebook.

This guide is the first in a series of two, which cover the complete area of the Italian Dolomites. Volume One covers the Eastern, Northern and Central areas of the Dolomites, taking in some wonderful mountain groups with a wide variety of via ferrata climbing routes from the very easy to the most difficult.

Volume Two covers the remaining areas, including the Southern Dolomites (with routes on Civetta, Schiara and Pala mountains) as well as the Brenta in the west, and additionally (not previously published in an English guidebook) routes around the Lake Garda area, where the mountains are generally lower and you can enjoy ferrata climbing over a much extended season.

John Smith and Graham Fletcher, 2002

Climbing action on the magnificent slab early on the Via delle Trincee route (Arabba Route 2) (photo: Collett's Mountain Holidays)

INTRODUCTION

Are the Dolomites the most beautiful mountains in the world? It is always difficult to make comparisons where so much natural beauty exists wherever you climb. However, the Dolomites are without doubt some of the most dramatic, spectacular and beautiful mountains you will find anywhere. With explosive shapes and unique colours they can be regarded as the crown jewels of the European alpine range. Via ferrata climbing is a way of enjoying the sheer magnificence of this awesome mountain environment in which you will be stopped in your tracks by amazing views and mountain situations.

Many via ferratas were originally built to aid the movements of alpine military units during the First World War, and now (although they also exist in Germany, Austria, France and Switzerland) they represent one of the major attractions in the Dolomites. They are, in effect, a range of protected routes, comprised of fixed cables, ladders and even gorge-spanning bridges, which aid ascent to places

The detached pillar on VF Tomaselli, which marks the escape route (Falzerego Route 1)

normally reserved for expert rock climbers. Routes are graded according to difficulty, and this is fully explained in the 'Safety' section of the Introduction.

In recent years, the old wartime routes have been restored and many more routes added to give a network of routes around the whole Dolomite region. Routes are regularly checked, maintained and waymarked by the Italian Alpine Club CAI (Club Alpino Italiano). You will also see reference to SAT (Societa degli Alpinisti Tridentini), which is the largest section of CAI and plays a major role in maintaining the Dolomite environment. To give you some idea of the scale, SAT has more than 20,000 members in 76 sections. They have 39 refuges and 12 bivouacs, and maintain over 6000km of paths, including via ferratas. Further background to the CAI is covered in the 'History' section of this Introduction.

HOW TO USE THIS GUIDE

This guide departs from the usual convention of listing routes by reference to the geological group in which they lie. Instead routes are grouped according to the best point of access to help you decide where to set up base. This has inevitably involved a few fairly arbitrary judgements, and it will be immediately obvious that many of the valley bases are sufficiently close together to enable you to tackle several different groups from

a single location. Information is also included on the availability of mechanical assistance (such as cable cars and jeep taxis), which can make getting to the start of the route considerably easier, and help conserve your energies for the climb.

The availability of maps is covered in 'Map Availability' below. Most via ferrata are indicated on the maps in popular use, although errors in location and naming are not unknown. You should also note that as the Dolomite mountains are characterised by such swooping, vertical faces, maps can often show only a fairly diagrammatic view of what is actually on the ground. This means that it is not always easy to visualise the vertical dimension of a route, especially the gradient to be encountered, nor is it easy to visualise the exposure involved until confronted by it! Even some of the technically easier via ferratas will take you into some extremely exposed situations, and an indication of exposure is therefore given in some route descriptions; this has been taken into account when grading the routes.

The route location diagrams for this guide are just that – diagrammatic. They are not all to the same scale, and their purpose is simply to help the reader locate the route on the appropriate map. They are not a substitute for a properly detailed map for use on the hill.

The times given in the guide assume a reasonable level of fitness

Looking back down to Passo Gardena from the Pizes de Cir V route (Corvara Route 2) (photo: Collett's Mountain Holidays)

on the part of the climber and, just as important, no undue congestion on the route. However, these timings are for guidance only, so whilst a fit and experienced via ferratist will frequently complete a route more quickly than our guide time, it is just as likely that the more popular and accessible routes will require twice as long.

Whilst 'via ferrata' is used as a generic term covering any protected route, there is other traditional nomenclature which you will see on local maps and signposts in the hills. 'Sentiero' (and its plural 'sentieri'), 'sentiero attrezzato', 'sentiero alpinistico', 'percoso attrezzato' and 'cengia' (which is Italian for 'ledge') are a collection of other route titles in general use across the Dolomites.

Incidentally, whilst the plural of 'via ferrata' is, of course, 'vie ferrate', this guide uses the anglicised form 'via ferratas'.

The guidebook follows the convention of using the local title for all routes. You will notice that some routes are referred to as 'sentiero'. What you will find is that sentiero routes are generally easier than via ferrata routes, and are in fact frequently extended traverses of mountainous areas. Whilst some of the sentieros are fully equipped with cables, ladders and stemples, a good many involve somewhat less challenging terrain, where the need for such equipment is limited to the more exposed passages encountered. However (and this is covered in the

Pull-up onto the summit of Pizes de Cir V (Corvara Route 2)

grading of routes and individual route descriptions), one thing you should note is that even though some of the easier sentiero routes have limited hands-on climbing, some do involve considerable exposure!

ROUTE GROUPINGS

Several guidebooks exist to via ferrata climbing, with each one seemingly having a different way of classifying routes into groupings, even though the fundamental geographic separations make some of these groupings almost the same, or at least very similar.

Although this book can be easily connected to a mountain area, the via ferratas are grouped into the valley base considered to be the most convenient place to stay or approach the route. As with all systems this leads to some anomalies (or at best overlaps) in deciding your attack point for each route. It is important to stress, however, that this is a **guide**book: given a map, some local knowledge and, most importantly, some time to spend enjoying the Dolomites, you too will work out variations on how to include a via ferrata route into your mountain day. We hope you have as much fun in the Dolomites as we have, and are sure you will relish poring over your maps and working things out for yourselves – enjoy! **For a detailed description of the grading system used in the guide, see the 'Safety' section.**

WHEN TO GO

There is no ideal time to go to the Dolomites, as there are a number of factors to consider. Much will depend on good luck with the weather, which (as in most mountain areas) is the major factor for a good trip. Via ferratas in the higher mountain areas can generally be climbed from middle to late June until the end of September/beginning of October. There is no hard and fast rule on this, though, with the preceding winter snows potentially lingering on routes well into June, and the onset of the next winter closing things down at the end of the season. Lower and south-facing routes will, as a rule, be in condition earlier than those at higher altitudes with north-facing sections.

However, as with many mountain ranges, the weather in the Dolomites can be extremely variable at any time in the summer climbing months, with snow at any time (even in August) not uncommon. Furthermore, August is an extremely busy month, when the majority of Italy seems to be on holiday! The plus side is that all the summer lift and bus services operate in August. The downside, especially if the weather is good, is that all the popular via ferratas are busy, and the cost of accommodation is, of course, at its highest. Mountain rifugios are also busy, and so a phone call to book beds in advance is recommended. Many rifugios can now be booked using the internet (see

The initial steep starting pitch of the VF Cesare Piazzetta
(Arabba Route 1)

'Accommodation' below for the web site of the Club Alpino Italiano).

TRAVEL TO THE DOLOMITES

The quickest way to get to Italy is to fly. Several airports give quick or reasonable access to the Dolomites: Venice, Treviso, Bergamo, Bolzano, Verona, Brescia, Munich and Innsbruck. The cheapest flights are generally those operated into Venice, Treviso, Bergamo and Brescia.

Cars can be hired at any airport, but note that car hire is cheaper in Germany, so the extra driving from Munich may be worthwhile financially, depending on time available.

Bus services run from all airports into the Dolomites, but are often infrequent (e.g. once a day) and some do not run on Sundays (see below, 'Local Transport').

Although not essential for most of the popular via ferratas, a car is very useful in getting around: dependence on public transport can take a sizeable chunk out of your climbing time. It is possible to drive from the channel ports into the Dolomites in one long day, but an overnight stay is generally a more desirable option. The German motorways are quick (and toll free), but there is a charge on both Austrian and Italian motorways. Austrian motorways require a 'vignette' sticker (valid for 10 days, 2 months or 1 year and available at border filling stations/shops or at tabacs if entering Austria by non-motorway routes). There are ticket-issuing points either on entry to or on Italian motorways,

Climbing action on the magnificent slab early on the Via delle Trincee route (Arabba Route 2)

Traversing a ledge past wartime buildings on the Via delle Trincee (Arabba Route 2) (photo: Collett's Mountain Holidays)

with toll-collection points again either on the motorway or at exit points. Driving over the Brenner Pass can be chaotic in high season, followed by the final part of the journey into the Dolomites on slow, windy mountain roads. Note that there is a separate charge for the use of the Brenner motorway, which can be avoided by using the old SS12 road, but that is a windy and slow option.

Inter-city trains can be used to travel across Europe. Services are quite reliable, but (as with air travel) connecting travel would have to be organised to get to the mountains. Depending on connections, journey time could eat into holiday schedules, and individual timetables should be consulted to confirm available options.

ACCOMMODATION

There is a wide range of places to stay in the Dolomites, ranging from the very basic to the height of luxury. The choice includes camping, mountain rifugios (including bivouac huts), self-catering apartments, guesthouses, hotels of all grades (including 'meubles', which are usually smaller hotels that do not provide evening meals; they can represent good value if you are content with a modest meal in a nearby pizzeria) and even catered chalets. All major towns, and even most small villages, in the Dolomites have helpful tourist information offices that will assist you in finding accommodation, though you usually have to make your booking direct with the place you want to stay. (The organisation of tourist offices is described in more detail at the end of this section.) Routes in this guidebook have been documented by area, which should assist in deciding where to stay.

There is an extremely good network of rifugios throughout the Dolomites, with many of them owned by the CAI, and a substantial number are privately owned. Most of the rifugios are very well appointed, and provide comfortable accommodation at reasonable prices, together with meals (usually substantial and generally of good quality) and, of course, drinks. Sleeping is usually in dormitories and, whilst blankets are generally provided, a sheet sleeping bag is required (although these can be hired at many of the larger rifugios). Washing facilities are provided, but these can be quite basic and hot water should not be expected. Full details of opening times can be obtained from local tourist offices or from the CAI web site, much of which is now translated into English (see www.rifugio.it).

Bivouac huts are often encountered, particularly in the more remote mountain areas. These are little more than emergency shelters, with very limited facilities – a few bunks and blankets at best. Anyone planning to use one for an overnight stay should carry all their needs, including food and water. Use is on an honesty basis:

Climber on the exposed ridge of Molignon, Via Ferrata Laurenzi (Val di Fassa Route 1)

there is no payment, but you should treat the facilities with respect, and leave the hut as you would expect to find it.

Italy has an excellent but quite complicated network of tourist information offices. The Italian State Tourist Board (ENIT) has offices in many capital cities, including London. Enquiries to these offices usually result in fairly generalised material, which is of limited practical help in planning your trip. It is much more productive to make enquiries directly to the local tourist offices in the area you plan to visit. Under the umbrella of ENIT, tourist offices are maintained at regional level, provincial level, and in most significant towns and villages in popular holiday areas. These offices are known either as APT (Azienda di Promozione Turistica) or EPT (Ente Provinciale Turismo). Many towns or villages which are not on the ENIT network maintain their own information offices, known as Assessorato al Turismo, and just to confuse even further you will also see 'Ufficio Turistico' signs, which may be the APT office anyway! An approach to any of these offices generally elicits a wealth of detailed material on matters such as accommodation, public transport and lifts in the area. Whilst most of the staff in the larger offices speak good English, this is not necessarily the case in some of the smaller offices. Consequently, if you make your enquiries by phone, prepare yourself with a few Italian phrases.

The following addresses and web sites might prove useful.

- ENIT London office: Italian State Tourist Board, 1 Princess Street, London W1R 9AY, Tel. 0207 3551557/73551439 or web site: www.enit.it/uk
- Italian Tourist Web Guide: www.itwg.com.

Both the above sites contain a huge amount of practical information, including links to local tourist offices, although not all the pages on the ENIT site are in English.

LOCAL TRANSPORT

Public transport in Italy is generally good and cheap, and many of the routes described in this book can be accessed by bus. There are two major operators, with well-integrated timetables, serving the area – Dolomitibus and SAD. A copy of their timetables will be useful even if you are using a car because some routes involve extensive mountain traverses that deposit you some miles from where you started out! You should note, however, that the services of both bus operators are reduced considerably on the middle weekend of September.

The Dolomites are well served by cable cars, and visitors used to Swiss prices will be pleasantly surprised at how cheap they are. Whilst a good many lifts operate only in winter,

A traverse across the slab above the stemple pitch on Colac (Val di Fassa Route 11)

those which cover the more popular mountain regions operate a good service throughout the summer months. Like the bus companies, the cable-car operators run reduced services at the beginning and end of the summer, although this depends on the individual companies and on unpredictable factors like the weather. As a general rule, most services operate from July through August, and will remain in place into the beginning of September, with more popular routes continuing into October in some cases. Local Tourist Information Offices (APT) are usually helpful in giving advice, and it is wise to check the services in advance to enable you to plan your climbing timetable accordingly. We have referred to bus and cable-car services throughout this guide, since changes have been very limited in recent years. It is, however, wise to check locally before finalising your itinerary for the day.

TELEPHONES

Telephoning Italy, or ringing home is simple. For calls *both to and within* Italy you need to dial the full telephone number, including the city code and leading zero (Italy's international access code is 0039). For international calls from Italy you need to drop the leading zero of your home number (UK International access code is 0044). Some mobile phones will now work across Europe – check with your operator before leaving home. Phone boxes in Italy now generally use phone cards rather than cash. Full instructions are often found in English, but this does not include directions to break off the corner of the phone card before its use (otherwise it won't work!). Phone cards can be bought from newsagents, tabacs, bars or even vending machines by the phone box.

Useful emergency numbers are: 113 (police); 115 (fire); 116 (ACI car rescue/repair); 118 (medical).

MAP AVAILABILITY AND PLACE NAMES

Visitors to the Italian Dolomites are well served by mapmakers, and any good book shop should provide a range of products. For general orientation and travelling around the region it is hard to beat the road maps produced by the Italian Touring Club (TCI) at a scale of 1:200,000. Of the road maps and atlases published in Britain (there are many available) you might consider that by the AA at a scale of 1:250,000, the Michelin Road Atlas of Europe at a scale of 1:1,000,000 or even a computer product such as Microsoft AutoRoute Express.

There is also a choice of the more detailed maps needed for exploration of the mountain areas, with accurate and well-drawn maps available at both 1:50,000 and 1:25,000 scale. The complex nature of the terrain requires the larger scale map out on the hills (despite the need to buy more maps to cover any given area),

Exposed view down to Punta Fiames, climbing VF Michielli Strobel (Cortina Route 3)

although the 1:50,000 maps are perhaps a better option back in the valley for gaining an overview of a particular area.

Availability is rarely a problem, even in fairly small settlements. Virtually all outdoor equipment shops, most newsagents and gift shops, and even many supermarkets stock local maps. To get hold of the relevant maps beforehand in order to plan ahead, contact the major UK-based map suppliers, such as Stanford's and the Map Shop in Upton on Severn (see Appendix 5). They can often provide what you need by return of post. Both of these companies also maintain good web sites, though maps will invariably be much cheaper if they are bought in Italy.

The two major publishers for the Dolomites are Tabacco and Kompass. Each has its adherents, but there is little to choose between them in terms of quality. Both offer good products which are easy to read, although neither can match the Ordnance Survey or Swiss maps for detail and accuracy. Neither series includes UTM (Universal Transverse Mercator) or latitude/longitude co-ordinates. Perhaps superior are the Freytag & Berndt maps, although these are not widely available locally and are only published at 1:50,000 scale. They do, however, include co-ordinates to satisfy aficionados of GPS. Probably best of all are the Alpenvereinskart maps, also including co-ordinates, but these are only available for the Brenta and for the Langkofel/Sella area. (**Note:** at the time of publication, the latest editions of the Tabacco 1:25000 series of maps are showing grid references. GPS users should set datum to European 1950, Eur50, ED50 or Europ).

Magnetic variation: Magnetic variation in this part of Europe is quite minimal (around one degree west) and is not generally referred to on maps. You may find this a little strange if you are used to using your compass

Climber at the start of VF Alfonso Vandelli (Cortina Route 15) (photo: Marion Smith)

The sign marking the start, and indicating the seriousness, of VF Cesare Piazzetta (Arabba Route 1).

for route-finding in the UK, but navigating with a compass is something you rarely need to do in the Dolomites. Even if you take your compass with you, you are more likely to navigate by getting your map, finding a path and following red markers, a valley, a ridge or (the reason for this guidebook) via ferrata cables!

Finally, a word of warning about the use of place names on maps. In those areas which were historically Austrian, many settlements and natural features such as mountains have both an Italian and a German-language name. Both appear on maps, and – depending on where you are and to whom you are speaking – Tre Cime di Lavaredo might well be referred to as Drei Zinnen. This guide gives both the Italian and German

names on first usage, but thereafter reverts to the Italian name only.

It is also worth noting that there is a wide variation in the way place names are spelled: maps produced by different publishers, or even different editions from the same publisher, frequently use different spelling forms. While this can be confusing, the authors cannot be held to account for any apparent variation in name forms.

WEATHER

As in all mountain areas, the weather in the Dolomites can be unpredictable. A commonly occurring pattern, however, sees days starting off clear and sunny, but later, as the day warms up, cloud increasing, with the possibility of afternoon thunderstorms. Note that in weather forecasts 'afternoon' can mean anything from midday to midnight! The forecasts (issued daily and available from tourist information offices and the offices of local mountain guides) generally give a good indication of what is to be expected, even over a two- or three-day period. You will also find accurate weather stations attached to the walls of shops and hotels in virtually all towns and villages in the mountains, with the barometer, in particular, being a useful guide to the weather patterns to expect.

Weather forecasts for the Dolomites are produced from the weather centre in Arabba. Their web site is www.arpa.veneto.it/csvdi, and a web cam can be found at www.svm.it/webarpav.

It is essential to keep an eye on at least the general forecast and try to plan routes (especially high-level mountain routes) when the weather is reasonably stable. If bad weather threatens later in the day, an early start can pay dividends; conversely, if the day starts badly the guide contains some shorter, more easily accessed routes that can be done in the afternoon.

Although wet rock is not ideal, via ferratas (especially in the easier grades) can be done in the rain, but beware if temperatures are low as icing can occur throughout the summer, and this can turn even the easiest route into a very serious exercise indeed.

Thunder and lightning presents an extremely serious problem. Being attached to a metal cable in a high, exposed mountain situation is not where you want to be! So if thunder is in the air, try to avoid climbs which lack reliable escape routes. If you do get caught in a thunderstorm on a route with no easy way off, there are some simple rules that should be followed to minimise the risk of being buzzed.

- If a storm is approaching (you will usually get some warning, seeing a build-up of towering cumulo-nimbus cloud or hearing thunder in the distance first) evaluate possible escape routes as soon as possible.
- If at all possible you should unclip from the cable and move a safe distance away. If an escape route is available, then use it. Otherwise, you may have no option but to sit it out. If you are on a cliff face, then a wide ledge might provide an adequate safety zone. If on a ridge, however, you should try to get off it as soon as possible.
- In a storm, stay out in the open if this is possible – **DO NOT** seek shelter under boulders or overhangs, or go into caves, as these can be the natural spark points as lightning tries to find its way to earth.
- Try to keep as low as possible. You should sit down to minimise your profile, and if the ground is

wet, as it probably will be, sit on your rucksack to avoid contact with wet ground.
- Try to keep your core as dry as possible by putting on your waterproofs without delay.

This may all sound rather frightening, and indeed it can be! However, remember that lightning strikes natural projections, such as mountain tops or rock pinnacles; so if you are unlucky enough to be caught, stay calm, make sound judgement and follow the good practice listed above, and the risks will be very small.

ROUTE GRADING

It is a truism that grading is a subjective matter and not an exact science. This is well illustrated by the fact that, of the various via ferrata guidebooks that have been published, no two use the same method of grading. The starting point in this guide, however, is the belief that any grading system should offer a view of the seriousness of a route as well as its difficulty. A route can be hard without being too serious.

In the mountains everyone experiences situations where their confidence and ambition prove to be misplaced and they have to back off a route and leave it for another day. On a route which is not only hard but also serious, things might not be quite so straightforward! Big routes on big mountains should be accorded a degree of respect, and factors like escape routes and even rescue access need to be considered. Other factors such as the weather and risk of stone falls can also result in a carefree day on the hill turning into an epic if unforeseen circumstances arise.

The Dolomites abound with via ferrata which are technically quite easy, but which negotiate terrain which needs to be taken seriously. Consequently, we want to ensure that the first-time visitor, perhaps a relatively inexperienced scrambler, does not get out of his or her depth by failing to appreciate the degree of mountain commitment involved in any particular via ferrata.

Each route in this guidebook is therefore **graded on a five-point scale of technical difficulty, with 1 the easiest and 5 the hardest grade**.

Additionally, because even some of the technically easy routes may involve long days in serious mountain terrain, we have assessed each route for its **seriousness**. The seriousness of a route takes into account the mountain commitment, accessibility, potential escape routes, level of required fitness and potential objective dangers. **The three-point scale of seriousness is shown as A, B or C, where C is the most committing**.

Technical difficulty
1. Easy routes, with limited via ferrata climbing, entirely suitable for the young and inexperienced.

Standard SAT and CAI safety notices

Requires no more than a head for heights and sure-footedness.

2. Straightforward routes for the experienced mountain walker or scrambler with a head for heights.

3. Rather more difficult routes, not recommended for the completely novice via ferratist. At this level complete freedom from vertigo and sure-footedness are required, as is complete competence in the use of via ferrata safety equipment.

4. Demanding routes, frequently involving steep rock faces and requiring a fairly high standard of technical climbing ability. Definitely not for the novice or those unsure of their confidence in mountain situations.

5. Routes of the highest technical standard encountered in via ferrata climbing, suitable only for the most experienced via ferratist.

Seriousness

A. Straightforward outings in un-threatening mountain terrain. Routes will have easy access and/or escape opportunities, will be virtually risk free in the event of a change in the weather, and be relatively free from the risk of stone-fall.

B. Routes where a degree of mountain experience is required. Access might be more difficult, and opportunities to escape from the route will be limited, so minor mishaps could develop

33

into quite serious situations. A change in the weather could potentially be more than merely inconvenient, and the climber needs to be aware of the risk of stone-fall.

C. Routes only for the experienced mountaineer. Such routes might lack any escape opportunities, be in remote areas, have passages of very exposed, unprotected terrain, or involve inaccessible situations where any mishap could have the most serious consequences. The threat of stone-fall might be a major consideration, or a change in the weather could add greatly to the problems posed by the route.

Route vital statistics

For each route an indication of the ascent, descent and length of via ferrata involved is given. Where a route involves extended traverses this can appear to give rather odd statistics where the length of the ferrata exceeds the ascent/descent figure (e.g. MISUR 4 VF De Luca Innerkofler).

EQUIPMENT

The basic equipment required to climb via ferratas safely is neither complicated nor expensive. The items below will suffice for all but the most demanding outings, but for the higher routes (and even lower ones early in the season) consideration needs to be given to additional gear such as ice axes and crampons.

Although some UK-based climbing shops do now stock (or can order) via ferrata equipment, it can be bought readily in the Dolomites. As well as being cheaper in Italy, a wider variety of equipment is also available.

Helmet: perhaps the single most important piece of equipment. This must conform to UIAA (Union Internationale des Associations d'Alpinisme) standard to protect the climber against rock-fall. To be effective it should be on your head, not in your sack, so be sure to put it on as soon as the risk of stone-fall is present. For example, the approaches to some routes negotiate gullies which can be raked by stones falling from above, **so don't wait until you are about to start climbing before reaching for your helmet**.

Harness: a full body harness will give you the best safety protection for climbing via ferratas. Many British visitors to the Dolomites will already own a climbing sit-harness; but, whilst this will generally suffice for tackling via ferratas, do remember that you will probably be carrying a loaded rucksack, so if you were to take a fall you run the risk of being turned upside down. Consequently, you can either invest in a full body harness, much more popular (and available) in continental Europe than in the UK, or supplement your sit har-

Full body harness showing Y-type self-belay system tie on

ness with a chest harness. *Whatever you choose to do, it is a totally personal decision and risk assessment.*

Via ferrata self-belay set: incorporating belay rope, KISA (see below) and karabiners. Like all climbing equipment, via ferrata self-belay equipment has improved considerably in recent years. The obvious problem with self-belaying on a vertical run of cable is that any fall will only be arrested when the climber reaches the attaching peg below him. With a long cable run, this can mean that a very high shock loading (anything up to 2 tonnes) will be generated. To help overcome this, a device called a Kinetic Impact Shock Absorber, or KISA, has been developed. There are several different models in use, but they all function in the same way, act-

ing as simple friction brakes which, in the event of a fall, absorb the energy generated, thus reducing the shock loading.

There are two different systems in use incorporating a KISA in the belay system. Each system contains the same components, albeit configured differently, which means that they must be used differently.

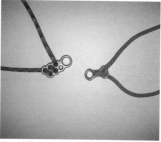

Two different types of KISA

35

a) The most commonly used type employs a single rope, about 2 metres long, which passes through the KISA and has a karabiner on each end. The KISA is then attached to the harness with rope or tape. With this system, only one karabiner should be clipped onto the cable, whilst the spare karabiner is clipped onto the harness or its gear loop. In the event of a fall, the loop of rope leading to the spare karabiner is pulled through the KISA under friction, thus absorbing much of the energy generated by the fall. On reaching a peg where the cable is attached to the rock face, the spare karabiner is removed from the harness and clipped into the next cable run. The original karabiner is then unclipped and attached to the harness. *It is only at the moment of leapfrogging over the peg that both karabiners are clipped onto the cable; otherwise the KISA cannot function (see illustration).*

lengths of rope, joined by a knot or stitched to form a Y-shape. There are several permutations on the theme, particularly regarding the means of attachment to the harness, but the principle of how this type works is as follows. The single length of rope (the leg of the Y) is threaded through the KISA to leave a spare loop of rope which becomes part of the system incorporated in the tie-on, or is attached to the side of the harness or gear loop. The KISA is then attached to the harness with rope or tape. In the event of a fall, it is the spare loop of rope which is pulled through the KISA under friction, thus absorbing the energy generated by the fall. With this method **both** karabiners can be clipped onto the cable: at the end of a cable run first one, then the other karabiner is leapfrogged over onto the next length of cable (see illustration).

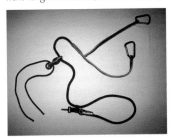

Petzl 'Zyper' Y-type self-belay system

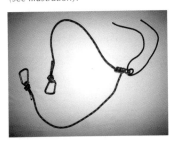

Simple 'straight through' self-belay system

b) In the alternative system, the karabiners are attached to two separate

Both methods are safe if used properly. The Y-type equipment is, arguably, slightly safer in that it is less likely to be misused! It is, however, more expensive, and one particular

Another roped variety of Y-type self-belay system

model (the Petzl Zyper, which uses tape rather than rope) has tails which are somewhat short, thus reducing the freedom of the climber to exploit the holds in the rock face.

A word of warning! DO NOT rely on a couple of slings in place of a proper self-belay system. Whilst these might give you a sense of security, they could well be useless if you were to take a significant fall.

Karabiners: if you buy a ready-made self-belay set, these will be included. However, there are quite a few different models available, not all of which are equally suitable. When buying your gear, pay close attention to the karabiners incorporated. Whichever type you have, they must always be the large sized D-type karabiners to clip over some of the thicker wire protection. As with any karabiners, locking gates are much stronger. However, conventional screw gates are hardly practical for use on via ferratas, where you will be clipping and

unclipping repeatedly. One suitable model has a spring-loaded gate, unlocked by simply pulling the gate-lock back with the index finger. A variation on this type needs to be both pulled back and twisted through 90 degrees before the gate is unlocked; this becomes frustratingly fiddly after a couple of hours! Small clips are also available to thread the rope through on the karabiner; these cost next to nothing but are extremely useful for holding the karabiner on the rope to stop it spinning round and potentially falling off. Best of all perhaps, but certainly the most expensive, is a model from Salewa, specially developed for via ferratas, where the rope is tied through a separately formed ring at the base of the karabiner, such that it cannot then spin round. On this type, the gate is released by pressure from the heel of the thumb, naturally applied as the karabiner is offered up to the cable, making for ease of use during a long day (see illustration for several commonly used types of karabiners).

A selection of four different types of karabiner

37

Gloves: specially designed gloves for via ferratas are readily available from gear shops in the Dolomites. They resemble cycling gloves, with padded palms and cut-off fingers. Whether you wear gloves is entirely a matter of personal preference. They can, however, be very useful when the weather is wet and cold, and they do protect hands against frayed cables. You might decide to keep a pair in your rucksack, where even a cheap pair of garden gloves may prove to be a useful accessory.

Refinements: An ice axe and crampons are suggested for several routes in this guide. A rope is another important accessory if climbing with someone with limited experience, and for some of the more demanding outings included in this guidebook. The authors favour carrying 20–30 metres of half-rope, a couple of tapes and a belay plate when climbing in such situations. A quick-draw can be useful when taking photographs and to facilitate a rest, for example in traffic jams or on unusually strenuous routes.

A useful source of information for the technically minded regarding safety equipment and shock loading is the Petzl web site found at www.petzl.com (see illustration).

Full body harness showing 'straight through' self-belay system

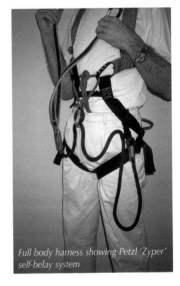

Full body harness showing Petzl 'Zyper' self-belay system

CABLE ETIQUETTE

The ferrata cables and their use can be a real debating topic, so here are a few words on that subject. Some climbers prefer to regard via ferratas as rock climbs which happen to have permanently fixed protection. On the other hand, there are those who feel no compunction about grabbing a handful of cable and hauling themselves up by dint of brute strength! The majority of us are happy to make our own compromises between these two extremes, climbing without use of the cable where we feel comfortable doing so, but using the cable for a boost when required. A technique which is recommended initially, until you have found your own point of compromise, is to climb with one hand on the cable, with the live karabiner sitting on top of the clenched fist and being slid up by it, whilst the other hand is used to exploit natural holds in the rock.

Many routes are busy, indeed overcrowded. Sooner or later, you will find yourself being pressed from behind (probably by a cable-grabber!). This feels rather like being tailgated on a motorway. The perpetrators are not only being discourteous, but are also putting both of you at risk. We have explained the principle of shock loading elsewhere in the Safety section, but should the upper climber fall he will probably take the lower climber with him, thus increasing the load on the protection far beyond that

which it is designed to withstand. Therefore, observe this simple rule. Do not clip into a length of cable until the climber above you has progressed to the next cable length.

WHAT TO WEAR?

Whoever you are, and wherever you have a day out in the mountains, what to wear is a matter of personal preference. Since readers are likely to have gained a fair bit of experience in the hills before embarking on a trip to the Dolomites, this is not an attempt to dictate what is acceptable and what is not. In fact, this being Italy, you will probably be amazed (and sometimes amused) at the range of gear that people wear on via ferratas. Neither are the Brits beyond creating a stir; we once met the archetypal UK rambler, happily bumbling along on an easy ferrata wearing a headscarf and carrying a plastic shopping bag.

Generally, the situation of the route (i.e. big remote mountain or short, easily accessible route) and the nature of the weather will dictate what you should take. In warm settled weather, travelling light and carrying a small pack will make for a more enjoyable day on the hill. The importance of checking the weather forecasts has been stressed elsewhere, but it bears repeating that you are in a high mountain environment with the potential for sudden and dramatic changes in the weather. You will get some advance warning of the

Traversing the main ridge of the Via delle Trincee route (Arabba Route 2)
(photo: Collett's Mountain Holidays)

approach of a storm, but be warned that a warm, sunny day with plus 20°C temperatures can quickly drop by 10° or more, and even in July and August hail or snow can be encountered down to 2500m. Do take this into consideration when you decide what to wear and what spare gear you carry on your via ferrata.

WEATHER/CONDITIONS IN THE MOUNTAINS

The route descriptions assume, as they must, that conditions are good and that icing-up is not a problem. Note, however, that even in midsummer weather can be extremely variable, with sudden thunderstorms particularly in the afternoons. Snow falls and ice formation can occur at any time of the summer in the Dolomites, and when considering route grading suggestions, you should therefore make the appropriate allowance for additional difficulties resulting from adverse conditions. The guide makes reference to those routes which are particularly prone to icing.

ACCIDENTS AND MOUNTAIN RESCUE

As in most mountain regions the police have responsibility for organising mountain rescue. If you are unlucky enough to be involved in an accident the **emergency contact number for mountain rescue is 118** (see Appendix 4).

SOME HISTORY

The history of the Dolomites, particularly recent history, has made dramatic and permanent changes to the very landscape itself. The area's rich and diverse culture is also a reflection of the sweep of historical events, this time over centuries. This brief survey of the region's history is therefore provided to add to the visitor's appreciation of this fascinating mountain region.

It is in the nature of things that mountain areas are boundaries rather than discrete political or economic entities. It is the plains which are the usual source of wealth, and thus power, with the adjoining mountain areas being mere hinterlands, acting as buffers between rival powers. For centuries, the Dolomite region has been just such a buffer, squeezed with various degrees of discomfort between the Latinate powers to the south and the Germanic powers to the north. For the greater part of history the area has been divided, with only relatively short periods of unification.

It was the Romans who first achieved unified control over the whole of the Dolomite region as their empire gradually extended northwards to encompass the greater part of Europe. Roman rule was generally quite benign and, as was the case throughout most of their empire, a fair degree of integration with the original inhabitants occurred. It was

Passo Gardena with Sassongher in the foreground on the right and the Sella massif with Piz de Lech in the foreground on the left. Routes CORV 1-3 are to the right and left of Passo Gardena.

this period which saw the origins of the Ladin language. This blend of Latin with the language of the indigenous people, the Rhaetians as the Romans called them, still survives today (see below). The gradual decline of Roman power allowed successive waves of attacks by the fearsome tribes from the north, such as the Huns, Goths and Astrogoths, leading to a disintegration of control and the fragmentation of government. Centuries of conquest and colonisation followed, by the 15th century resolving itself into confrontation between the House of Hapsburg and the Venetian Republic. By this stage the differences between the Germanic culture (in the north and west of the region) and the Italian culture (in the

south and east) were well established, although the earlier Ladin culture survived in the more remote valleys.

The Napoleonic Legacy

This uneasy balance of power was turned upside down by the Napoleonic wars and the tide of revolutionary thought which spilled out across the continent. Whilst Napoleon's reign was relatively short-lived, his rule in Italy was to have profound consequences and sowed the seeds for the creation of the modern state of Italy. The Congress of Vienna in 1815, which attempted to return Europe to a pre-Napoleonic status quo, gave Austria control of the Dolomite region together with the formerly independent territories of

Venice. The rest of Italy was broken up, with control handed to foreign powers. However, the philosophy and ideals of the French revolution had taken a firm hold, making such casual geopolitics no longer tenable. Italian nationalism was born.

It took over 50 years of insurrection and uprising, and military assistance from France and Prussia, before Italy was finally united in 1870. United, that is, except for the Italian-speaking territories of the Dolomite region, which remained under Austrian control. To the Italian nationalists, this was a potent piece of unfinished business, and helps explain Italy's role in the Great War, which was shortly to plunge Europe into chaos.

In 1914 Italy, as a young country with an ill-prepared army, chose not to enter the war. Instead, it spent the first year of hostilities negotiating with the two sides to see which would offer the most favourable terms in a post-war settlement. Its aims were clear and ambitious: in addition to power over the whole of the Dolomite region, it sought the port of Trieste and the Dalmatian coast to ensure future control over the Adriatic. In 1915, judging that its interests would be best served by an alliance with Britain, France and Russia, Italy declared war on Austria. Italy's entry into the war was prompted significantly by considerations about frontiers, and can be seen as the final stage of Italian unification.

The Mountain War

When Italy entered the war, Austria was heavily committed on the Russian front. Consequently, the maintenance of its border with Italy was unrealistic, and the Austrians chose to retreat to geographically defensible mountain tops and passes. Previously Austrian towns such as Cortina d'Ampezzo and San Martino di Castrozza now found themselves behind enemy lines and occupied by Italian troops in the summer of 1915. The so-called Mountain War had begun (see also Falzarego section).

Whilst this was a war between nations, in the Dolomite region it was also a war between two ethnic groups. German-speaking mountain folk fought in the Austrian Alpenjager, whilst their Italian-speaking neighbours, sometimes friends, opposed them in the ranks of the Alpini. Here was the particular poignancy of a civil war. However, being unusually remote from higher authority and enduring a shared hardship of survival in the mountains, troops on opposing sides are known to have fraternised and exchanged supplies. There are even accounts from the Cortina area of Italian soldiers delivering messages to the families of Austrian soldiers who were unable to visit their home villages, now behind Italian lines.

Initially, the Italian army made slow and uncertain advances, probably over-estimating the actual strength of the Austro-Hungarian forces when,

One of several well-preserved wartime buildings built into the rockface on VF Ivano Dibona (Cortina Route 6)

as is now known, the Italian strength in the Sud-Tyrol was much greater. However, this delay gave the Austrians time to organise their defences. From late spring 1915 to November 1917, the Austrian troops and their Italian counterparts fought a war of fixed positions, with the front line remaining essentially stationary. Troops frequently slept within earshot of their enemy, and hand-to-hand combat was common. This was a war of attrition, with both sides seeking to establish positions as high as possible, often on mountain summits. Fortifications established in spring, summer and autumn were maintained through the harsh winters at great cost. The winter of 1916 proved to be particularly bitter, with a record snowfall of 10 metres. More than 10,000 men, from both sides, lost their lives from avalanches during that winter alone. In one incident, at the Austrian barracks below the summit of Gran Poz on the Marmolada, some 400 soldiers died in a single avalanche.

Neither side was able to break the stalemate which ensued, so both turned to an underground war of tunnelling and mining. Considerable ingenuity went into the creation of extraordinary excavations, leaving an extensive legacy of tunnels and galleries. Both sides were ingenious in establishing their positions, with trenches, observation posts and literally thousands of metres of tunnels and galleries being constructed. The

mining campaign resulted in vast explosions, literally changing the landscape. At Col di Lana an Italian mine forever altered the shape of its summit, whilst probably the best-known and most conspicuous testimony to this phase of the Mountain War is the Lagazuoi Piccolo, overlooking Passo Falzarego. Here, three huge explosions changed this mountain face dramatically (see route FALZ 2 for a more detailed description).

Perhaps the most remarkable legacy of the war is the so-called 'City of Ice', now being exposed by the retreating Marmolada glacier (see 'The Mountain War' in the Falzargo section for more details).

The cost in human lives of the Mountain War was overwhelming, particularly given the relatively small populations from which the combatants were drawn. At least 60,000 soldiers died in avalanches alone (this statistic, thought to be somewhat conservative, comes from the research of Heinz von Lichem in his outstanding three-volume study *Gebirgskrieg 1915-1918*, published 1980, 2001). To put this in perspective, a far smaller number of troops, 25,000, were killed by poison gas on the Western front.

The Mountain War ended and the stalemate was eventually broken when in late 1917 the Austrians, aided by German forces, broke through the Italian lines at the village of Caporetto, north of Trieste. The Italians retreated from their mountain-top positions to form a last line of defence on the River Piave, north of Venice. This line was held, with the assistance of British and French troops, but the Italian front was now little more than a sideshow to the major events being played out elsewhere and which resulted in the armistice in 1918.

The Aftermath

Neither side won this tragic war in the mountains. The final political resolution took place at the bargaining table, far from the battle zone, and with little recognition of the events on the ground. Peace was cemented in 1919 by the treaty of San Germain which, among other things, established Italy's present borders. The ambition of Italy's war aims has been noted, and it has to be acknowledged that she was a major beneficiary of the peace settlement. In addition to the whole of the Dolomite region, Italy also secured the port of Trieste, although less of the Dalmation coast than had been sought. Altogether, some 1.6 million new Italian citizens were acquired, many of whom could not speak Italian! Many families will tell of older relatives who were born Austrian, but died Italian.

Despite their Italian nationality, the people of the northern Dolomites generally retain German as their first language and demonstrate many expressions of their cultural traditions. Road signs, newspapers, restaurant menus and even the architecture all suggest to the visitor that he has strayed over the border into Austria. Unsurprisingly, separatist sentiment can be found not far beneath the surface within the German-speaking community. To a degree these pressures were defused by the granting of special status to the Trento-Alto Adige region, within which much of the Dolomites fall. This has been reinforced by generous tax benefits and grant aid, cementing the position of the region as one of the richest in the country. Tensions, nonetheless, remain, and the Italian constitution strikes a delicate balance between the powers of the central government and those of the regions; indeed, any attempt to impose strong central control would run the risk of the country tearing itself apart.

What of the Ladin community in all this? Attempts by successive regimes to Germanise or Italianise them were sternly resisted, and, whilst numerically they represent a small fraction of the population of the Dolomites, they retain a fierce pride in their culture. Roughly 50,000 people now define themselves as Ladin, with the greatest concentration living in the valleys which radiate out from the Sella massif, and particularly in Val Badia. For such a tiny population, they are extraordinarily successful at maintaining their individuality, with Ladin cultural institutes, newspapers and even daily Ladin-language broadcasts from Bolzano. Travellers in the Dolomites soon become used to see-

Climbers below the wartime ladders at the start of
VF Tomaselli (Passo Falzarego Route 1)

Approach to the Santner pass ferrata (Val di Fassa Route 5)
(photo: Collett's Mountain Holidays)

ing road signs with both Italian and German place names; in Val Badia these are often joined by a third, with old Ladin names for villages refusing to be squeezed out.

Information is available on the internet site of the Great War Society: www.worldwar1.com/itafront/

Museums can be found at Passo Fedia and on the Marmolada, as well as Passo Padon, but the via ferratas themselves give an outstanding example of the stupidity of war and the harsh environments in which it is sometimes fought.

History of the CAI and Refugios

Prior to the First World War mountain huts were built across the Alps, including the Sud-Tyrol, by the then joint alpine club the German and Austrian Alpine Club (or DuOAV). In 1920, following the end of the First World War, the Sud-Tyrol was handed over to Italy under the Treaty of St. Germain. As a result the huts (now 'rifugios') were taken over by the CAI. However, many of the huts were either destroyed or used by Italian soldiers in their attempts to stop insurgency, and during the period 1922 to 1973 the Austro/Italian border was effectively closed to climbers. Since 1973 there has been free access, and many huts have been rebuilt or renovated (see also 'Accommodation' section above).

GEOLOGY

The name 'Dolomites' is derived from a French geologist, Deodat Guy Sylvain Tancre de Gratet de Dolomieu, a scholar who in 1789 was so fascinated by the carbonate rock that he sent samples to Switzerland for classification. When they were returned as of a previously unknown composition, they were named after him. In the 19th century it was mainly English mountaineers who applied the name 'Dolomia' to the area in recognition of the geological discovery.

Dolomite rock is made up of stratified calcium magnesium carbonate, with some areas of true limestone, some containing more stratified and folded rock than others depending on the area. Limestone has a reputation for loose rock, the Dolomites being no exception. Interestingly enough the colour of the rocks gives an indication of the firmness or friability. As a general rule, grey and black rocks are firm (though the black colour also indicates possible wetness), yellow- coloured rock is reasonably firm and red rock is the loosest.

FLORA

Flora – flowers, plants, trees, vegetation – are a wonderful complement to the mountain environment! The present landscape in the valleys of the Dolomites is a result of man's work

49

over the years (and with ski developments this is now the case on the hills as well). Initially the scree and glacial debris taken from the peaks into the valleys was stony and barren, and in the Dolomites this initial stage can still be seen in vast areas. However, with time the organic remains in the earth allow vegetation to grow, and it is amazing to see the array of flowers that the Dolomites has to offer in even the most bleak of landscapes.

Vegetation on the mountainside includes all aspects of plant life. Trees such as beech, fir and larch grow in the valleys, with hardier pines on higher ground. In valleys, and particularly in woods, many varieties of fungi can be found, but collecting them, as well as being a specialist subject, is a restricted pastime. On the high-level plateaus only flowers and mosses have managed to adapt to the environmental conditions.

Alpine flora is a generic term referring to plants growing above the tree line in the Alps, but is a term used around the world for plants growing in mountain areas, and is also abbreviated to alpines. In the Alps and Dolomites the growing areas are known as the high alpine zone (2000m–3000m), montane zone (1000m–2000m) and sub-montane zone (below 1000m). The sub-montane zone includes all vegetation from coastal areas upwards, with the montane zone being wooded and the high-altitude level being that above the tree line. Even within the separate

zones there are sub-zones at different altitudes, with particular alpines growing at quite specific altitudes. Many factors (temperature, light, soil, wind, rain, snow, ground slope) create complex environments and help determine which plants adapt to different habitats by developing distinctive characteristics. Many plants grow in thick tufts to protect themselves against thermal fluctuations, and another common adaptation is for plants to grow a protective covering of hairs, which act as a thermal cushion. Where soil is thin, on exposed rock and crevices, plants develop long root systems. Snow cover in the winter has a big impact on plant life, and it is truly amazing in spring or early summer to see flowers appearing even as the snow melts!

A wide variety of alpine flora exists in the Dolomites: Edelweiss, Soldanella, Ranunculus (alpine buttercup), Saxifrage, Gentian, Geranium, Anemone, Violet and Primula, to name but a few. Some species are endangered and protected, but your general rule should always be DO NOT PICK FLOWERS, however abundant they may appear to be.

WILDLIFE

Among the animals you are likely to see in the mountains are: chamois (a type of goat which can seen at high levels above the tree line; they graze on the scant grass among the rocky scree); stambecco (a long-haired

Profile of the Punta Serauta slab and ridge from Porto Vescovo (photo: Collett's Mountain Holidays)

mountain goat – not as common); roe deer (seen in the valleys, on hillsides and even by the side of the road – you will even see road signs to this effect); and marmots (generally shy animals that live burrows in colonies above 1600m – you are more likely to hear them shriek/whistle than to see them, although in more populated areas they are now becoming more used to human traffic and will sometimes sit and pose on their hind legs as you pass by).

It is interesting to think that until the end of the nineteenth century bears commonly inhabited woods in the Dolomites, but hunting and de-foresta-tion have taken their toll, and the bears were thought to have been extinct for many years. However, there has been some suggestion recently that bears may have migrated back towards the Dolomites from Slovenia, though this is a long way from the main areas where via ferratas are found.

Birds include eagles, buzzards, mountain choughs (swarms of which seem to arrive on every summit as soon as a sandwich is unwrapped!), woodland grouse or capercaillie (at home in woods and undergrowth), white ptarmigan (which changes its plumage in summer to a brown colour), crows, woodpeckers, owls, alpine tree creeper, jay, skylark and many species of finch.

Snakes are often encountered on warm, sunny afternoons basking on paths. They are often adders, easily recognised by the chevron pattern along their back. Tread carefully, and do not disturb any snake, remember-ing that it will be more frightened than you are. Just leave it alone!

Some of the surviving WWI timber ladders on VF Della Scalette, Torre Toblino
(Misurina Route 2)

PEDRACES/LA VILLA

Maps:
Tabacco Carta Topographica 1:25,000 Sheet 07 or
Kompass Wanderkarte 1:25,000 Sheet 615/616

Tourist Information Office:
APT Pedraces, 39036 Pedraces, Alta Badia, Italy
Telephone: (0471) 839695, Fax: (0471) 839573
Internet: www.altabadia.it
E-mail: altabadia@dolomitisuperski.com

Val Badia is scenically spectacular, being dominated by the mountains of Puez-Odle Natural Park to the west and the Fanes Natural Park to the east. It is also very much the heart of Ladin culture; so don't be surprised by the sight of road signs in **three** languages!

Pedraces is just one of several busy villages in Val Badia (Gadertal) which make good bases for mountain excursions. The road up the valley from Brunico (Bruneck) is a convenient route into the Dolomites for visitors from northern Europe, and there are good bus services up to where the valley divides at La Villa.

Pedraces and La Villa have Tourist Information Offices and a good range of shops, banks and restaurants to suit all pockets. Hotel and guesthouse accommodation is readily available in here and in other nearby settlements; there is a campsite at San Cassiano. There is also an indoor swimming pool available in La Villa.

None of the routes in this section is at all technically challenging. They do, however, take you into the heart of the two Natural Parks, so you will be assured of grand mountain days in splendid scenery. One of the routes is accessible from the Pedraces chairlift, although a car is essential for the others.

Although Pedraces and La Villa are north of the Sella massif and many of the other areas described in this book, there are many other routes within an hour's drive: see Corvara, Falzarego, Cortina–Tofane and Arabba particularly.

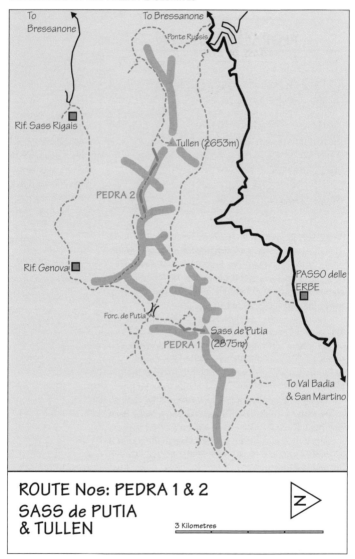

To
Bressanone

To Bressanone

Ponte Russis

Rif. Sass Rigais

Tullen (2653m)

PEDRA 2

Rif. Genova

PASSO delle
ERBE

Forc. de Putia

Sass de Putia
(2875m)

PEDRA 1

To Val Badia
& San Martino

ROUTE Nos: PEDRA 1 & 2
SASS de PUTIA
& TULLEN

3 Kilometres

N

PEDRA 1:

SASS DE PUTIA

Grade:	1, Seriousness: A
Departure point:	Passo delle Erbe
Ascent:	900m
Descent:	900m
Via ferrata:	80m
Approximate time:	4 hours (or with additional option 5½ hours)
Highest altitude:	2875m

Sass de Putia (Pieterkofel) is a good mountain to climb for the commanding views of the area, but has only a small section of via ferrata climbing.

The wire protection is on the final 70–80m ascent to the summit; it takes about 15 minutes up and 10 minutes down. It is a very easy ferrata and does not necessarily require the use of equipment (depending on experience and your head for heights, the wire can simply be used as a handrail for security to scramble to the summit).

Access to Sass de Putia can be gained from the Rif. Genova, but the simplest approach is from the car park at Passo delle Erbe. From Passo delle Erbe follow path 8a to Forcella de Putia, 2357m (joining path 4 at around 2100m); this takes about 75–80 minutes. Then follow the signposted path to Sass de Putia, which zigzags up to the start of the ferrata in about another hour. Total time from car park to summit is around 2½ hours.

Descent is back to Forcella de Putia, where you can either return directly to Passo delle Erbe or complete the Circuito de Putia on paths 35 and 8b. Direct return from the forcella takes about an hour, and completion of the circuit about 2½ hours.

PEDRA 2:

TULLEN AND GUNTER MESSNER PATH

A good mountain
day with some
limited ferrata
sections along
the way.

Grade:	1, Seriousness: B
Departure point:	Ponte Russis (Russis Bruke)
Ascent:	1000m
Descent:	1000m
Via ferrata:	200m
Approximate time:	8 hours (plus ¾hr for Tullen ascent)
Highest altitude:	2653m

The Gunter Messner Path is a clearly marked round, way-marked 'GM'. It is best completed as a circuit from Ponte Russis (1735m), taking around 8 hours, including 2½ hours along the crested ridge of Monte Odle di Eores. Prior to starting the ridge traverse there is an optional extension of around 45 minutes which includes a round-trip to the summit of Tullen (2653m).

At the Ponte Russis road junction (1735m) there is ample parking, and the round-trip is started by walking 5 minutes down the road to pick up a path signposted 32a and GM. This path goes steeply uphill through the forest for around 30 minutes, when a traverse path rises to the right (west) at around 1960m, with good views north across the lowlands between the Dolomites and the Austrian Alps. The path rises gradually to a shoulder (2114m), and turns east and then north-east as the view returns to Dolomitic scenery south across Val di Funes into the Puez Odle National Park. A good path rises up through a spectacular sunken valley to the junction signposted to Tullen; this is about 2 hours from the start of the walk.

The ascent of Tullen (2653m) takes about 30 minutes up and 15 minutes down; there is a summit cross, a route book and a commanding view. Return to the sign-post; the GM path continues on an easterly traverse and in 5 minutes there is some wire protection in a stepped gully (no exposure). Then a zigzag path leads in a further 10 minutes over an exposed ridge and descends to a col. A short, easy, but exposed wired section now leads to the summit of Walschering (2590m), which has a small wooden cross. The Gunter Messner Steig now continues as a high-level traversing path (mostly on the south side of the mountain), which has only occasional ferrata wires in the most exposed places. About an hour from the Walschering summit a 10m ladder is ascended; fol-lowing a short section of wire, the path continues down and joins path 4 to Forcella de Putia. Total time from the start to here is about 5½ hours.

From Forcella de Putia you descend steeply to the north-west on path 4 until path 8a branches off to the right (north-west). Here you continue to descend on path 4 until another junction at around 2000m, where GM is signposted to the left (west), with path 4 continuing down to the right. You now follow the GM path on an undulating traverse on the north side of the ridge, pass-ing below the summit of Tullen before descending through the forest and back to the road. Total time from the Forcella de Putia to the road is around 2½ hours.

PEDRA 3:
MONTE CAVALLO

Grade:	1, Seriousness: B
Departure point:	Pedraces/Rifugio San Croce
Ascent:	900m
Descent:	900m
Via ferrata:	150m
Approximate time:	6 hours
Highest altitude:	2907m (3026m for extension)

An easy scrambling route with some very exposed walking.

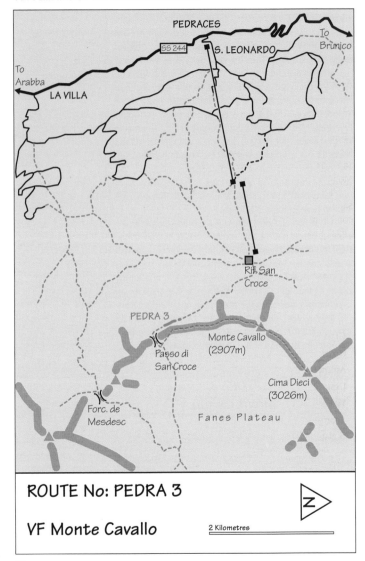

ROUTE No: PEDRA 3

VF Monte Cavallo

2 Kilometres

The route follows waymarked path 7 to the Passo di San Croce, then continues along the ridge to the summit of Monte Cavallo (Helikreuzkofel), with an added option of going along the ridge to Cima Dieci (Zehnerspitzen).

Approach using the chairlift from Pedraces (only the lower chair operates from the middle of June to the end of September; it closes over lunchtime). From the top of the chair walk uphill for 30 minutes, past the 14 Stations of the Cross, to the church and Rif. San Croce (good food). Path 7 is clearly signposted and waymarked from San Croce. Follow it along the ridge to the summit of Monte Cavallo (2907m).

You can descend by the same route or, from Passo di San Croce, make the walk into a long mountain day by continuing along path 7 onto the Fanes plateau until the junction with path 12, and then returning on path 12 to Forcella de Mesdesc and down to La Villa. •

• **Extension:** It is possible to extend your day by continuing north along the ridge from the summit of Monte Cavallo to Cima Dieci and then returning back the same way. This is an exposed ridge with superb views across Val Badia to the Puez Odle Natural Park and the Sella massif. You should allow about 1½–2 hours for this round-trip extension, which includes around 150m of additional ascent and descent.

PEDRA 4:
PIZ DE LES CONTURINES

Grade:	1, Seriousness: B
Departure point:	Capanna Alpina
Ascent:	1350m
Descent:	1350m
Via ferrata:	100m
Approximate time:	8 hours
Highest altitude:	3064m

This is a big mountain walking day with only a 100m ferrata to climb to gain the summit of Piz de les Conturines (Cunterinesspitze).

This route could be done just as a walk (excluding the via ferrata), with La Lavarella (3055m) being climbed as an alternative summit. Strong walkers should allow around 7–8 hours. Do not be put off by the prospect of returning along the same path – it is easy walking with spectacular views, and the wooded section is particularly pleasant.

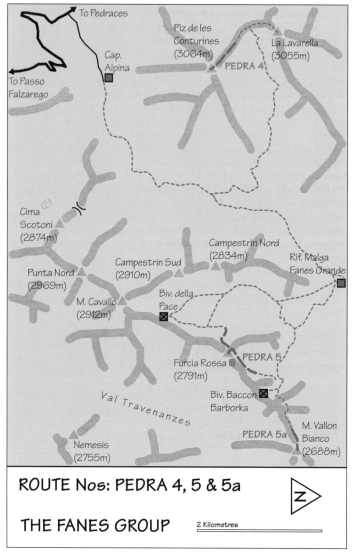

To Pedraces

Piz de les
Conturines
(3064m)

La Lavarella
(3055m)

PEDRA 4

Cap.
Alpina

To Passo
Falzarego

Cima
Scotoni
(2874m)

Campestrin Nord
(2834m)

Rif. Malga
Fanes Grande

Campestrin Sud
(2910m)

Punta Nord
(2969m)

M. Cavallo
(2912m)

Biv. della
Pace

Furcia Rossa III
(2791m)

PEDRA 5

Val Travenanzes

Biv. Baccon
Barborka

M. Vallon
Bianco
(2688m)

PEDRA 5a

Nemesis
(2755m)

ROUTE Nos: PEDRA 4, 5 & 5a

N

THE FANES GROUP

2 Kilometres

Approach by driving up the mountain road to Cap. Alpina at 1720m (this road leaves the La Villa to Passo Falzarego road above Armentarola). Follow path 11, which climbs steadily up to Col De Locia through attractive conifers in around 50–60 minutes, and then follow an open (fertile) glacial valley along a fairly level path until reaching a signpost in a further 30 minutes. The path now leads up to the left, rising up through a series of glacial bowls with some easy walking in between. The ridge between Piz de les Conturines and La Lavarella is reached at point 2885 metres, about 2 hours after leaving path 11. This is an outstanding viewpoint with San Cassiano and La Villa directly below and a great panorama of the Sella massif. The path to Piz de les Conturines is clearly waymarked along the ridge to the start of the ferrata – a large wooden ladder! There are some wires and other wooden aids as the route climbs a series of ledges to the summit, which is a truly wonderful viewpoint in all directions. Note that the ferrata is on the northern side of the mountain at 3000m, and in cold weather can be liable to icing.

Descent is made by reversing the ascent route back to Cap. Alpina, in around 3 hours. •

• To climb **La Lavarella** (either as well as, or as an alternative to, Piz de les Conturines), take the path that zigzags steeply up from point 2885m, then goes around a rock ledge to the right with very easy scrambling leading to the summit in around 30 minutes. This summit is also a truly wonderful viewpoint in all directions.

PEDRA 5:
VF FURCIA ROSSA –
CIMA FURCIA ROSSA III

Grade:	2, Seriousness: C
Departure point:	Capanna Alpina
Ascent:	1200m
Descent:	1200m
Via ferrata:	300m
Approximate time:	8 hours
Highest altitude:	2791m

Whilst this is anything but a demanding via ferrata, it is as good a mountain day as one could wish for. The terrain is fascinating, the geological interest is great, and the scenery is stunning.

The remoteness of this route makes it a fairly serious under-taking, and it is not to be recommended in poor weather; quite apart from the potential for route-finding problems, it would be such a missed opportunity!

The route is in the Fanes Natural Park and is relatively remote. It can, however, be approached from three directions. The quickest approach on foot, although it will probably involve a fairly long drive from your base, is to leave Alta Badia at St Vigil and drive up Val Tamores to Rif. Pederau (1540m), where a jeep taxi can be taken to Rif. Fanes (2060m). The longest walking approach is from the Cortina side (east), following path 10 along Valle de Fanes (limited parking at the Visitors' Centre, just off the SS51, as described in CORT 1). The third (rec-ommend) option, described below, is from Cap. Alpina (1720m), clearly signposted 2km south-east of San Cassiano; there is a large car park just before the bar and restaurant at Cap. Alpina.

Follow path 11, well graded as it climbs through conifers to Col de Locia (2069m) and then levels out to cross an attractive glacial plain to Passo Tedega (2157m). The path now goes slightly downhill towards the junc-tion with Valle di Fanes and meets a path to the right (south-east) signed as VB-17, some 5 minutes before Rif. Malga Fanes Grande. Allow about 2 hours to this junc-tion from Cap. Alpina; you might enjoy the short diver-sion to the rifugio for some refreshments.

Follow path VB-17, climbing steadily through an area of impressive limestone pavements, in 30 minutes reaching the point where path 17 heads up to Monte Castello. This, incidentally, would be a straightforward descent route at the end of the day, although the descrip-tion below suggests a more interesting alternative for your descent. Your route, now waymarked VB, continues to the left (east), going slightly downhill before making a long rising traverse, with an impressive cirque rising up to your right (south). After this, an apparent junction is reached, some 45 minutes after you first embarked on path VB-17, and at an altitude of about 2350m. At this point, there is a small rock-fall, and a rather half-hearted attempt to block off the path which continues slightly to the left. You should take the path to the right, which is indicated by a rather faded arrow. This path almost immediately turns back sharply to the left and leads into a series of well-constructed zigzags. About 10 minutes up these zigzags, at an altitude of about 2400m, and at one of the sharp right-hand turns of the path, you will pass the remains of a group of old wartime buildings on your left. A few minutes later, some 10m above these ruins, look out for a large

Furcia Rossa, the rather ramshackle ladders encountered in descent

boulder on the left-hand side of the path. This bears a plaque reading 'ERBAUT COSTRUITO Nel 1915 ERNEUERT RIPRISTINATO Nel 1973'. This is in recognition of the reconstruction, in 1973, of the original First World War path, dedicated by an Austrian, Walter Schaumann, as the Via della Pace (Friedensweg), or Path of Peace. Painted on this boulder (albeit very faded) are two arrows: one, pointing uphill, reads VB; the other, pointing slightly downhill, reads FR. This is the key to the rest of the day, and you must be sure to take the latter route in order to reach Furcia Rossa III (the route ahead, up the zigzags, leads up to VF Monte Vallon Bianco; see PEDRA 5a below).

Your path leaves the zigzags at this point and goes off to the right (south) on a shelf which runs along the foot of a rock wall. Whilst the route is not initially very easy to pick out, waymarking soon confirms that you are on course. For the next 30 minutes or so, continue to make progress along this shelf, climbing to an altitude of about 2560m and passing a couple of large natural caves in the rock wall to your left.

By now it is clear that you are heading for the broad col at the head of the cirque, which you crossed earlier. Your way is barred, however, by a 20m rock wall below you to the right. The waymarking leads you to an obvious weakness – a wide broken chimney which is descended with the aid of a cable, leading to a series of three timber ladders. The path, still waymarked, now leads up the cirque and on towards the col, where a ruined observation post provides a quite astonishing view down into Val Travenanzes, some 700m below, with Tofana di Mezzo and Tofana di Rozes straight ahead.

The path now traverses, a little below the col, to the rock wall which forms the upper south-west wall of the cirque. Once at the wall, recently renewed cables lead in easy zigzags up to a further series of timber ladders; a memorial plaque at the first ladder commemorates the building of the route in 1974. From the top of the wall, the track takes a course up a scree slope and along a shelf, traversing to the right (north-west) below a further wall. This is soon climbed with the aid of stemples, safeguarded by cables. The stemples lead into a broad scree-filled gully, the right wall of which, some 10m high, is ascended without difficulty. At the top of the wall, by now at an altitude of about 2720m, the path leads in easy zigzags onto the boulder-strewn slope of the summit plateau. Within a few minutes you will notice waymarking indicating VB back the way you have just come and Passo Limo off to the north-west (this latter route would be a quicker way off the mountain in deteriorating weather, but is not shown on maps and is probably a less secure route back into the lower reaches of Vallon Bianco).

The Furcia Rossa III summit cairn and cross soon come into view above you to the left, as the path continues on a gently rising traverse to the south. The foundations of an old building mark a junction in the path. Painted signs indicate VB back the way you have come; CAST (Monte Castello) to the right, which is your descent route for later; and FR to the left, leading up to the summit, some 5 minutes away. On a clear day, the views that greet you on your arrival are amongst the finest in the Dolomites, and will more than repay the 4½ hours or so you have taken since leaving Cap. Alpina. However, you are now at an altitude of 2791m, and still have over 3 hours of descent before you, so keep an eye on the time!

Return to the junction just mentioned, and take the path leading towards Monte Castello. You now zigzag down steep scree, picking a way easily down a series of short vertical steps until a more demanding obstacle is reached, in the shape of a 10m wall. This is descended, with the aid of cable and ladders, onto a steep scree slope running down to an airy little forcella at about 2700m. The path, still clearly waymarked, now contours generally southwards on a shelf overlooking the barren upper reaches of Vallon Bianco, down which your descent route runs. You now reach the final protected passage of the day, in the shape of a series of rather ramshackle timber ladders winding down a 40m rock wall. Exposure is minimal, given the way the ladders are set into an artificially widened natural rake in the wall, although head room is limited in places! At the foot of the ladders, at an altitude of about 2660m, a memorial plaque, identical to the one passed earlier, marks the end of the ferrata.

The path continues generally southwards, heading for Bivacco della Pace, but you can see your return route in the valley below you heading in the opposite direction. A rock step below you, on your right, precludes a more direct course for home, so you must continue for a further 10 minutes or so until you can descend a scree slope to reach the floor of the upper part of the valley at about 2550m, about an hour after leaving the summit. Once on the path you spotted from above, head northwards down the valley until you reach an obvious junction. Whilst there are no signs to help you at this point, the left-hand course is the preferred route, since this both cuts off a large corner and leads through a delightful area of thin pines and limestone pavement; old yellow waymarking guides the way back to path 11 at its junction with VB-17. Were you to continue straight ahead (at the junction without signs), you would reach the point where path 17 becomes VB, where a left turn brings you back to path 11. Whichever option you choose, your day ends with a straightforward walk back to Cap. Alpina along the path (11) you took at the start of your day. Allow 3½ hours from the summit back to Cap. Alpina.

PEDRA 5A:
VF MONTE VALLON BIANCO –
PATH OF PEACE

Although there are some short sections of cable and a narrow bridge (with damaged and incomplete handrails), this route cannot be regarded as a climber's ferrata, even though it is named via ferrata and is shown as such on maps and signposts.

Grade:	1, Seriousness: C
Departure point:	Capanna Alpina, Val di San Cassiano, but see alternative options in PEDRA 5
Ascent:	1180m
Descent:	1180m
Via ferrata:	100m
Approximate time:	7½ to 8½ hours
Highest altitude:	2688m

With a good head for heights you can climb this route without the need for ferrata kit. You could climb the Monte Vallon Bianco only (an easier alternative to completing the entire Furcia Rossa III route (PEDRA 5)) or climb it in addition to

Furcia Rossa (in which case allow an extra 2 hours for the ascent and descent from the route junction at 2410m).

To climb Monte Vallon Bianco on its own allow at least 4 hours ascent from Cap. Alpina, plus 3 hours for the return. The approach is the same as that for the Furcia Rossa III route (PEDRA 5) as far as the large boulder with the Path of Peace memorial plaque at about 2410m; this is where the Furcia Rossa III route follows the FR way-mark. For Monte Vallon Bianco you follow waymark VB and continue climbing the well-constructed zigzag ledges until, 20 minutes after the boulder with the plaque, you arrive at a battered sign indicating 'via ferrata Mt Vallon Bianco' to the left and 'FR 15 mins' painted on a rock to the right (2560m). •

Continuing your ascent of Monte Vallon Bianco from the battered sign, follow the ledge to the left (north-east), descending slightly to 2520m before climbing to reach the damaged short bridge (6m long) spanning a deep gorge. You now continue on a good but narrow path as it zigzags up and traverses along ledges to the summit of Monte Vallon Bianco. The stairways of the path are very well built, and particularly around the summit there are a lot of wartime remains, so although easy, the route does have a lot of interest. On the summit is an old wooden cross sporting a shiny stainless steel box with the inscription 'Berg Heil, September 1992 Monte Vallon Bianco 2688m Via della Pace'. The views are fantastic, especially those plunging down into Val Travenanzes and across to the impressive north faces of Tofana di Dentro and Tofana di Rozes.

Your descent is by retracing the ascent route, although this is definitely a summit you will want to linger on if the weather is clear. However, if your day out includes climbing Furcia Rossa as well, then retrace your steps back to the plaque at 2410m more quickly, as you still have a long day ahead of you.

• **Note:** if you follow the FR route from here it climbs a ledge towards Bivacco Baccon Barborka (2620m). A visit up to there is a worthwhile diversion for the spectacular views down into Val Travenanzes and across to Tofane di Dentro and di Rozes. However, this path then makes its way to the summit of Furcia Rossa I, and it is NOT possible to make the link to the Furcia Rossa III traverse (described in PEDRA 5 above) from here (even though Kompass maps indicate the existence of a path, which is very misleading).

SELVA

Maps:
Tabacco Carta Topographica 1:25,000 Sheet 05 or
Kompass Wanderkarte 1:25,000 Sheet 616

Tourist Information Office:
APT Selva. Telephone: (0471) 795122, Fax: (0471)
794245

Internet: www.val-gardena.com
E-mail: selva@val-gardena.com

Selva (Wolkenstein), a rather straggling village, is the largest settlement in the upper reaches of Val Gardena (Grodnertal), a valley which displays the classic V-shape common to many in the Dolomites. It is also one of the few Dolomite destinations featured by British package holiday companies, which might be of interest to those who prefer to have their travel plans made for them.

As a popular holiday destination, Selva is inevitably very busy, particularly so in August. It has a wide variety of shops, banks, restaurants and places to stay, together with a Tourist Information Office. Despite the rather commercialised feel to the village, it is a very convenient base for trips into the surrounding mountains, as it is served by a number of bus services and has three cable cars operating throughout the summer. Of the four routes described in this section, the two in the Puez-Odle Natural Park (SELVA 1 and SELVA 2) are best described as good mountain days, whilst the other two are somewhat more technically demanding.

SELVA 1:
VF Est and VF Sud – Sass Rigais

Est (ascent):	Grade: 2, Seriousness: B
Sud (descent):	Grade: 1, Seriousness: B
Departure point:	Col Raiser gondola (Santa Christina)
Ascent:	1000m
Descent:	1000m
Via ferrata:	800m
Approximate time:	7–8 hours
Highest altitude:	3025m

Sass Rigais is a 3000m peak with two via ferratas; climbed together, these make a good traverse of the mountain.

The route up the east side is the harder of the two routes, and so it is best to ascend VF Est and descend VF Sud. Either way there are no real technical difficulties, but it is a fairly long and committing day (even by using the Col Raiser gondola lift for access). If you are planning an overnight stay Rif. Firenze (also shown on maps as the Regensburger Hutte, and sometimes known as the Geisler Hut), a few minutes away from the top lift station and downhill to the east, makes a good base.

The Col Raiser gondola opens mid-June, closes early October, and is open all day from 0800 to 1700. There is reasonable amount of parking at the lift station, but it is best to be early, particularly in peak season, as the car park fills up quickly. Note that there is a small charge for parking.

From the top of the gondola, you head north on path 2 and follow signs to 'Via Ferrata', which then pick up path 2a. Now follow path 2a east, eventually passing the sign for Ferrata Sud (your descent route) to ascend Val della Salieres to Forcella Salieres. You should allow 2–2½ hours to this point from the top gondola station, and then VF Est will take you a further 1–1½ hours to the summit.

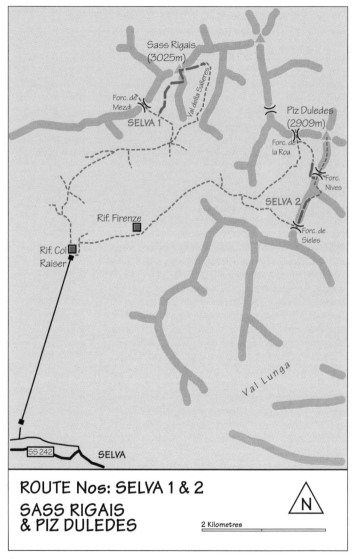

ROUTE Nos: SELVA 1 & 2

SASS RIGAIS
& PIZ DULEDES

2 Kilometres

The first wire protection starts about 10–15 minutes above the forcella at the top of the valley, but comes to an end quite quickly and is followed by an airy section on exposed ground with no protection. After a few minutes of exposure the wires start again with a high reach and a steep stemple pitch. Protection is now good, until the last 150m or so to the Sass Rigais summit, which is unprotected but is clearly waymarked by red paint. The summit, with its interesting cross, is a good viewpoint for Sasso Lungo and the Sella massif.

Your descent follows VF Sud, which initially heads south-east along a quite airy broken ridge, turns south and then descends in a generally south-westerly direction with intermittent wires and unprotected scrambling. Continue to follow waymarks across a combe until a last section of wires leads down steeper ground into a broken gully, where the path, still going down steeply, turns south-east to return to path 2a and the Ferrata Sud sign you passed on your way to VF Est. From here you retrace your steps along path 2a and then path 2 back to the gondola station. Allow 2½–2¾ hours for your descent from the summit of Sass Rigais.

SELVA 2:
PIZ DULEDES

Grade:	1, Seriousness: A
Departure point:	Col Raiser gondola (Santa Christina)
Ascent:	900m
Descent:	900m
Via ferrata:	150m
Approximate time:	6 hours
Highest altitude:	2909m

Not really a via ferrata day as such, but a good mountain walk with some wire protection in the most exposed places.

Easy access to and from this ferrata can be gained using the Col Raiser gondola in Santa Christina; this is open from mid-

June, closes early October, and operates from 0800 to 1700. There is a small charge for parking, which is controlled.

From the top of the gondola follow a well-made path slightly downhill to Rif. Firenze (Regensburger Hutte), and then path 2/3 towards Forcella de Sieles along a wide glacial valley. About 45–50 minutes from the rifugio, path 3 branches to the left (north-east) and heads up towards Forcella de la Roa. Go almost to the forcella, ignoring signs after about 20 minutes for Alta Via 2, which leads back to the right (the Alta Via sign is a triangle with a 2 inside it). Near the top of the zigzags leading up to the forcella (which can quickly be visited for the view) a path leads off to the right to the start of the wire protection.

The route goes up a series of broken gullies and ledges with four short sections of wire, a short ladder and then a final fifth wire before attaining the ridge; this is very easy and takes around 20 minutes. Turn left at the ridge to follow an easy path to the summit of Piz Duledes in a further 20–30 minutes. The summit is an excellent viewpoint and takes about 3 hours from Rif. Firenze.

Descent is made by retracing steps back to Forcella Nives, and then following a well-waymarked path to the south along a high-level plateau until the path leads down a ridge to the east before traversing to Forcella Forces de Sieles (about 1 hour from the summit of Piz Duledes). On this traverse there are four short sections of wire, but exposure is minimal and there is a good path all the way. From here path 2, then paths 2/3, lead back to Rifugio Firenze in around an hour. Consult the map for other options to extend the day or vary the return/approach; depending on time available, you could have an overnight stop in a rifugio.

SELVA 3:
VF Oscar Schuster - Sasso Piatto

Grade:	3, Seriousness: B
Departure point:	Passo Sella
Ascent:	700m
Descent:	1200m
Via ferrata:	300m
Approximate time:	6 hours
Highest altitude:	2964m

An interesting ferrata, which makes a good mountain round-trip.

The climbing is not especially difficult on this route, but protection is quite minimal and in places a steady head is required for some very exposed scrambling.

Approach the route using the Sasso Lungo gondola from the Gardena side of Passo Sella to Rif. Tony Demetz; this operates all day from the middle of June until early October. An early start is to be recommended in peak season, as parking around the lift station can be hectic. From Rif. Demetz path 525 descends to Rif. Vicenza, passing an interesting memorial to a recent helicopter crash. At Rif. Vicenza simply turn left and follow a way-marked path up into the combe (fairly rough going through a boulder field) to the start of the route. It is possible that there maybe snow in the combe early in the season.

The route starts high up on the right-hand side of the combe, but the initial protection doesn't last for long and some care is then required in following the painted way-marks whilst doing some fairly exposed scrambling without protection. Another point to note is that the wire ropes are (at the time of writing) quite old, frayed and not always attached. Keep following the waymarked route to the summit of Sasso Piatto (Plattkofel). The route is north facing and subject to icing and residual snow patches early in the season.

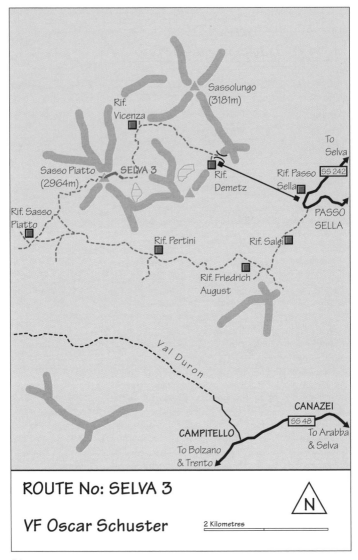

ROUTE No: SELVA 3

VF Oscar Schuster

2 Kilometres

N

Descent follows the traditional walking route, way-marked with cairns and paint, which zigzags down over steep stony ground towards the Rif. Sasso Piatto. There is no need to go all the way down to the hut as a fairly obvious south-easterly traversing path descends to the Friedrich August Way, cutting the corner off. Continue generally east along a very pleasant waymarked path, which follows contours and has little height loss or gain. Refreshments can be had at the Rif. Sandro Pertini, then continue following Friedrich August Way back towards Passo Sella and return to your car.

This is a route for fairly experienced mountaineers and it is not recommended in poor weather conditions.

SELVA 4:
VF DELLE MESULES –
PIZ SELVA

Grade:	4, Seriousness: C
Departure point:	Passo Sella
Ascent:	800m
Descent:	800m
Via ferrata:	500m
Approximate time:	6–7 hours
Highest altitude:	2942m
Note:	long sling or short rope advised

Overall this is a long alpine day, requiring stamina, sure-footed climbing skills, a head for exposure and route-finding skills; it is therefore a route for experienced mountaineers. For those without technical rock climbing experience some of the moves may prove challenging.

VF delle Mesules (also known as the Possnecker path) is recognised as the oldest protected rock path in the Dolomites. Protection on the ferrata is not especially good, with some long runs between anchors. The route, which ends on top of a remote summit with some distance to cover across the Sella plateau, is committing and not recommended in poor weather conditions. The 1:25,000 map is essential. Depending on the choice of descent a second car can be left in the car park below Passo Gardena, as used for the

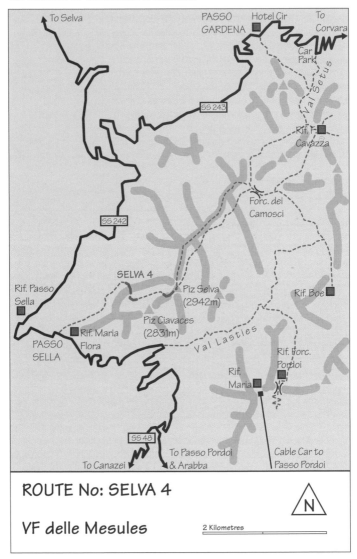

ROUTE No: SELVA 4

VF delle Mesules

2 Kilometres

Brigata Tridentina (route CORV 4), or at the end of Val Lasties where path 656 meets the road below and east of Passo Sella. (Parking here is limited, and hitching back up to the top of the pass may also be possible.)

Approach the route from Passo Sella. An early start is to be recommended in peak season, as parking around the pass is hectic. Path 649 from the pass is easy to follow; it goes past the third Sella tower, and then the start of the route is obvious up a dark, water-streaked wall. After a steady start, an exposed ledge leads to a smooth, polished and frequently damp chimney. This is ascended on widely spaced stemples, some requiring big steps. There is no separate protective side-cable as found on most stemple pitches, so you must clip onto the stemples themselves. At the top of the chimney there is an unprotected 5m or so in an exposed position where a long sling (or short rope) can provide useful aid for anyone not happy with the move out onto a detached pillar. The route continues from the pillar with a short (and not too reassuring) ladder, where the cables are loosely anchored and there are some long runs between the anchors. On this section there are a number of airy moves, which require care and confidence. The climbing becomes progressively easier but some unprotected movement is required on exposed sections.

The main section is completed with a waymarked walk onto a flat area of ground with a small lake (sometimes dried up) under the rock face of Piz Ciavaces (this is a good place for lunch). Continuation (a necessity, not an option, unless you want to reverse what you have just ascended) follows waymarks to the final section of the via ferrata. Progress is made up a broken rock face, then into a gully (with a possibility of snow early in the season) and eventually follows waymarks on exposed ground to the summit of Piz Selva. This final section of the route is not completely protected and seems quite exposed in places; it takes around an hour.

Descent is made by following path 649 to the northeast either across the plateau or over a series of summits (which involves a lot of ascent/descent). Again note the possibility of snow on the plateau early in the season (or in cold weather at any time), which can cover the way-marks. The choice of descent occurs at the Forcella Dei Camosci (junction of 649 and 676/7 paths). To return to Passo Sella follow 649 to the south-east, before turning back to the south-west on 647 and eventually 656 down Val Lasties and back to the road (paths well waymarked throughout). If you have chosen to return to Passo Gardena, then follow path 676 (677 is also an option), which leads into Valun di Pisciadu, by means of a short section of protective cable where you might well encounter snow. This path takes you on to Rif. F. Cavazza, from where you should swing to the north-west on path 666 for 5–10 minutes before descending into Val Setus (this is the descent route described in CORV 4) and down to the car park. Both descent options take around 3 hours, making an overall time of 6–7 hours.

CORVARA

Maps:
Tabacco Carta Topographica 1:25,000 Sheet 07 or
Kompass Wanderkarte 1:25,000 Sheet 616

Tourist Information Office:
APT Corvara – Colfosco, Via Col Alt 36, Cap 39033
Corvara, Italy. Telephone: (0471) 836176, Fax: (0471)
836540
Internet: www.altabadia.it
E-mail: corvara@dnet.it

Many readers will have heard of the Sella Ronda, the
classic winter ski tour round the Sella massif, which
negotiates the four passes of Gardena (2115m),
Campolongo (1875m), Pordoi (2239m) and Sella
(2244m). The tour is even more popular in summer,
although coaches, cars and motor cycles are the
favoured mode of travel. A hardy few undertake the trip
on foot, using cable cars to aid progress; this can even
be arranged through the tourist information office.

Corvara (1568m) is a large and attractive village,
which is situated at the north-eastern corner of the Sella
Ronda and has the towering Sassongher as its backdrop.
It is the largest village in Val Badia (Gadertal), and is well
provided with all the usual facilities such as banks,
restaurants, cafes and shops, including a number selling
sports equipment. Sport Kostner and Sport Alfredo are at
the top end of the main street and are both worth a visit.

Accommodation of all standards is in plentiful sup-
ply, and for those on a tighter budget there is a campsite
just outside the village on the way to Colfosco.

Corvara also has the only outdoor swimming pool in
the area. This is very attractively set amongst splendid
mountain scenery, but don't be deceived by its beauty as
the water is heated naturally (i.e. by the sun) and is often
on the chilly side of cold!

Note: at the time of writing, VF Vallon (see CORV 7) has been closed for three seasons (1999–2001) due to a bridge collapse. Since this route can be incorporated in a splendid circuit of the Sella group it is worth checking locally to see if it has been reopened.

The village is quite well served by public transport, with buses along Val Badia to Brunico, and an occasional service over Passo di Campolongo to Arabba and over Passo Gardena to Selva. Access to some of the routes in this section is aided by the two-stage lift from Corvara to Rif. Vallon in the Sella group. A jeep taxi, which used to run from Colfosco up to the top station of the Col Pradat lift, is unfortunately no longer operating. Whilst a summer service on the lift has been promised for some time, it had still not materialised at the time of going to press.

The seven routes listed in this section provide a good variety of via ferratas in the lower and middle grades. They are generally of good quality, with good protection, and are readily accessible. These routes are consequently very popular, and queues are quite common during August. So if your stay coincides with the peak period, you might want to think about either an early or late start if the weather forecast permits. Whilst you should not attempt routes when there is thunder in the air, don't be put off by cold weather or a bit of drizzle, as this can be when the locals stay by the fire and you can have a very quiet day on the hill!

CORV 1:
GRAN CIR

A very easy route and a suitable first outing for someone with little experience of mountain scrambling who is, nonetheless, keen to try their hand at climbing via ferratas.

Grade:	1, Seriousness: A
Departure point:	Passo Gardena
Ascent:	450m
Descent:	450m
Via ferrata:	100m
Approximate time:	2½ hours
Highest altitude:	2592m

This route is more of an exposed walk than a true via ferrata, but nonetheless useful for familiarisation with equipment

Gran Cir viewed from Passo Gardena

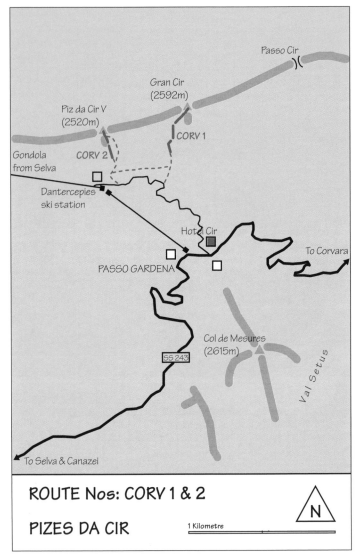

ROUTE Nos: CORV 1 & 2

PIZES DA CIR

1 Kilometre

N

and sampling Dolomite exposure. Indeed, one often finds mountaineering parents teaching their small children the rudiments of rope work on this route.

Access from Passo Gardena is very straightforward, although parking there can be hectic, particularly during August. The easiest approach is to follow the vehicle track adjoining the Hotel Cir. This is the access road to Dantercepies, a few hundred metres to the north-west, the top station of the gondola lift from Selva. The path to Gran Cir (Grosse Tschierspitze), which is waymarked in red, is signposted from this track; a good landmark to look for is a large white marble cross (sadly, now broken by stone-falls). The path goes up the unpleasantly eroded gully to the right of the cross. Allow about 30–40 minutes to the start of the route.

The route begins with an easy-angled ramp, which is protected by a section of wire for about 100m. Next comes a slabby corner, which takes a little drainage and can therefore be slippery. It is, even so, very straightforward. After this short protected section the route leads onto a waymarked narrow path, which then zigzags up the hill. There is a second short section of wire (less than 50m, about half-way up, again very easy), and the path then continues to the summit. Whilst the descent involves reversing the ascent route, passing other parties presents no problems. The round-trip, up and down from the pass, takes around 2½ hours.

Although it is a very easy route, Gran Cir is the highest peak in this group, and thus has a slightly wider panorama. It provides a splendid viewpoint, both north into the Puez National Park, and to Piz Boe and the Sella group to the south. The route can easily be combined with Piz da Cir V (Tschierspitze V; see CORV 2) in the same day (or even in the same afternoon). To do so, take the pleasant little track which traverses across the scree to the grassy rib mentioned in the route description below.

CORV 2:
PIZ DA CIR V

Piz da Cir V
(Tschierspitze V) is
an excellent little
route and a really
good introduction to
the sport. It is easily
accessible, the
protection is totally
sound, and the rock
is reassuringly solid.
Furthermore, the
route is quite short,
and so not
particularly
demanding.

Grade:	2, Seriousness: A
Departure point:	Passo Gardena
Ascent:	450m
Descent:	450m
Via ferrata:	100m
Approximate time:	2½ hours
Highest altitude:	2520m

The initial approach to Piz da Cir is the same as that for Gran Cir (see CORV 1) from Passo Gardena. Both routes can be climbed in the same day, though this (the more difficult of the two) is the recommended route for all but the most inexperienced of mountain scramblers.

Access is from Passo Gardena, where parking can be hectic, particularly during August. The easiest approach is to follow the access road adjoining the Hotel Cir. This leads to the Dantercepies ski station to the north-west of the pass, which can also be reached by the gondola lift coming up from Val Gardena. There is a rifugio and toilet at the ski station. The path to the via ferrata is waymarked in red and follows the grassy rib which ascends directly north behind the ski station, past a radio mast. When the grassy slope runs out, continue the ascent to the route by the left-hand gully (the start of the route can also be reached by the right-hand gully, but this is particularly badly eroded). It is now a 5 minute scramble over large and uneven boulders to the start of the climb, which is on a pleasant belvedere from which the route starts up a short ladder.

The climb is fairly short, but on good rock and in good situations. The pleasant rib above the ladder levels out after a very few metres to a small platform, next to

Short ladder at the start of the Piz da Cir V

• Note: if you keep
your eyes open, as
you zigzag down the
descent gully after
the wire ends, you
will spot a small
track traversing out
of the right-hand
side of the gully; this
gives you an option
to return back to the
belvedere at the start
of the route, and
descend back to the
ski station by the
gully you climbed
earlier.

which a Madonna statuette guards the route. The main section of the route is followed, from the end of the wire, by a brief walk to the final section of about 10m, which leads to the splendid little summit where there is room for about 10 people at the most. This short summit pitch has to be reversed in descent.

It is, in fact, far more satisfying to down-climb the whole route. However, the only drawback of this excellent little ferrata is that, due to its accessibility, it gets quite busy, which makes for difficulties in crossing other climbers. Consequently, unless it is quite late in the afternoon and there are no other parties on the way up, it is better to continue from the descent of the summit pitch down the gully to the east. The upper half of this gully has wire protection, which provides a useful handrail. When the protection ends it is a matter of picking the easiest way down the gully, which is somewhat loose in places, until a zigzag path leads down to the grassy slope below. If you are doing only the one route then continue down the path to the right of the gully and round to the first part of the ascent path, back to the ski station and on down to the pass. If doing the Gran Cir as well, then continue on the zigzag to the left (east) to pick up the path which traverses round to the white marble cross referred to in the CORV 1 route description above. •

CORV 3:
SASSONGHER

A straightforward
ascent with great
views. More a
protected walk than
a true via ferrata,
with wires in
exposed places.

Grade:	1, Seriousness: A
Departure point:	Colfosco, Col Pradat
Ascent:	1000m
Descent:	1000m
Via ferrata:	100m
Approximate time:	6–7 hours
Highest altitude:	2665m

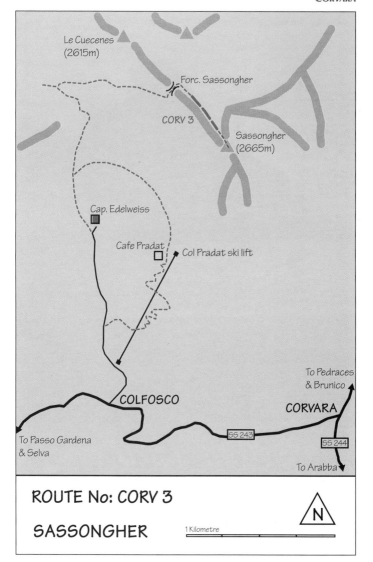

Le Cuecenes
(2615m)

Forc. Sassongher

CORV 3

Sassongher
(2665m)

Cap. Edelweiss

Cafe Pradat

Col Pradat ski lift

To Pedraces
& Brunico

COLFOSCO

CORVARA

To Passo Gardena
& Selva

SS 243

SS 244

To Arabba

ROUTE No: CORV 3

SASSONGHER

1 Kilometre

N

The village of Corvara with its stunning backdrop of the Sassongher

Cars can be parked in Colfosco in the Col Pradat ski-lift car park. Unfortunately, the lift does not run during the summer, and the jeep taxi, which used to operate up to a point a little above the Capanna Edelweiss, has been suspended. It is, however, worth checking at the Tourist Office whether this has been reinstated or, better still, the long awaited summer lift service introduced. In the meantime, you can take the path which zigzags up alongside the gondola to Col Pradat, and then swings round to the left (west) to meet path 4 leading up from Capanna Edelweiss. The route now climbs quite steeply to a fork just beyond a small shrine. Turn to the right (east) here and follow path 7 upwards to Forcella Sassongher (2435m). The protected section, which involves scrambling rather than climbing, is encountered between the forcella and Sassongher summit. The route has a little exposure but presents no difficulties. There are, however, some spectacular views, especially from the summit.

Descent is via the same route, but with the option of a variation in the lower section for a change of scenery.

CORV 4:
VIA FERRATA BRIGATA TRIDENTINA

Grade:	3, Seriousness: B
Departure point:	Car park below Passo Gardena on the Corvara road
Ascent:	750m
Descent:	750m
Via ferrata:	400m
Approximate time:	5–7 hours (depends on traffic)
Highest altitude:	2585m

There is only one thing wrong with this route – its popularity! It is very near to the road, very well protected, is on very good rock, has super views and ascends to a hut serving drinks and good food!

The route involves 750m of climbing, with one possible escape after the short first section, with the only other

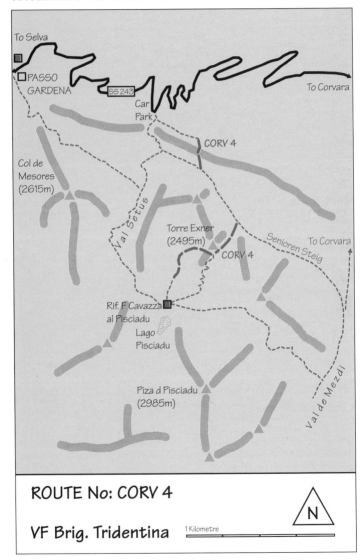

To Selva

PASSO
GARDENA

SS 243

To Corvara

Car
Park

CORV 4

Col de
Mesores
(2615m)

Val Setus

Torre Exner
(2495m)

CORV 4

Senioren Steig

To Corvara

Rif. F Cavazza
al Pisciadu

Lago
Pisciadu

Piza d Pisciadu
(2985m)

Val de Mezdi

ROUTE No: CORV 4

VF Brig. Tridentina

1 Kilometre

N

potential escape route being towards the top. Consequently, it is not to be taken too lightly.

Start from the large car park six or seven bends below Passo Gardena on the Corvara side (this car park can be reached by bus from Corvara). Your via ferrata kit can be put on here, as the first part of the route is only 10 minutes walk from the car park. Follow a marked path through the undergrowth to the obvious start of the route. Ascend first on stemples, then traverse using wires and good holds across a slab that takes drainage and is therefore usually damp. The only area of loose rock on the route is then encountered as you ascend a corner to the end of the first section (about 100m). Continue to the left between two very large boulders, and a 15–20 minute walk is made on a good path to the main section of the climb.

The route is unmistakable. Follow the wires (and probably the people) upwards, past the waterfall and on superb rock, for about 1½ hours depending on the weight of traffic. Eventually a large open bowl is reached below Rif. F. Cavazza al Pisciadu. The signposted and waymarked path to the left side of the bowl leads up to the rifugio, and offers the last opportunity to escape from the route. The rock now steepens, and the route becomes more difficult as it continues up a section with stemples, a ladder and finally a spectacular bridge (which you can see from the road as you drive up from Corvara). Finally, follow the red waymarked track to the rifugio, where you can treat yourself to a well-deserved drink.

Descent can be made quite simply with a direct route back to the car park in around 1–1½ hours. Go north on path 666 for 5–10 minutes and descend Val Setus. As there is some wire protection for the first couple of hundred metres, it is worth keeping your via ferrata kit on initially. Following the end of the wire, the path develops into a clear zigzag down the gully. As the season progresses this becomes a much better path than it looks, either from above or from down in the car park. Early in the season, however, you are likely to encounter some old snow in the upper reaches of the gully.

An alternative descent which, whilst longer, is much quieter than the more direct return to the car park can be made following path 676 eastwards from the rifugio. This would also be the route to take if you had started the day with a bus ride from Corvara. The track, which offers splendid views of the upper stretches of the climb, descends into the dramatic Val de Mezdi, where it swings left (north) on path 651 back towards Val Gardena. A good track will now lead you back to Corvara in less than an hour. However, if you are returning to the car park, you should take care not to descend too far down Val de Mezdi. About 10 minutes after joining path 651, take a left (north-west) fork onto a track (marked 'Senioren Steig' on some maps) along the broad shelf which is formed between the foot of the main line of cliffs and the smaller, lower crags. The route leads

pleasantly to the track above the first, short pitch of the via ferrata. Whilst this can be down-climbed, it can also be avoided by continuing to walk north-west back towards Passo Gardena and the car park.

Upper stemple pitch on the Tridentina, with the escape route below

CORV 5:
PIZ DA LECH

A good route, which can be climbed in a fairly short day by the use of lifts.

Grade:	3, Seriousness: B
Departure point:	Vallon chairlift
Ascent:	350m
Descent:	350m
Via ferrata:	200m
Approximate time:	3 hours
Highest altitude:	2910m
Note:	ascent/descent and timing assumes use of Vallon chairlift

Starting from Corvara, the Boe Gondola and then Vallon chairlift take you to within 15 minutes or so of the start of the route. However, it is also possible to park at Passo Campolongo and walk up to the bottom station of the Vallon lift in around an hour (the return fare on the Vallon lift is only slightly more than a one-way ride, whereas the return fare on the gondola from Corvara is significantly more expensive). The lifts run from the beginning of July to around the middle of September (operating times are 0900–1215; 1400–1710). However, the Vallon chairlift is closed on Tuesdays, which can make for a very quiet day on what is otherwise a very popular route.

From the top of the Vallon lift (note that Rif. Vallon, shown in this location on some maps, no longer exists) the path is well waymarked off to the right, and then goes left around the combe to the start of the route in about 15–20 minutes. The approach is eased somewhat if, about 50m after the second signpost from the top of the chairlift, you branch right uphill above a large boulder field to climb the slope diagonally to the bottom of the route. The route starts in a broken gully left of an overhang and a large vegetated ledge.

There is some loose rock on the route, especially on

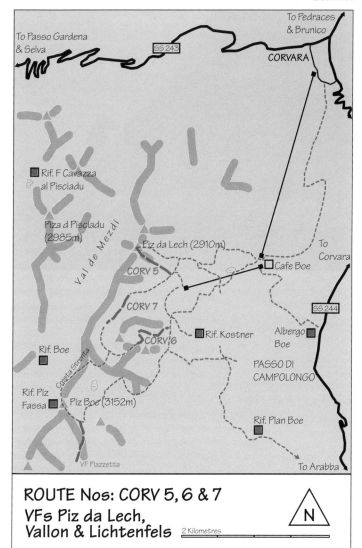

**ROUTE Nos: CORV 5, 6 & 7
VFs Piz da Lech,
Vallon & Lichtenfels** 2 Kilometres

N

A fairly delicate traverse section on the Piz da Lech

the first part of the climb, so be aware of other climbers above and below. However, it is a pleasant route, which has easy sections interspersed with some short, steep and entertaining pitches, but is always well protected albeit with a thinner cable than is usual, which tends to encourage proper climbing rather than cable hauling.

After about 30–40 minutes of climbing there is a steep section with an exposed move up to the left followed by an easy walk to an impressive wall of about 30m. (The broad, broken shelf below the wall provides the only escape route from the climb; old waymarking and a painted arrow indicate a way off to the right, leading into the scree-filled gully below. If you need to take this escape route, the descent is easier if you stick to the right-hand side of the scree as it approaches the point where the gully divides.) The wall is climbed on two 15m ladders with a short wire section in between. Protection is good throughout, but the move off the top of the second ladder is quite exposed and tends to push you outwards as you move up.

The exciting ladder pitches at the top of the Piz da Lech ferrata

After this the route eases off and the protection ends. There is now a waymarked walk to the Piz da Lech (Boeseekofel) summit, where there is a large cross and good views across the Sella plateau and Val de Mezdi to the Rif. F. Cavazza al Pisciadu at the top of Via Ferrata Brigata Tridentina (see CORV 4).

The descent follows the well-waymarked path 646 down rock and scree until a short protected section with wires and stemples is reached (so it is worth keeping your via ferrata kit on until this is past). After the stemples, at a signposted junction, follow the path to the right rather than going straight on. This leads to another short section of wire down an open gully below a rock wall and almost back to the starting point. From here you can return directly to the chairlift or walk across the plateau to the Rif. Franz Kostner for some sustenance. Depending on where you started, it is also possible to walk all the way down to Corvara or Arabba to extend the day.

CORV 6:
LICHTENFELSER STEIG – PIZ BOE

This is not really a via ferrata in terms of climbing or exposure, but provides an excellent scrambling route up or down Piz Boe via the Cresta Strenta.

Grade:	1, Seriousness: B
Departure point:	Vallon chairlift
Ascent (to Piz Boe):	600m
Descent:	600m
Via ferrata:	200m
Approximate time:	4–5 hours
Highest altitude:	3152m

Lichtenfelser Steig is waymarked path 672; it is clearly signposted from the junction of paths below the Rif. Franz Kostner.

Approach can be made using the Vallon chairlift (see route CORV 5 above for full details of opening/closing), and the route can be included as an option in various rounds in this area. But if using path 638 to descend from Piz Boe, make sure that after the first 200m or so of descent you follow the waymarks north-east towards Rif. Franz Kostner and Vallon, and not south-east down a ridge to the top of VF Cesare Piazzetta (route ARAB 1), which is a top-grade ferrata!

Warning: Some editions of the 1:25,000 Tabacco and Lagir Alpina maps show Lichtenfelser Steig in the wrong place! (Note survey (print) date of maps 21.7.86 and 24.9.96, respectively, and check out locally.) See below for details of Ferrata Vallon (CORV 7), which is actually to be found where Tabacco and Lagir Alpina show Lichtenfelser Steig, and which is Grade 2, definitely NOT Grade 1!

CORV 7:
FERRATA VALLON – PIZ BOE

Grade:	2, Seriousness: B
Departure point:	Vallon chairlift
Ascent (to Piz Boe):	600m
Descent:	600m
Via ferrata:	200m
Approximate time:	4–5 hours
Highest altitude:	3152m

Ferrata Vallon has the same approach as Piz da Lech (route CORV 5).

At the time of going to press this route is closed, as the bridge half-way up the route has collapsed. It is signposted from above the Vallon chairlift and continues, following waymarks, past the start of VF Piz da Lech into the combe. At Rif. Franz Kostner you may be told that the bridge is going to be mended (next week even!).

However, this has been the reply for at least the last two years, so don't hold your breath.

If the bridge is rebuilt, the route ascends the watershed gully at the head of Il Vallon, first on the left of the waterfall, then across it, and finally on the right of the waterfall to the top. Prior to the waterfall the climbing is fairly easy, although there is some loose rock and the wire was not always firmly anchored. The wall on the right is short but has pleasant climbing to the top of the rock wall and the end of the protection. To reach the summit of Piz Boe, take path 672 along the Cresta Strenta. However, if time is insufficient or if the weather is deteriorating, a very short round can be completed by swinging to the south and then east round Piz Vallon to join path 672, which becomes the previous route (CORV 6), which can then be reversed to lead back to the Vallon chairlift.

ARABBA

Maps:

Tabacco Carta Topographica 1:25,000 Sheet 07 or
Kompass Wanderkarte 1:25,000 Sheet 616

Tourist Information Office:

APT Arabba, 32020 Arabba, Italy

Telephone: (0436) 79130, Fax: (0436) 79300

Arabba occupies a strategic location at the foot of Passo
Pordoi and Passo di Campolongo, and on the route over
from the eastern Dolomites via Passo Falzarego. Its situation makes it a splendid base for exploring a wide area
of the surrounding mountains, although it is still better
known as a centre for winter sports. The village is situated on the south-eastern corner of the Sella Ronda, the
famous circuit described in the Corvara section.

This small, friendly village is markedly less commercialised (and therefore less costly) than many other
Dolomite villages, and is all the better for that. Arabba
nonetheless provides for all the needs of the visitor, with
facilities including banks, a Tourist Information Office
and a good variety of shops, including one selling sports
equipment. There are restaurants of all standards and a
fairly small, but good range of accommodation.

Whilst there are occasional bus services over Passo
Pordoi and Passo di Campolongo, a car opens up a much
wider area and makes this is an excellent jumping-off
point for mountain exploration. The Porta Vescovo cable
car climbs straight from the village to the ridge of La
Mesola to the south, making light work of the approach
to one of the most popular via ferratas in the Dolomites.

There are just four routes in this section, but two are
amongst the definitive via ferratas in the Dolomites.

ARAB 1:
VF CESARE PIAZZETTA – PIZ BOE

This is a wonderful route that lives up to its hard and strenuous billing, especially for the first 100m. It also keeps going at a good standard throughout its length.

Grade:	5, Seriousness: C
Departure point:	Ossario del Pordoi
Ascent:	900m
Descent:	900m
Via ferrata:	500m
Approximate time:	5–6 hours (return by cable car)
Highest altitude:	3152m
Note:	safety rope advised

Approach the route from the mausoleum Ossario del Pordoi (2229m) along a fairly level side road leading from Passo Pordoi. The pass can also be reached by bus if you do not have a car. The parking area is reserved for the use of visitors to the mausoleum, but there is plenty of space on the verge to the approach road, where parking does not appear to be a problem. You may feel it is worthwhile spending an eerie few minutes inside the mausoleum, which is a monument to the Dolomites' war victims – a chilling reminder of how wars are fought in even the most beautiful places.

Go uphill from the mausoleum on the waymarked path, traversing right at a rock spur, then again continuing up the gully on a good zigzag path all the way to the imposing rock walls above. The route starts 200–300m along a path to the right once you reach the rock walls; this approach will take you about 1–1½ hours from the mausoleum.

Although the climbing is strenuous (and gear sometimes has to be clipped under pressure, which is unusual on via ferratas) the protection is good and there are resting points if you look for them. At the end of the really strenuous section (i.e. after the iron steps and bulging slab) there is a big ledge where you can rest and have a

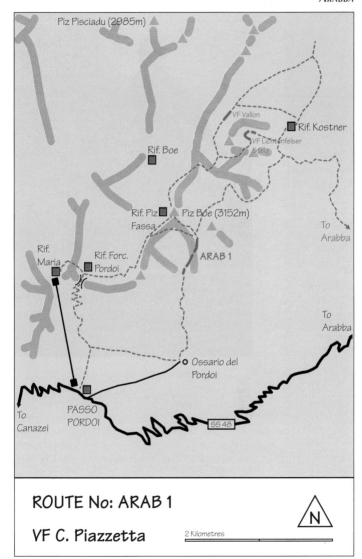

Piz Pisciadu (2985m)

VF Vallon

Rif. Kostner

Rif. Boe

VF Lichtenfelser Steig

Rif. Piz Fassa

Piz Boe (3152m)

To Arabba

Rif. Maria

Rif. Forc. Pordoi

ARAB 1

To Arabba

Ossario del Pordoi

To Canazei

PASSO PORDOI

SS 48

ROUTE No: ARAB 1

VF C. Piazzetta

2 Kilometres

N

*VF Cesare Piazzetta.
The bridge without
planks!*

drinks stop; this is very important if the day is sunny, as
the route faces south and it can be very hot even if you
have made an early start. At the end of the ledge there is
a short, shiny and often wet chimney, which needs a bit
of a thrutch to get up it (a big rucksack is a real disad-
vantage here). This marks the end of the steepest part of
the route; from here, the angle of the rock falls back
noticeably, and the climbing becomes less strenuous.
You then reach the bridge which, unlike some, has no
planks, so you need a good head for heights as you look
down into the abyss in order to place your feet on the
rungs for the crossing!

After the bridge the route continues with good, well-
protected climbing. Eventually there is a short break in

the protection before the final sting in the tail, which the route has kept for those climbers who thought they could relax. This is a newly cabled and quite strenuous section on good rock, which has replaced some unprotected scrambling on loose, steep rock, where the old paint waymarks and belay pegs are still in place. After this there is still some unprotected climbing (including one quite airy traverse). For this reason, and the sustained and steep nature of the route, carrying a safety rope is recommended as a useful back-up.

The via ferrata ends when a rock is reached with the painted notice 'Forcella Pordoi 30 mins, Piz Boe 40 mins'. At this point a number of options open up. If you decide not to visit Piz Boe summit, then follow the way-marked traverse to the left, round a large scree-filled bowl, to join paths 638 and 627 leading to Forcella Pordoi. However, the top of Piz Boe can be reached in about half an hour from the top of the via ferrata, which makes for an appropriate finale to a fine route. From Piz Boe you could walk all the way back to Arabba via Vallon (this makes a really long but satisfying day). Most climbers will, however, choose to return to Forcella Pordoi and make the 15 minutes' climb up to the cable car station in order to take the speedy ride down to Passo Pordoi (operates May to October).

An alternative descent is possible by means of the scree gully from Forcella Pordoi, which is steep at first, with the wire on the side of the gully fixed so high up the rock that it is not really of any use at all. There is potentially a good scree-run in the middle part of the gully, but be careful and aware of others both above and below you in the gully. Eventually a good zigzag path continues down the scree and then, at the end of the scree, there is a good traverse line (no path or waymarks) across the grassy plateau with a direct descent back to the car park at the mausoleum. Allow about 1½ hours for the descent from the forcella (which makes the total time for the day 6–7 hours).

Via ferratists take a rest when they can on a steep section of the VF Cesare Piazzetta

ARAB 2:
VIA DELLE TRINCEE – LA MESOLA

Grade:	4, Seriousness: B
Departure point:	Porto Vescovo cable car
Ascent:	500m
Descent:	500m
Via ferrata:	300m
Approximate time:	6–7 hours (plus 1½–2 hours without cable car)
Highest altitude:	2727m
Note:	torch essential

Although highly graded, this route is easily accessible by cable car (15–20 minutes), and the hardest climbing is done in the first 30m of the climb.

The rock on this ridge is volcanic, and consequently the climbing has a different character and requires different techniques to the limestone routes which predominate in the Dolomites. Good protection is now in place throughout the route, and, even though the climbing on the first wall is noticeably steep and footholds limited, once you have done the initial haul the route becomes easier. In fact, because there are two good escape points along the ridge, you could tackle the route with some degree of comfort, even if a break in the weather is forecast later in the day. Note that the final section of the route negotiates a series of tunnels, for which a torch is essential.

The Porta Vescovo cable car runs from early July until early September, with longer operating hours during the peak month of August; it is closed at lunchtime. A return ticket makes a worthwhile round (see details of descent route below). When the cable car is not running, the approach to the route makes for a longer, more tiring day. However, you will have the considerable bonus of finding the route all but deserted – a rare treat! Whilst the walk up from Arabba is perfectly feasible, it is far better to drive or take the bus up towards Passo Pordoi,

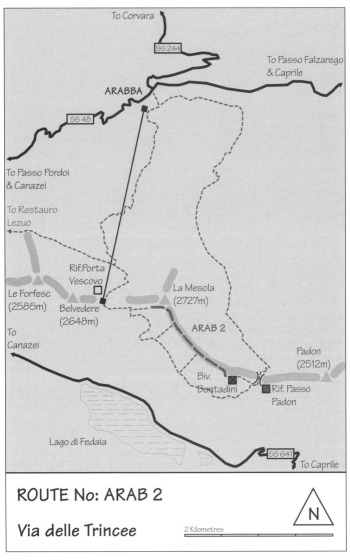

ROUTE No: ARAB 2

Via delle Trincee

2 Kilometres

N

stopping short at Restauro Lezuo, where limited roadside parking is available. About 50m back down the road towards Arabba, a path leads off across the hillside (way-marked 680). After a couple of kilometres, you join the dirt access road which leads to the top station of the cable car, which you will reach in about 1½ hours from your starting point.

Generally the route is quite sound with little danger of loose rock, but watch out for some loose pebbles at the top of the first steep section; these are retained by a piece of timber shuttering. After the strenuous start, go along a ledge and move up and across a really superb slab and round a corner. The route continues up to the ridge, with its superb views all the way back down to Arabba. Follow the ridge and then cross the bridge; the route book which used to be stored here has been removed and not replaced. The route now continues along the ridge and eventually descends to a broad col, the end of the first section and the first escape point.

After the first section a short walk (clearly way-marked) leads uphill to some First World War buildings; this is about an hour or so from the start of the via ferrata,

View of the Via delle Trincee from Passo Campolongo

and so is probably a good place for a lunch stop. If the weather has turned bad, there is a straightforward descent to the south-west to join the path which traverses back to the cable car station.

The second section of the route continues along some ledges, with more wartime buildings, and then descends quite awkwardly down some stemples and wire, with a couple of helpful artificial footholds. Protection is good throughout, but this passage is exposed and feels somewhat insecure since you are down-climbing. The wire now leads round a corner and then down, again somewhat awkwardly. This is the end of the second section, where you arrive at a path leading across a steep grassy slope to yet more wartime buildings and the second escape point. This is another good place to stop for a break. If an escape is required, descent can be made on the south side of the ridge and back to the cable car. Indeed, many climbers seem to regard this as the end of the route, but they are missing out on a really interesting part of the day, which earns the route its name 'Way of the Trenches'. This is where a torch is essential.

To complete the excursion, continue towards Padon on the path along the lovely airy crest straight ahead of you. This leads to the next section of cable, which leads down to the south side of the ridge. After about 10 minutes, follow waymarks past a bricked-up tunnel and continue the traverse. In a further 5 minutes, a big cave is passed and the cable leads back up to the ridge. Then descend on the north side and into the first short tunnel, where at the first junction of tunnels you take the left branch. (The tunnel system you are now entering contains a number of junctions and side galleries. They are, however, well waymarked, but do keep a sharp eye out for them since they can be easily missed in the gloom.) On leaving the short tunnel, follow waymarks through another short tunnel and then along some trenches on the side of the hill. About 30 minutes after entering the first tunnel, the last of the protective cable heads uphill again before going into a long uphill tunnel section. This

Ferratists on the bridge and the ridge of the Via delle Trincee

offers splendid views of the Marmolada to the south from the old lookout points.

The route ends when you emerge from the last tunnel at the Bivouac Bontadini; then take a clear path down to Rif. Padon, where refreshments can be had. Also at Padon there is a small but interesting wartime museum, which is open from mid-July to the end of August. Allow about 5 hours for the whole of the route through to Padon, including some time for lunch stops.

Whilst a descent can be made from Passo Padon direct to Arabba in about 1½ hours (on paths 699 and 698), this goes down the winter ski pistes and is not recommended. A better option is to follow the waymarked path from Padon back to the cable car. The path initially descends to the west from Rif. Padon along pleasant grassy slopes. After passing through a collection of very large boulders, and as the path rises steadily uphill, ensure that you keep taking the right-hand forks which you come across, since there are a number of animal tracks which look appealing but will take you on a traverse line well below the cable car. The path also provides a good view of the line of the route, including the bridge which you crossed several hours earlier. Allow about an hour from Padon back to the cable car.

ARAB 3: SASS DE ROCIA

Whilst this hardly qualifies as a via ferrata, it is included since it incorporates a visit to an interesting little summit and is a delightful spot for a day off, perhaps whilst you recover from the bigger routes.

Grade:	1, Seriousness: A
Departure point:	Ronch
Ascent:	100m
Descent:	100m
Via ferrata:	30m
Approximate time:	2 hours to as long as you want!
Highest altitude:	1620m

This is a grand spot to make the most of an improving afternoon. Sass de Rocia is an out-of-the-way place for climbers,

Climbers in the big gully on Sass de Roccia (photo: Collett's Mountain Holidays)

with a large number of bolted climbing routes. However, there are only a couple at Grade V, a couple at Grade VI, with the rest Grade VII and above!

Access is from the Pieve to Caprile road, just south of Digonera. Drive up a narrow, windy road to Laste, where the road becomes even narrower, and on to Val, where a (signposted) left turn takes you up to Ronch. Despite the narrowness of the road, there is a good parking area where it ends.

Approach can be made from the parking spot following a well-marked grassy track to Sass de Rocia, or from a path (rather inconspicuously signposted) which heads uphill from just below the last house, about 200m down the approach road. The upper path takes you towards the north of Sass de Rocia and the climbing areas. The way to the via ferrata is through a distinctive gash in the rocks (note the bolted climbing lines alongside). This leads into an impressive gorge, where, if you look directly above, you will see a bridge that will be crossed shortly. Turn left here, walk past the Madonna perched on a rock on your left, and climb the stemples up the left-hand wall. This leads to a small footbridge, which was not so readily apparent from below. A cable now leads to a lovely track, first over the footbridge you spotted from below, then through pines and over a third footbridge. The track now takes you through more pines to Bivacco Pian delle Stelle, with its veranda equipped with benches and picnic tables: a lovely spot! It will take you about 45 minutes to reach here from the car park.

Behind the bivouac, a pretty track leads in less than 5 minutes to a summit (not quite the highest in this pleasant little group of rocks). On the way, take care to avoid the deep, narrow cleft over which you must step.

Return to the gorge by the same route and now go downhill. The slope is at a relatively easy angle, but a cable is attached to the left wall for security. The deep gloom of the gorge makes this seem rather like open-air pot-holing! At the end of the cable a set of fairly steep stemples leads down to a path which takes you back to the road at the alternative approach referred to above.

This route is the only one in the book without a sketch map; if you want a bit of easy fun in a lovely, relaxing spot, take a map, have a look round and enjoy!

ARAB 4:
COL DI LANA

Col di Lana lies on the same seam of volcanic rock as La Mesola (see ARAB 2, Via delle Trincee), a little to the south-west.

Grade:	1, Seriousness: A
Departure point:	Corte/Sief
Ascent:	800m
Descent:	800m
Via ferrata:	100m
Approximate time:	4–6 hours
Highest altitude:	2452m

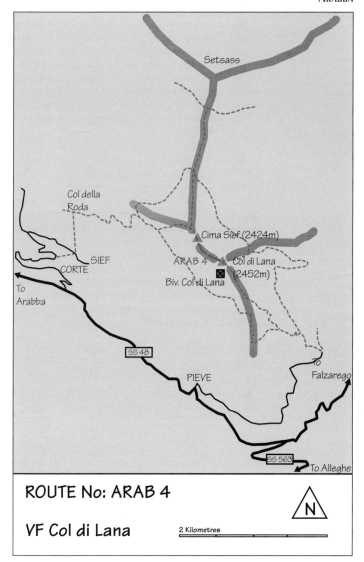

Setsass

Col della
Roda

Cima Sief (2424m)

SIEF

ARAB 4

Col di Lana
(2452m)

CORTE

Biv. Col di Lana

To
Arabba

SS 48

PIEVE

To
Falzarego

SS 563 To Alleghe

ROUTE No: ARAB 4

VF Col di Lana

2 Kilometres

N

Col di Lana was the scene of particularly intense fighting during the mountain war; indeed, it shares with nearby Lagazuoi the dubious distinction of having its profile completely altered by the detonation of huge quantities of explosives. Today it is a lovely place and a fine viewpoint, with numerous opportunities for walks either traversing or circumnavigating the summit. It is particularly worthwhile to continue off to the north to visit the impressive pinnacles of the Settsass ridge.

The traverse offers a stretch of easy scrambling which, whilst not particularly exposed, is protected by several lengths of cable, hence its inclusion in this guide. There are several possible approaches, the one providing easiest access to the ferrata section being from the hamlet of Corte near Arabba, ascending via Sief to Cima Sief and on to Col di Lana. A somewhat longer outing, from Pieve, offers the opportunity of a visit to a small museum with an interesting display of wartime memorabilia and contemporary photographs (signposted from Pieve). Whichever route is chosen, make your return by simply reversing your ascent.

VAL DI FASSA/CANAZEI

Maps:
Tabacco Carta Topographica 1:25,000 Sheet 06 or
Kompass Wanderkarte 1:25,000 Sheet 686

Tourist Information Office:
APT Alba. Telephone: (0471) 836176, Fax: (0471)
836540
Internet: www.valdifassa.it
E-mail: info@valdifassa.it

Canazei is a pleasingly bustling village at the head of Val di Fassa, another classic V-shaped valley. Flanked on all sides by mountain ranges, including the Latemar to the south, the Marmolada further to the east, the Catinaccio (Rosengarten) peaks and the Sella group at its head, it is as dramatic a location as you will find.

The valley has long been a favourite jumping-off point for trips into the mountains, with the nearby settlements of Moena, Pozza, Vigo and Campitello also serving as good bases. Canazei itself provides a good range of shops, including several selling sports equipment, with cafes and restaurants of all standards, a tourist office and banks. It also boasts a good-sized indoor swimming pool. Accommodation of every type, from smart hotels to campsites, is readily available. It is, however, a very popular area, with August particularly busy.

The village is quite well served by public transport, with several buses a day travelling up the valley from Bolzano and back, and the occasional service running over Passo Pordoi and Passo Sella. Whilst a bus service to Lago di Fedaia provides access to the Marmolada routes, many of the routes described are relatively distant from this, the main valley, and so a car is virtually essential to exploit the full potential of this area. Indeed, because of the wide geographic distribution of these routes, involving several different mountain groups, this section is sub-divided for ease of use.

Some, but by no means all, of the routes in this section can be approached by summer cable car (or chairlift) services, which take the sting out of the effort required. There are currently four such operations: two from the western side of the Catinaccio, the Ciampac cable car about 3km south-east of Canazei, and the Marmolada lift from Lago di Fedaia. Another useful transport service is a return minibus operation, which runs from Pera di Fassa to Rif. Gardeccia, giving easy access to the Catinaccio group.

A wide range of routes is accessible from Canazei. Many are amongst the easier grades – not offering challenging outings for those interested mainly in the harder routes, but nonetheless providing grand mountain days. Some, however, are serious undertakings, with the Marmolada routes amongst the best the Dolomites can offer. They are particularly dependent on good weather, and also require familiarity with the techniques involved in negotiating glaciers.

CATINACCIO – SCILLAR

Routes FASSA 1 and 2 (see below) are fairly remote from Val di Fassa. In mountain group terms, they overlap with the Scilliar Natural Park, and one of the possible approach routes is from the north. However, whichever way you choose to climb these routes, they will involve fairly long days in the mountains. One of the routes (FASSA 2) is relatively easily graded (though an exposed mountain day), the other one, FASSA 1 VF Laurenzi, is one of the more serious via ferratas to be found in the Dolomites. Enjoy.

FASSA 1:
VF LAURENZI – MOLIGNON

Grade:	4, Seriousness: C
Departure point:	Campitello, Val Duron, but see other options below
Ascent:	1350m
Descent:	1350m
Via ferrata:	850m
Approximate time:	8–10 hours
Highest altitude:	2852m
or	
Grade:	4, Seriousness: C
Departure point:	Gasthof Dialer – see below
Ascent:	930m
Descent:	930m
Via ferrata:	850m
Approximate time:	8 hours
Note:	safety rope advised

This is a fairly serious and, from Val di Fassa, a relatively remote route.

You can complete the route from Campitello in a single (but long) day, but by using a mountain base you could complete FASSA 2 (Sentiero Massimiliano) in one afternoon and then FASSA 1 the following day. For an overnight base and to check route conditions, contact Rif. Alpe di Tires (2440m, tel. 0471 727958). For a more expensive (even luxurious) option, try Gasthof Dialer (2145m, tel. 0471 727922). Approaches to Rif. Alpe di Tires are set out below, but if you choose to stay at Dialer (shown on maps as Casa del Scillar TCI (Touring Club Italia)) you are allowed to drive there from Alpe di Suisi along roads which are closed to general traffic.

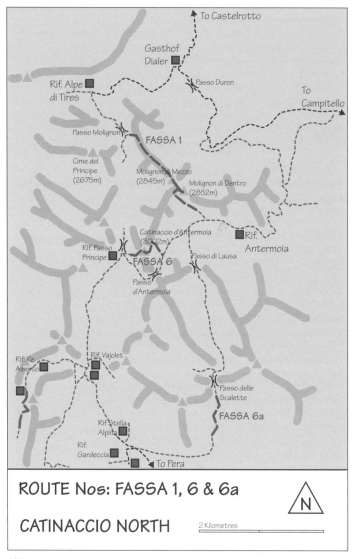

ROUTE Nos: FASSA 1, 6 & 6a

CATINACCIO NORTH

2 Kilometres

There are four approaches to Rif. Alpe di Tires:

* from the west, via Tires/Lavina Bianca and Val Ciamin/Tschamintal, 3½ to 4 hours,
* from the north, using the Panorama chairlift (June to October, 0900 to 1700) from Compaccio in Alpe di Siusi (charge for parking), 2½ hours,
* from the east via Campitello and Val Duron, 2½ hours if using the jeep taxi, and
* from the south, in 2½ hours from Rif. Vajolet.

Although it is potentially one of the longest options, the eastern approach from **Campitello Val Duron** is recommended, as this enables you to either simply climb this route and return the same day, or do both FASSA 1 and FASSA 2 over two days.

It is possible to arrange for a jeep taxi in Campitello to take you up Val Duron by contacting either by Prinoth Leonado (tel. 0462 750241) or Taxi Volpe (tel. 0336 352881). You can meet the taxi pick-up in the village. Alternatively you can drive up Val Duron on a narrow metalled road to a parking point at about 1500m (this is the limit for public vehicular access), and be picked up by the taxi from there. The jeep taxi fare as far as Rif. Micheluzzi (1860m) is inexpensive; the journey takes 10 minutes and will save you an hour's walking (Rif. Micheluzzi was being renovated at the time of writing).

Follow a path to the right of and behind the rifugio (signed Alpe di Suisi/Antermoia), and in 15 minutes there is a small bar at Lino Brach. Continue on the good track (path 532) along Val Duron to pass the junction of path 578 (your return route from VF Laurenzi) in a further 10 minutes. The track continues along the pretty valley with the walls of Molignon, whose ridge VF Laurenzi traverses, rising vertically at the head of the valley. Follow the track up to Passo Duron (2204m) and then continue along track 4 to Rif. Alpe di Tires (2441m), where you can stop for well-earned refreshment. This is a total climb from Campitello of over 900m and takes about 2 ½ hours (allow an extra hour if not using the jeep taxi).

However, if you are happy with a bumpy hour in the jeep taxi and don't mind the more expensive fare, it is possible to negotiate a ride from Campitello up to Rif. Alpe di Tires.

Whilst this is a long day, involving a good deal of walking, it is in an area of extraordinarily attractive mountains. It will also provide you with exposed situations to take your breath away during the traverse of the Molignon ridge! For this reason, and the intermittent nature of the protection on some of the most airy passages, we urge you to consider carrying a safety rope, particularly if any member of your party has limited experience of via ferrata climbing. The route can be, and is, climbed in either direction, although a traverse from north to south is recommended.

If starting from **Gasthof Dialer**, take the service road up to Rif. Alpe di Tires (this will take you about 45 minutes), where the large wind turbine comes as a surprise in this setting, particularly as it stands on the very boundary of the Scilliar (Schlern) Natural Park.

To approach the route from Rif. Alpe di Tires, head south on path 3a-554 and on up the easily angled slabby wall protected by a rather unnecessary cable. The track turns left (south-east) at the top of the slab and continues along a broad, rounded ridge, heading towards the main Molignon ridge. At Passo de Molignon (2598m), the main path continues southwards into the heart of the Catinaccio group, whilst Via Ferrata Laurenzi is signposted up to the left (east). An easy scramble up the slope takes you to the start of the route, with its standard format CAI sign about safe use of equipment. You are now at an altitude of about 2650m, and will have taken about 45–50 minutes from Rif. Alpe di Tires.

The climb begins with an easy scramble up a broken rib, protected by about 20m of cable. The protection ends as the angle eases slightly up to the pleasantly airy ridge above. The ridge soon widens out into a fairly broad plateau, and whilst the track is waymarked and cairned, it is no place to be in poor visibility or unstable weather. About 20 minutes after the start of the

Climbers on the exposed ridge of Molignon, Via Ferrata Laurenzi

via ferrata, a couple of closely adjoining subsidiary summits rise out of the plateau at an altitude of about 2750m. The second of these overlooks a broken saddle with an airy ridge beyond; this is the start of the real action! The protection resumes to safeguard the descent into the saddle, which is immediately very exposed, although technically quite straightforward. The exposure continues unabated for the traverse of the ridge beyond, the key to which is to select footholds at a comfortable level rather than be tempted to climb too high. This section of the route will occupy some 20–30 minutes before the difficulties ease and the protection becomes intermittent, although the scrambling is as airy as it comes!

The protection resumes once more as you embark on the next difficult passage, an undulating traverse through a succession of small broken pinnacles, some of which are bypassed on the east, and some on the west side of the ridge. This passage of the route culminates in the descent of a 30m buttress; the climbing is steep and not always well provided with holds. Whilst the protection is good, relatively inexperienced climbers might welcome the security of a top rope for this rather awkward descent. You now find yourself in a narrow little gap, from which the route continues across a broken slab. Whilst there is no cable to safeguard the traverse, a line of metal hoops drilled into the rock provides adequate security. A few metres beyond the slab, a shallow cave at an altitude of about 2700m contains the route book. From the start of the ferrata to this point will have taken around 1½ hours; more if any ropework has been employed.

A slope of broken rock now leads to yet another passage of relatively easy, but strikingly exposed, ridge walking cum scrambling. Once more the cable has deserted you, but occasional steel bolts, recently installed, provide belay points if you need to get the rope out again.

An easy trudge up to the summit of Molignon di Mezzo (2845m) follows, so you can now begin to appreciate the superb views which have been unfolding in all directions. Excluding any extra time for rope work, you will have been climbing for about 2 hours since the start of the ferrata. This is not quite the highest point of the ridge; a 5 minute stroll will take you on to Molignon di Dentro (2852m), past the waymarked route down to your right (south-west) which you must take next for the descent. This begins with a steep and exposed zigzag path, waymarked, but again devoid of any protection. As the descent steepens, intermittent lengths of cable safeguard the more difficult steps on what is now a very broken broad rib. This passage culminates in a very steep, and quite difficult, descent of a buttress on excellent rock. Whilst the protection is good, this is another passage where a top rope might be appreciated by less experienced climbers. You are now at about 2700m, and a CAI sign about safety confirms that you are at the end of the via ferrata, having taken about 20–30 minutes from the summit.

Below you, in the broad Vallon de Antermoia, path 584 is clearly visible. This runs eastwards to Lago de Antermoia and its adjoining rifugio, although neither is visible at the moment. Waymarks now lead down a broken rib, with an easy-angled scree-filled gully alongside to your left. Where the rib steepens uncomfortably, take to the gully and make your way down to the valley bottom, aiming for the large, prominent boulder adjoining the main track. Once there, at an altitude of about 2520m, you will find a signpost for VF Laurenzi to guide those who choose to do the route in reverse and make a clockwise circuit, with a south to north traverse of the ridge. This approach to the route would be up the left hand of the two closely adjoining gullies. A 10 minute stroll now takes you past the lake and on to the rifugio (2499m, not 2599m as some editions of the Tabacco maps claim); by now, you will feel a drink is more than justified! However, you now have either a 2 hour walk to get back to your car at the guest house, or a walk-out down Val Duron to Campitello in about the same time. The route is straightforward enough, however, utilising path 580 as far as Passo

Ciaragole (2282m) and path 555 down to the floor of Val Duron. The sting in the tail, if you are heading back to Gasthof Dialer, is the 160m trudge up the rough track to Passo Duron (2168m), overlooking the guest house. If your destination is Rif. Alpe di Tires you have a further 270m to climb! Either way you will have enjoyed an unforgettable mountain day.

FASSA 2:
GRANDE DENTE DI TERRAROSSA AND SENTIERO MASSIMILIANO

Although this is an easy route, it is quite spectacular and definitely not for the faint-hearted, as there are some tricky unprotected climbing moves in very exposed positions along the ridge.

Grade:	2, Seriousness: B
Departure point:	Campitello, or Lavina Bianca, or Alpe di Siusi
Ascent:	1300m
Descent:	1300m
Via ferrata:	200m
Approximate time:	6–10 hours (or 3 hour round-trip from Rif. Alpe di Tires)
Highest altitude:	2655m

This route is in the Val di Fassa section as it is best climbed from Rif. Alpe di Tires (see approach details in FASSA 1 above).

From the back of Rif. Alpe di Tires (2441m) the route is signposted Maximilian Way, initially ascending the Grande Dente di Terrarossa 2653m (around 200m of ascent) in about 30–40 minutes. First of all a short walk leads to a short section of cable, then further walking and more cables lead to a col, where there is the first stunning view down to Alpe di Suisi. From the col, cables continue up to the left and then onto an unprotected airy crest leading to the summit, from which there are great views.

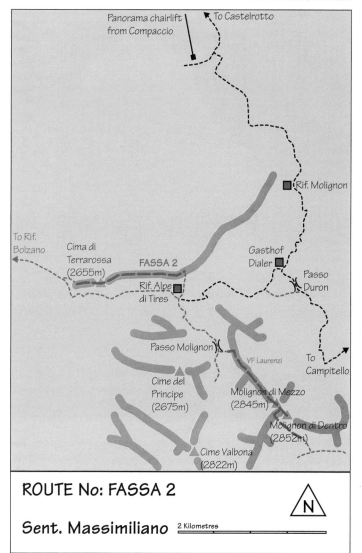

Panorama chairlift
from Compaccio

To Castelrotto

Rif. Molignon

Gasthof
Dialer

Passo
Duron

To Rif.
Bolzano

Cima di
Terrarossa
(2655m)

FASSA 2

Rif. Alpe
di Tires

Passo Molignon

VF Laurenzi

To
Campitello

Cime del
Principe
(2675m)

Molignon di Mezzo
(2845m)

Molignon di Dentro
(2852m)

Cime Valbona
(2822m)

ROUTE No: FASSA 2

Sent. Massimiliano

2 Kilometres

N

Descending through the rock gap on Grande Terrarossa

To get to Sentiero Massimiliano (Maximilian Way) descend west down zigzags and through a rock archway to climb steeply down wires for about 25m and then along the airy, unprotected ridge! A few minutes along the ridge a 5m chimney is down-climbed on good rock, but with only a single metal ring for protection. At the end of the ridge pass a sign 'Notausteig/Rientro d'Emergenza' (this is an emergency escape route down to Rif. Alpe di Tires, and should only be used as such).

From here a mixture of free climbing and wire protection ascends to the summit of Cima de Terrarossa (2655m); this takes about 1½ hours and involves around 150m of decent and ascent.

What protection there was is now over, and from the summit of Cima di Terrarossa descend about 100m (5 minutes) to the junction of path 3–4. If you have used either the westerly or northerly approaches, this path goes west to give a return to Alpe di Siusi and then either on to Rif. Bolzano for a return to Lavina Bianca or north along Sentiero del Turisti to Compaccio. However, to return to Rif. Alpe di Tires head south-east on path 3–4, descending a further 100m and traversing back to the rifugio in around 30 minutes. At Rif. Alpe di Tires you can either stay the night to complete Via Ferrata Laurenzi (FASSA 1) the next day, or return directly to Val Duron by retracing your ascent route down paths 4 and 532. Your return time for the descent from Rif. Alpe di Tires to the car park in Val Duron 1500m will be about 2½ hours.

FASSA. PASSO COSTALUNGA – CATINACCIO

Passo Costalunga is the southern limit of the Catinaccio Group. In winter it is a pleasant skiing area with access by means of the Super Dolomiti ski pass, and the area therefore provides plenty of accommodation. To the west is the Trentino valley, producer of fine wines, and Bolzano, an interesting town and home of the Ice Man. The preserved body of Otzi, the Ice Man, was discovered in the Otztal Glacier, where he had remained since he fell into the glacier several thousand years ago. The body can now be seen in the museum at Bolzano. The three routes in this section are accessed from Passo Costalunga. None is especially hard, but all provide interesting outings and fine mountain days in both spectacular and famous scenery. The only drawback is the area's accessibility and popularity, which tends to make it fairly busy in peak season.

FASSA 3:

FERRATA MASARE

Although there are a number of places where some slightly technical down-climbing is required, the ferratas are essentially a way of enjoying a good mountain day along a ridge without any long uphill climbs. It is not especially difficult at any point, but there are some quite exposed sections to negotiate.

Grade:	2, Seriousness: B
Departure point:	Hotel Alpenrose, Passo Costalungo (Karer Pass)
Ascent:	900m
Descent:	900m
Via ferrata:	400m
Approximate time:	7½ hours with Roda de Vael option, or 4 hours if climbed on its own
Highest altitude:	2727m (2806 with option)

An excellent combination of routes, which are recommend as an excellent long day out, although a choice of options is outlined if you require a shorter day. The end-to-end route of Ferrata Masare and ascent of Roda de Vael works its way along, up and down a series of mountain ridges over a period of 3–3½ hours from the first summit at Punta Masare to Passo di Vaiolon.

Approach the route using the Paolina chairlift from Hotel Alpenrose below Passo Costalunga (chairlift opening hours June to October are 0800 to 1215, and 1330 to 1800; reductions for members of OeAV, DAV, CAI). From the top of the chairlift follow signs to Rif. Roda de Vael along path 539/549 (the chairlift ride and walk to Rif. Roda de Vael take about 45 minutes). From the rifugio Ferrata Masare is clearly signposted, and the path works its way up towards the left-hand (south) end of Punta Masare – at first, through a large boulder field, and then by zigzags up to the first wire protection (about 30 minutes from the rifugio).

The ferrata route is easy to follow, although protection is not continuous and there are some unprotected

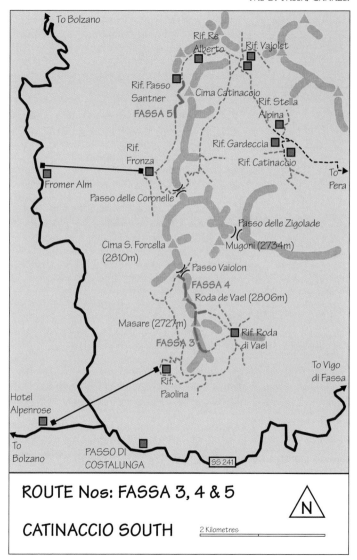

To Bolzano

Rif. Re Alberto

Rif. Vajolet

Rif. Passo Santner

Cima Catinacojo

FASSA 5

Rif. Stella Alpina

Rif. Gardeccia

Rif. Fronza

Rif. Catinaccio

To Pera

Fromer Alm

Passo delle Coronelle

Passo delle Zigolade

Cima S. Forcella (2810m)

Mugoni (2734m)

Passo Vaiolon

FASSA 4

Roda de Vael (2806m)

Masare (2727m)

FASSA 3

Rif. Roda di Vael

To Vigo di Fassa

Rif. Paolina

Hotel Alpenrose

To Bolzano

PASSO DI COSTALUNGA

SS 241

ROUTE Nos: FASSA 3, 4 & 5

CATINACCIO SOUTH

2 Kilometres

N

moves in quite exposed, airy situations. The majority of people seem to favour the south to north traverse, which involves more down-climbing than travelling north to south, but has the advantage of going with the flow of others doing the route. After about 2 hours and a significant loss of height Ferrata Masare comes to an end, and there is a walk along a path on a steep grassy hillside. At this point there is a possible escape route, involving another down-climbing ferrata, with a direct return to Rifugio de Vael, which takes about 30 minutes.

Continuing onwards and upwards to VF Roda de Vael (again clearly signposted) the route climbs on a zigzag path to Forcella del Diavolo (2560m), where you will see an amazing hole (complete with an enclosed metal cross) in the rock wall to the right of the path. At the top of the grassy slope left of the hole in the rock the ferrata descends steeply to the right, with some testing moves, down to a col with dirty, broken rock and steep gullies to either side. After an awkward first move out of the col, there is a short ladder followed by unconnected sections of wire protection before the angle of ascent eases and Roda de Vael summit (2806m) is reached by a zigzag path directly to the summit cross and route book. Time required from leaving the junction at the escape route point to the summit is about 1–1¼ hours.

Descent from the summit has good protection and continues north down to Passo di Vaiolon in about 30 minutes. From Passo di Vaiolon descend west down path 551; this zigzags down an impressive gully until turning left and traversing below some awesome rock walls. Continue the descent, following waymarks downhill and generally west until path 549 is reached. Follow path 549 south on an excellent undulating traverse until a path zigzags downhill on a grassy slope directly to the chairlift (about an hour from Passo di Viaolon). Your overall round-trip from Rif. Paolina will be around 7–7½ hours.

An alternative shorter day from Rif. Roda de Vael would be to climb Ferrata Masare or Roda de Vael individually. For Ferrata Masare use the ascent described

above but return direct to Rif. Roda de Vael and then retrace path 549 to the chairlift (5–5½ hours). For options on climbing Roda de Vael direct, see route FASSA 4 below.

Climbers on the VF Masare ridge (photo: Collett's Mountain Holidays)

FASSA 4:
VF RODA DE VAEL

Grade:	1, Seriousness: B
Departure point:	Alpenrose Hotel, Passo Costalungo (Karer Pass)
Ascent:	700m
Descent:	700m,
Via ferrata:	200m
Approximate time:	4 to 4½ hours
Highest altitude:	2806m

Roda de Vael can be climbed on its own or (the recom-mended option) combined with VF Masare to make a full mountain day – see FASSA 3 above. In fact even climbing Roda de Vael alone, which is a very easy ferrata, provides two options.

The better of the two options for climbing Roda de Vael is to make an ascent from the northern side of the moun-tain. Starting from the top of the Paolina chairlift, take a zigzag path directly behind the chairlift station until it joins path 549. Follow path 549 generally north on an excellent undulating traverse for about 1km, until path 551 branches north-east to zigzag steeply uphill to Passo di Vaiolon (about 1½ hours). From Passo di Vaiolon fol-low a waymarked path south and again steeply uphill; this leads to good protection on steep but easy ground, reaching the summit in around 1 hour from the pass. Descend from the summit reversing the ascent back to the north down to Passo di Vaiolon and back to the Paolina chairlift; this will take around 4½ hours in total.

The other option for climbing Roada de Vael is ini-tially the same as for the approach to VF Masare (FASSA 3 above), but avoids the full traverse of the ridge. Follow signs from the top of the chair to Rif. Roda de Vael along path 539/549 (from the bottom of the chairlift to Rif. Roda de Vael in about 45 minutes). From the rifugio, ascend a waymarked path to the north-west to Forcella del Diavolo (2560m). From here, at the top of the grassy slope left of the hole in the rock (see FASSA 3 above), the ferrata descends steeply to the right with some testing moves down to a col with dirty, broken rock and steep gullies to either side. After an awkward first move out of the col, there is a short ladder followed by unconnected sections of wire protection before the angle of ascent eases and Roda de Vael (2806m) summit is reached by a zigzag path directly to the summit cross and route book. Allow a time of about 2 hours from Rif. Roda de Vael to the summit. Descent from Roda de Vael is detailed in FASSA 3 above.

FASSA 5: SANTNER PASS

Grade	2, Seriousness A
Departure point:	Frommer Alm, 1743m to Rif. A. Fronza 2339m
Ascent:	900m
Descent:	900m
Via ferrata:	300m
Approximate time:	6 hours (return from top of chairlift)
Highest altitude:	2734m

Although the via ferrata element is easy and rather limited, this is a good mountain round-trip which can be completed in around 6 hours.

Access to the start of the route is gained by using the Laurin chairlift from Frommer Alm on the road from Passo Costalunga towards Passo Nigra; this operates from the beginning of June until mid-October, with longer operating times in July and August (0800 to 1215, 1330 to 1800). A return trip on the chairlift is recommended (reductions for OeAV, DAV, and CAI club members); note that it is a long ride, taking 20 minutes each way. Because of the easy access, this is a very busy route in high season.

*Climbers on the
Santner pass ferrata
(photo: Collett's
Mountain Holidays)*

Rif. A. Fronza is at the top of the chairlift, and from here path 542/550 leads directly uphill, with some scrambling and a very short section of wire, to where (in a few minutes only) the paths divide. Path 542 leads off to the left (north) and in around 30 minutes reaches an ascending ramp with some fairly exposed (but easy) scrambling. The route is obvious and well waymarked as it climbs through a series of interesting gullies until (after climbing a short ladder) more continuous wire protection is reached (over an hour from the start). The route passes through a cleft between two rock walls and then descends to cross a wide gully; this gully can be full of hard packed snow in early season, and later on is an area of loose broken rocks and earth. A final section of wire leads up from this gully to Passo Santner (total time around 2 hours, but will take longer if the route is busy).

From Passo Santner a good path (542) leads quickly down to Rif. Re Alberto (Gartlhutte) with panoramic views of the famous Vajolet towers. Path 542 continues downhill from here towards Rif. Vajolet on steep ground with some wire ropes, which are useful handrails. Path 542 need not be followed all the way down to Rif. Vajolet, as at about 2300m a path (not signed, nor on maps) traverses to the right immediately below a rock buttress; this leads around the southern side of Catinaccio. The descent from Passo Santner to here takes about 45 minutes.

The traverse path is quite narrow and exposed at first, with one particularly airy corner, before it ascends through some boulders to join path 541, which comes up from Rif. Vajolet. Path 541 now continues uphill, heading south, until it joins path 550 and Passo Coronelle is clearly signposted. Path 550 heads steeply uphill on zigzags to Passo Coronelle, and then continues down, again steeply, directly back to Rif. A. Fronza and the chairlift. The total return time from Passo Santner is 3–3½ hours.

FASSA. POZZA DI FASSA – CATINACCIO

Catinaccio d'Antermoia is the main mountain of this group, and the only one (just!) over 3000m. As mentioned in the introduction to the FASSA group, there are many places to use as a base to tackle these via ferratas, and Pozza is just one of them. Pozza has its own section in the guide because it is the easiest point of attack for Catinaccio's highest peak and via ferratas; the rest is fully explained in the route descriptions that follow. Rising above Pozza to the south-east is Sasso Dodici, the other route in this section, which is approached from the beautiful Valle San Nicolo.

FASSA 6:

CATINACCIO D'ANTERMOIA

Although an easy ferrata, there are some exposed, unprotected sections, particularly the final 50m along the ridge to the summit of Catinaccio d'Antermoia.

Grade:	2, Seriousness: B
Departure point:	Pera
Ascent:	1150m
Descent:	1150m
Via ferrata:	600m
Approximate time:	6–8 hours
Highest altitude:	3002m

The route can be climbed either west to east or east to west, with the favoured way appearing to be west to east, as described below (see map p.120). Note that Cima Catinaccio is a separate peak to the south-west of Catinaccio d'Antermoia above Passo Santner (see FASSA 5).

Reasonably easy access to and from this ferrata can be gained using the Bus Navette Gardeccia, which departs from Pera in Fassa from mid-June to mid-September. The uphill service runs from 0730 to 1230 and 1400 to 1830, and the downhill service from 0830 to 1230 and 1430 to 1900. This saves 600m of ascent and descent, with the cost of the return fare being a small price to pay for the effort saved (one-way tickets can be bought if required).

From Rif. Gardeccia follow path 546 up to Rif. Vajolet, and then path 584 to Passo Principe; this takes

2–3 hours and is very busy in high season. From Passo Principe an arrow on the right indicates the path up to the start of the ferrata, which is reached in about 5 minutes.

Just above Passo Principe, the route initially traverses off to the left along a ledge under an overhang, and then climbs unprotected, exposed ground until a short down-climb on a new (secure) ladder. The route follows cables (new in 2000) and waymarks, with alternating sections of protected and unprotected climbing, until the exposed summit ridge is reached. The total time for the ascent from Passo Principe will be around 1–1½ hours.

The descent is down the east ridge, and again follows new cables and waymarked, unprotected sections until the end of the ferrata at the head of Val d'Antermoia (50–60 minutes). From here there are two options for the return to Rif. Gardeccia.

- Ascend path 584 south-west to Passo Antermoia to return to Passo Principe and then continue south on path 584 back to Rif. Gardeccia (2–3 hours).
- Via Passo di Lausa and Scalette Path ferrata (see also FASSA 6a below): continue the descent into Val d'Antermoia and then follow path 583b up to Passo di Lausa; this is an obvious path, but it is not well waymarked until joining path 583 near the pass after about 30 minutes ascent.

From Passo di Lausa the route descends into an expansive glacial valley enclosed by impressive rocky ridges, one of which screens a second glacial valley which appears, after a while, on the right. The path then crosses a bridge (dam wall) and has a short ascent to Passo Scalette. From here the descent continues down a wide, rocky gully with a very short (less than 10 minutes) protected section; this is not particularly exposed and is quite easy to descend. At the end of the gully the path ascends slightly and then traverses through pine woods back to Rif. Gardeccia. Time from Passo Scalette to Rif. Gardeccia is about 1½ hours.

FASSA 6A:
SCALETTE PATH

Not really a ferrata route, although its ascent to Passo Scalette and on to Passo di Lausa gives a good walk with a short section of none too difficult scrambling, for which ferrata equipment is not essential. This route is quieter than that up to Passo Principe.

Grade:	1, Seriousness: A
Departure point:	Pera
Ascent:	400m
Descent:	400m
Via ferrata:	60m
Approximate time:	The route is only 1 hour from Rif. Gardeccia
Highest altitude:	2700m

The Scalette path is path 583 from Rif. Gardeccia. The short protected section would be reached (in ascent) in under an hour from the rifugio. By combining the descent of the Scalette path with an ascent of Catinaccio d'Antermoia, one can have a really satisfying mountain day (see map p.120); this is fully described above in route FASSA 6 above.

FASSA 7:
VF FRANCO GADOTTI –
SASSO DODICI AND SASS AUT

This is a fairly easy ferrata but a really good mountain day out, with superb panoramas of Catinaccio, Val di Fassa, Marmolada and the Sella Massif.

Grade:	2, Seriousness: C
Departure point:	Malga Crocifisso
Ascent:	1100m
Descent:	1100m
Via ferrata:	400m
Approximate time:	7–8 hours
Highest altitude:	2637m

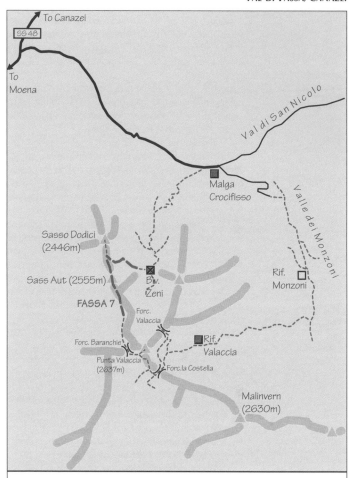

To Canazei

SS 48

To Moena

Val di San Nicolo

Valle dei Monzoni

Malga Crocifisso

Sasso Dodici (2446m)

Sass Aut (2555m)

FASSA 7

Biv. Zeni

Forc. Valaccia

Rif. Monzoni

Forc. Baranchie

Punta Valaccia (2637m)

Rif. Valaccia

Forc.la Costella

Malinvern (2630m)

ROUTE No: FASSA 7

VF Franco Gadotti

2 Kilometres

N

A plaque dedicates this ferrata to 'Franco Gadotti, Trento, 9.1.1955 to 20.7.1976'. The seriousness of this route is more indicative of the strenuousness and sometimes exposed nature of the path, rather than any via ferrata difficulty.

Approach by car from Pozza di Fassa towards San Nicolo along a minor tarmac road. There is good parking by the chapel at Malga Crocifisso, where the road splits for Val di San Nicolo and Valle dei Monzoni.

Although not shown on maps, path 615 bis starts about 200m back down the road below Malga Crocifisso. You then head steeply uphill to the south, with the path well waymarked as it zigzags up through pine forest to join the main path 615 coming up from Soldanella. In about 45 minutes from Malga Crocifisso you continue straight on uphill, with path 635 crossing from east to west. After passing some large boulders, 10 minutes further on at around 2000m, there is a short cabled section (water course when wet), which serves as a useful handrail for a short climb. In a further 20 minutes Bivacco Donato Zeni is reached, and 5 minutes further (up to the right) is the start of the ferrata, about 1½ hours from the car park.

The ascent is a mixture of protected sections and walking unprotected up narrow zigzag paths on steep ground. On the ferrata sections there are a couple of exposed moves, but the route is easy technically and the protection is very good. The wires appear to be fairly new (year 2000), though there is a notice at the start asking climbers to check the condition of the wires before climbing! At a wind-gap the route descends slightly to the left before following a rising traverse path around a classic glacial bowl. From the start of the ferrata to the Sasso Dodici ridge takes about an hour, and if it is clear the extra 10 minutes of ascent to the summit cross of Sasso Dodici are well worthwhile for the wonderful views down to Val di Fassa and beyond.

Retrace your steps back to the ridge heading south from Sasso Dodici, and the route (signposted 'Forcella Vallacia') leads up along ledges, with more ferrata sections and some unprotected walking leading onto grassy slopes and the summit of Sass Aut. Alternatively there is a traverse path, which leads around the eastern side of Sass Aut, giving a choice of avoiding the summit. From Sass Aut waymarks lead south to a large muddy gully, which has wire protection on its right. After about 100m of descent the wires lead down through a spectacular hole on the left through an enclosed gully beneath enormous wedged boulders with some steep down-climbing (always well protected). The descent continues for a further 100m until (at about 2400m) the wires come to an end and the via ferrata is over; this is about 50–60 minutes from the summit of Sasso Dodici.

A rising traverse now leads upwards, continuing in a southerly direction, with large rock walls on the left, until a wind-gap is reached. The path (well waymarked) now turns to the left (east), climbing up to the summit of Punta Vallacia (2637m) in about 45 minutes from the end of the ferrata. Again the panoramic views from the summit are superb, and total time for the ascent so far is 4–5 hours.

Descend to path 624, at first retracing your steps then continuing east down a ridge until a signpost (indicating several directions) shows that path 624 descends north into the open grassy bowl on the left. After a short while Rif. Vallaccia is passed, then path 603 is joined, which takes you past Rif. Monzoni (which has an amazing collection of various objects). Your final descent is easy walking down the road back to Malga Crocifisso, with the total time for descent from Punta Vallaccia (assuming you don't hang around) being less than 2 hours.

Fassa South-East – Moena and Falcade

Two of these routes, FASSA 8 and 9, are quite close to Moena, the main town at the southern end of Val di Fassa. FASSA 10 is rather remote and can also be accessed from Moena or, if you are based further east, from Agordo or Belluno (routes in these areas are covered in volume two of this guide). None of the routes in this section is especially difficult, though they are quality outings; and because these mountains are not quite as popular as some of the others in the guidebook, you may have a relatively quiet day. The views from Cima Bocche (FASSA 8) are as good as you will find anywhere in the Dolomites.

FASSA 8:
VIA ATTREZZATA DEL GRONTON

This is a very easy excursion, which follows an old First World War protected path over Cima del Gronton (2622m). There are some good cables, as the route follows ledges and staircases, but exposure is minimal, and it is arguable whether the cable is needed at all, except as perhaps a reassuring handrail in some places.

This route also requires the use of Tabacco sheets 22 and 14.

Grade:	1, Seriousness: A
Departure point:	Passo di Lusia
Ascent:	600m
Descent:	600m
Via ferrata:	250m
Approximate time:	4–4½ hours (plus 1 hour option to Cima Bocche)
Highest altitude:	2622m (plus option 2745m)

The views from Gronton and Cima Bocche must rate as some of the best in the Dolomites, with a tremendous panorama taking in Pale San Martino, Latemar, Catinaccio, Sasso Lungo, Sella towers, Piz Boe, Marmolada, Pelmo and Civetta. So for an easy and very pleasant mountain day do this route in clear weather and enjoy it, even though the ferrata is one of the easiest you will find.

The route is approached from Passo di Lusia, above Moena; this can be reached in two ways, either by car or by gondola. By car take the SS346 east from Moena for about 2km, and then it's a 5km drive up (quite steeply at times) a bumpy gravel road, which is actually path 621 on the map starting at 1298m. It's first gear nearly all the

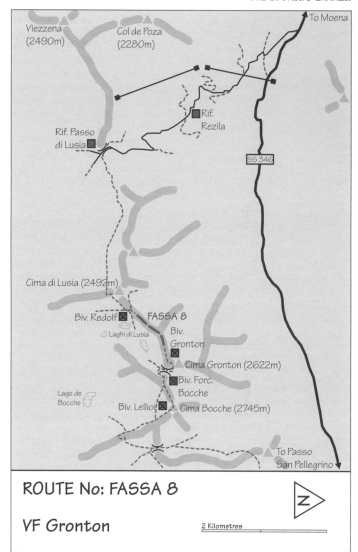

Viezzena (2490m)
Col de Poza (2280m)
To Moena
Rif. Rezila
Rif. Passo di Lusia
SS 346
Cima di Lusia (2492m)
Biv. Redolf
FASSA 8
Biv. Gronton
Laghi di Lusia
Cima Gronton (2622m)
Biv. Forc. Bocche
Lago de Bocche
Biv. Lellioi
Cima Bocche (2745m)
To Passo San Pellegrino

ROUTE No: FASSA 8

VF Gronton

2 Kilometres

N

way and takes about 25 minutes – passing places are minimal. Using the two-stage gondola, Funivia Lusia, takes you to 2272m above Passo di Lusia, and a wide track (path 614) leads down to the pass; this 200m descent has to be reclimbed at the end of the day, so using the gondola will add about 45 minutes to the timing from Passo di Lusia. Funivia Lusia operates from the end of June to the middle of September from 0830 to 1200 and 1430 to 1800.

From Passo di Lusia (2055m) ascend path 633 for around an hour in a north-east then east direction to arrive at spot height 2425m, where a sign points to Laghi di Lusia straight ahead and left uphill to Cima di Lusia. The short ascent to Cima di Lusia, spot height 2492m, is worthwhile for the view down to Moena, but you must return to the sign to continue towards Laghi di Lusia. Just before reaching Bivacco S Redolf 'Via Attrezzata' is signed to the left. As mentioned in the introduction this is a cabled route, but use of ferrata equipment is not really necessary except for the very unsure. The route leads along ledges and stairs on the north side of Cima Gronton (2622m), ending just below the actual summit.

Descend from Gronton to Forcella di Bocche (2363m), having taken 3 hours from Passo di Lusia. It is possible to return directly from here to Passo di Lusia, but if time permits (an additional hour required), the ascent (and return descent) of Cima Bocche (2745m) will reward you with the unparalleled view of the Dolomites mentioned above. Return from Forcella di Bocche (generally south-west) back to Passo di Lusia along path 633 in 1–1½ hours.

As with many ferrata routes you could work out other options on this day. One of those which may appeal, if using bus and gondola ascent from Moena, would be to continue from Cima Bocche on path 626, and then descend north on path 628 to reach Passo San Pellegrino, where you could return to Moena by bus, or even stay overnight in order to do Via Ferrata Bepi Zac (FASSA 9) the next day. Check bus times locally.

FASSA 9:
VIA FERRATA BEPI ZAC –
CIMA DI COSTABELLA

Grade:	1, Seriousness: B
Departure point:	Paradiso chailift, Passo San Pellegrino
Ascent:	900m
Descent:	900m
Via ferrata:	250m
Approximate time:	5–5½ hours (return from top of chairlift)
Highest altitude:	2762m
Note:	torch useful

Another easy ferrata which follows the ridge of Cima Costabella (2762m).

A more difficult option of extending the day by climbing Cima d'Uomo (3010m) should be available in the future (see note at the end of this route). Via Ferrata Bepi Zac has recently been restored; it follows the line of one of the main Austrian front lines of the First World War, where thousands of lives were lost as the Austrians managed to stop the Italian advance into Val di Fassa. A number of fortifications are passed en route.

From Passo San Pellegrino the day is made easier by taking the Costabella chairlift to Rif. Paradiso (2150m); this operates from the end of June to the middle of September from 0830 to 1220 and 1420 to 1750. From the top of the chair follow path 604 to Rif. Passo le Selle (Bergvagabunden Hutte); this is a pleasant, easy climb which takes about an hour. You could, of course, go to Passo le Selle and stay the night at the rifugio (which has 20 bed spaces, tel. 0437 4039331) for an early start the next morning.

At the pass there is a monument to the First World War with a Madonna, various memorabilia and an eerie

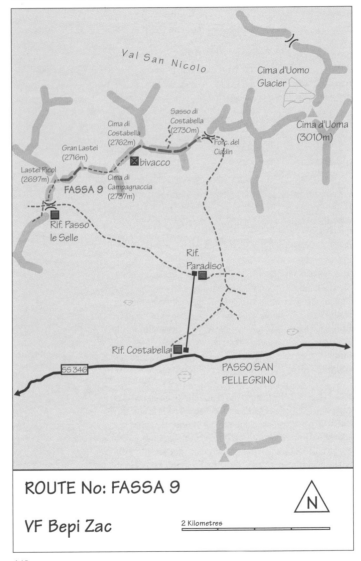

Val San Nicolo

Cima d'Uomo
Glacier

Cima di
Costabella
(2762m)

Sasso di
Costabella
(2730m)

Cima d'Uoma
(3010m)

Gran Lastei
(2716m)

Forc. del
Ciadin

☒bivacco

Lastei Picol
(2697m)

Cima di
Campagnaccia
(2737m)

FASSA 9

Rif. Passo
le Selle

Rif.
Paradiso

Rif. Costabella

PASSO SAN
PELLEGRINO

SS 346

ROUTE No: FASSA 9

VF Bepi Zac

2 Kilometres

N

barbed-wire cross as its centre-piece. Just beyond this is an impressive plaque in honour of mountaineer and fer-rata builder Bepi Zac. The path 637 Costabella Bepi Zac heads uphill to the north, climbing fairly steeply to Lastei Picol (2697m) in 15–20 minutes. The first cable is now reached, but at this point the path is wide with not much exposure, so it's a useful handrail only.

The route now continues easily along the ridge to Gran Lastei (2716m) and on towards Cima di Campagnaccia (2737m), passing through a short tunnel. A torch would be useful in some of the tunnels later on the ridge, but most of them are short and so the torch is not a necessity. 10 minutes from the first tunnel a second one is reached, and this leads to a ledge where a wartime bivacco has been restored (it would have been a grim place to have to spend the winter equipped with the gear of 1915). Ferrata kit is useful now as an exposed descent leads down to a section of easy walking, follow-ing waymarks and passing extensive areas of wartime trenches to reach quite a long tunnel in about 45 min-utes from the restored bivacco.

After this tunnel a descent on a 50m stretch of cable leads down to a sign at Cresta di Costabella (2715m). Path 637 descends north into Val San Nicolo, but VF Bepi Zac continues along the ridge towards Forcella del Ciadin, signposted 10 minutes. However, after only a couple of minutes walking a large rock buttress (Sasso di Costabella, 2730m) towers above you, with a big hole high up on its face; this was a wartime look-out point. An easy path leads around the rock on its left (north) side, but it is much more interesting to ascend the ferrata signed '637 bis Variante Osservaterio S di Costabella' up a gully on the right. This leads up to the observatory, where you look out through the big hole in the rock and appreciate what a strategic look-out point it must have been.

From the observatory, the ferrata continues down the other side, on good cables, leading into a steep downhill tunnel which has a series of wooden staircases at the bottom before rejoining the easy path which comes

Reconstructed wooden ladders on the Bepi Zac route

round from the side of Sasso di Costabella. From here a short descent leads to Forcella di Ciadin (2664m), having taken 2–2½ hours from Passo le Selle (or even longer if you have spent more time exploring the First World War ruins).

To complete the return, descend south on a steep zigzag path, then steep scree towards Passo San Pelegrino. The path continues through scattered limestone boulders and then meadows, reaching Rif. Paradiso and the top of the chairlift in an hour from the forcella. Either return by the chair or walk down to Passo San Pelegrino in a further 30–40 minutes.

Note

Work is taking place to install ferrata protection for the ascent of Cima d'Uomo, thereby making it possible to extend the VF Bepi Zac day to climb Cima d'Uomo or even to climb Cima d'Uomo on its own. From Forcella Ciadin (see above) there is a waymarked route, Itinero Alpinisto, which leads along ledges, first up then down and through a narrow gap, continuing on steep ground to reach a very unpleasant gully on the left. At the top of the gully (2720m) the path goes across steep ground (subject to early season snow retention) to the left, and continues upwards before descending to a col and the final ascent of Cima d'Uomo. There are cables for 200–300m on the final ascent to the summit, an ascent which has to be reversed as the way down. This route is not graded, nor can advice be given on its condition until the ferrata is completed. Updated information should be available from the Costabella chairlift.

FASSA 10:
VF PAOLIN-PICCOLIN –
CIMA DELL'AUTA ORIENTALE

Grade:	3, Seriousness: B
Departure point:	Colmean
Ascent:	1300m
Descent:	1300m
Via ferrata:	300m
Approximate time:	7–8 hours
Highest altitude:	2624m

This outlying route is reached from the Moena to Cencenighe road (SS346) via Passo San Pellegrino by turning

This ferrata is a long mountain day with 1300m ascent and descent; it is fairly steep most of the time, with very little level walking. The ferrata is relatively easy, but has some interesting sections, and the descent by the Via Normale is exposed and steep in places.

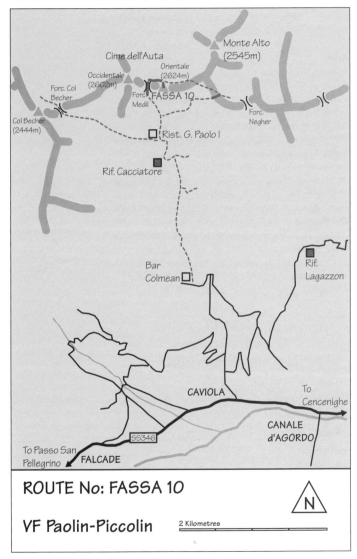

Monte Alto
(2545m)

Cime dell'Auta

Occidentale
(2602m)

Orientale
(2624m)

Forc. Col
Becher

Forc.
Medil

FASSA 10

Forc.
Negher

Col Becher
(2444m)

Rist. G. Paolo I

Rif. Cacciatore

Bar
Colmean

Rif.
Lagazzon

CAVIOLA

To
Cencenighe

CANALE
d'AGORDO

SS346

To Passo San
Pellegrino

FALCADE

ROUTE No: FASSA 10

VF Paolin-Piccolin

2 Kilometres

N

off in Caviola and driving up to the hamlet of Colmean. There is a good car park at the roadhead, close to Bar Colmean. From the summit there are some wonderful views, particularly of the south wall of the Marmolada.

From the car park follow waymarked path 689 which leads up (at times steeply) through the pine woods to Rif. Cacciatori in around 50–60 minutes. The rifugio is only open during August, so don't rely on refreshment here. Continue uphill to the left, following the path signposted 'Cime dell'Auta Via Ferrata and Via Normale M2602'. In a further 10 minutes Rif. Giovanni Paolo 1 is reached (a simple log cabin, and again no refreshments!), and the path to the ferrata is waymarked to the right just below the rifugio. The path continues uphill, and in about 45 minutes (on steep and stony paths) the route for the via ferrata is signposted to the left (along with Forcella Col Becher) and 'Normale Cima Auta 689' to the right (the descent route returns to this point). From here the ferrata is reached in about 20 minutes, first up a tedious scree slope and then by traversing to the left under some rock walls. The total time from car park to the start of the ferrata is around 3 hours.

From the sign 'Ferrata delle Auta Paolin-Piccolin' 1969 ascend a ladder and then some stemples, with a couple of awkward moves on a steep wall (note that the stemple pitch does not have a separate ferrata wire alongside to clip onto). After the first 50m on good rock, the route then follows the left side of a loose scree gully, where care and awareness is required if there are other people on the route. Some new cable takes the route off the scree on the left-hand side of the gully and follows a line up a steep chimney, which takes drainage after rain. The route continues on rocks on the left side of the gully, arriving at Forcella Medil about 45 minutes from the start of the ferrata.

From Forcella Medil follow waymarks heading east on the ridge towards Cima dell'Auta Orientale; this leads quickly to a short ladder and further ferrata protection to climb directly up slabs on good rock until a ledge leads to the left, past a small cave, to a small saddle. The summit of Cima dell'Auta Orientale is reached up to the right in a few more minutes. For the total ascent from car park to summit allow 4–5 hours.

Descent is made by Via Normale, returning to the saddle and going over a small summit on the right. There is some wire protection as the route descends to the east on the north side of Cima dell'Auta; this is often a steep, narrow path and feels quite exposed in places. In about 30 minutes a helicopter pad (down to the left) is passed, and the path continues with a short ascent before going to the right of some crumbling basalt (volcanic looking) towers. Via Normale is now signposted down to the right descending 'Sentiero Attrezzato Attilio Bortolli 1983', initially down a steep, loose slope and then along a narrow path under large rock walls to the right to rejoin the ascent route in about 50 minutes from the summit. From here you retrace the ascent route, returning to the car park in around 2 hours, giving a total descent of around 3 hours.

FASSA. CANAZEI – MARMOLADA

Canazei is the main town at the head of Val di Fassa and is covered in detail in the introduction to this section. Marmolada, at 3343m, is the highest mountain in the Dolomites. Punta Serauta is one of the four Grade 5 routes in this guidebook. This section hosts some of the best that the Dolomites has to offer. You will appreciate on reading each of the more serious route descriptions that you will need some luck with the weather if you are going to climb these via ferratas, as well as mountain experience and fitness.

FASSA 11:
VF DEI FINANZIERI – COLAC

Grade:	3, Seriousness: C
Departure point:	Alba, then top of Ciampac cable car
Ascent:	700m
Descent:	700m
Via ferrata:	600m
Approximate time:	4 hours plus possible extension (see FASSA 12)
Highest altitude:	2715m

Although a long and fairly strenuous ferrata, this route is not a long day; it is, however, a serious undertaking and should not be taken lightly.

The route is easily approached using the Ciampac cable car from Alba, which runs from the end of June until early September from 0830 to 1700. As the ferrata faces north-west it may be cold (even icy) early in the day (and even all day, as it stays in the shade). Descend the skiing piste on the left as you come out of the cable car and then take a marked path to the right which leads past a small reservoir and then up scree to the start of the route.

The route was completely re-cabled (during 1999–2000), but despite the improved protection there are still large sections of the route with loose rock (and the occasional loose peg!), so care is needed, especially if there are a lot of people on the route. Also, due to the risk of stone-fall on this route, a helmet is absolutely essential.

At the start there is a short cable, then a path leads to the main cable. The route rises up a slabby corner (often damp), which takes drainage even after several dry days. Rounding the corner there is a steep slab, with some stemples, which leads up to an even steeper series of stemples (which have replaced some old ladders) with a very exposed feeling, even though you are well protected. Although the route then eases off a little after this, the

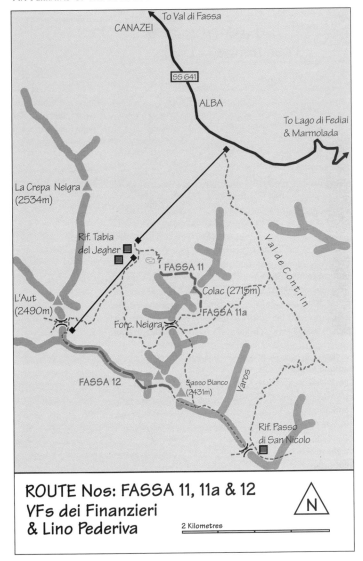

ROUTE Nos: FASSA 11, 11a & 12
VFs dei Finanzieri
& Lino Pederiva

2 Kilometres

View up the slab pitch of Colac, which can be subject to icing

ascent keeps on going, giving a sustained ascent of around 2 hours. The summit has an airy feeling with good views of the Marmolada massif.

Descent is waymarked and painted with 'Ciampac' and arrows which lead down to the right through a gap in the rocks. The route then follows a clearly marked combination of wired and unprotected sections into a wide scree-filled gully, where the wires end and a path goes round to the right and on to the Forcia Neigra. The possible extension to Sasso Bianco (see FASSA 12) would make a much longer day with a lot of walking but little additional climbing, whereas the return to the cable car and (Rif. Tobia del Giagher for some refreshment per- haps) is an easy waymarked descent down path 613.

FASSA 11A:

ASCENT OF COLAC BY THE FERRATA

DESCENT ROUTE

Grade:	1, Seriousness: B
Departure point:	Alba, then top of Ciampac cable car
Ascent:	700m
Descent:	700m
Via ferrata:	200m
Approximate time:	4 hours
Highest altitude:	2715m

Quite simply this is the reverse of the descent route described above in FASSA 11. It is included as an easy via ferrata option for those who want to climb to the summit of Colac, but may not feel up to the technical difficulties involved in climbing Colac using the Finanzieri route.

From the top of the Ciampac cable car follow path 613 south past the rifugios and up to Forcia Neigra. Then follow the traverse path round the hillside to the left (north-east) and follow waymarks and cables to the summit of Colac; this will take around 2 hours. The descent is made by reversing the same route that you ascended, so you need to be confident of your down-climbing ability in order to make your return to the cable car.

Climbers on the descent from Colac

FASSA 12:
SENTERIO ATTREZATO LINO PEDERIVA – SASSO BIANCO

This route is little more than an exposed walk, with only short sections of protection on the more exposed passages. It is, however, a grand ridge, with superb views of the less familiar south side of Marmolada, and is well worth visiting if you feel like an easy day.

Grade:	1, Seriousness: A
Departure point:	Alba, then top of Ciampac cablecar
Ascent:	600m
Descent:	600m
Via ferrata:	200m
Approximate time:	4 hours
Highest altitude:	Ridge circa 2500m

Unusually, the ridge incorporates both dark volcanic rock as well as Dolomite limestone. This makes for a particularly wide variety both of wild flowers and of the butterflies which feed on them. There is also a wealth of wartime fortifications on Sasso Bianco and the Varos ridge, so the outing offers a good deal of interest to compensate for the lack of technical climbing difficulties.

The route can be undertaken as part of a circular walk from the top station of the two-stage Ciampac lift system, returning to the valley down Val de Contrin, which can be reached either by path 646 or 648.

Whilst this route is amongst the easiest in this guidebook, the basalt rock can be very slippery in wet conditions, so care is still needed.

If time permits, it is a splendid way of rounding off a day on Colac. If this is your choice, descend south-east from Forcia Neigra on path 613, passing below Croda Negra. On reaching the Sasso Bianco ridge, path 613b turns to the right (north-west) and leads along the ridge. Continue along the ridge to the top station of the chairlift and then head down on paths 613 and 644 back to the Ciampac cable car station.

View from the western end of the Sasso Bianco ridge with the Marmolada in the background

FASSA 13:

MARMOLADA WEST RIDGE TO PUNTA PENIA SUMMIT

This route is a high-grade via ferrata; it goes to the highest summit in the Dolomites and is regarded as a serious mountaineering excursion, with conditions subject to icing and quickly changing weather. Ice-axe, crampons and a full rope are essential companions on this route and after new snowfall, which may conceal crevasses. Previous experience of glacier crossing is recommended.

Grade:	4, Seriousness: C
Departure point:	Lago di Fedaia, Rifugio Plan del Fiaconni
Ascent:	850m
Descent:	850m
Via ferrata:	400m
Approximate time:	6 hours
Highest altitude:	3343m
Note:	ice axe, crampons and rope essential

Approach can be made by making an overnight stay in Rif. Contrin and then climbing north-east to Forcella Marmolada on path 606 in around 2 hours (with some protection on the final approach to the forcella). However, an easier way is recommended to complete a circuit in a day, including reaching the summit of Punta Penia (3343m) by approaching Forcella Marmolada on path 606 across the small glacier (ice-axe and crampons required) on Marmolada's north-western side. At the western end of Lago Fedaia, which can be reached by bus from Canazei, follow the road south around the lake to a busy spot with cafes, souvenir shops and a large parking area. From here (2074m) take the Marmolada Seggiovia lift (a rather aged system with small metal boxes to stand in) to Rif. Plan del Fiaconni (2650m). In summer, the lift operating hours are continuous from 0800 to 1700. Note also that there is a small museum at the lift departure point, and although all displays are labelled in only Italian or German, a visit is well worth the small cost of entry to appreciate the war on the glacier (see 'Marmolada: City of Ice', below).

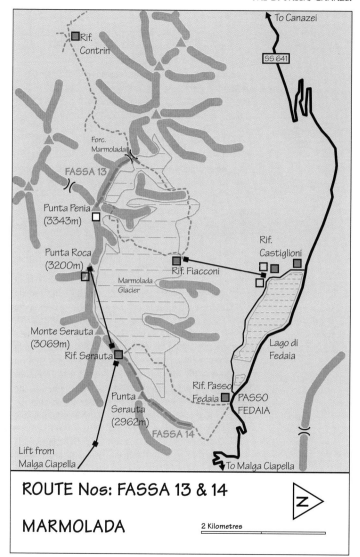

To Canazei

SS 641

Rif.
Contrin

Forc.
Marmolada

FASSA 13

Punta Penia
(3343m)

Punta Roca
(3200m)

Rif. Fiacconi

Rif.
Castiglioni

Marmolada
Glacier

Monte Serauta
(3069m)

Rif. Serauta

Lago di
Fedaia

Punta
Serauta
(2962m)

FASSA 14

Rif. Passo
Fedaia

PASSO
FEDAIA

Lift from
Malga Ciapella

To Malga Ciapella

ROUTE Nos: FASSA 13 & 14

MARMOLADA

N

2 Kilometres

From the top of the lift descend to the right following waymarks to 'Ferrata' and path 606. The path descends west through slabs and glacial moraine to about 2500m, where it goes around a rock spur and heads uphill towards Forcella Marmolada. The path zigzags towards the middle of a small glacier, as it works its way up the middle of the ice-falls and then to the right (uphill) of the glacier to the beginning of the ferrata protection just bellow the Forcella Marmolada. Allow about 1½–2 hours to here.

The west ridge now takes around 1½–2 hours to the summit of Punta Penia. The ferrata is well protected throughout, and follows a series of ladders and stemples as it works it way up the west ridge. When conditions are good, and the route is dry and free from ice it is a relatively simple, though spectacular, ascent. However, a considerable distance of the ridge is north facing and above 3000m, and is much more serious in (or after) a period of bad weather. Sections of the wire may be buried by fresh snowfall, and crampons may also be needed on the ferrata. The wire protection ends around 3300m, and a zigzag path leads from here up the final section of the ridge; this can be covered in snow at any time of the year. There is a small rifugio on the summit which serves hot drinks and food, and if caught in a storm it provides a very welcome shelter.

Crampons and ice-axes are needed for the descent, which is made by following a snow fan down the curving ridge to the north until a marker post is reached, indicating the top of a rock wall; this is down-climbed to the main glacier. The rock wall is unprotected, and, although the holds are good, it is exposed and requires climbing skill and a good head for heights. There are, however, some pegs in place, which can be used for abseil, if required. The descent across the glacier is initially across to the right (downhill, east), and then works its way through a steep ice-fall with some large crevasses. Again the route is easy to follow during spells of settled weather (due to the amount of traffic), but can quickly become a serious undertaking after fresh snow. The glacier ends around 2700m, with a short walk back to the top station

Marmolada, 'City of Ice'

On the Marmolada, remnants of the so-called 'City of Ice', once an 8 mile labyrinth of tunnels, are slowly emerging from the mountainsides surrounding the Marmolada glacier in the Dolomites, on what was the Austro-Italian border, as the glacier shrinks at a rate of 7 metres a year. Most of the original structure remains intact, with Italian specialists clearing away ice to reveal a network of communication tunnels, including sleeping space for 300 troops, an officers' mess and a hospital. During the excavations, several of the wooden huts, built inside the glacier, have been found, together with munitions, uniforms and the occasional body – perfectly preserved in sub-zero temperatures. From 1915 to 1917 the Marmolada was a key military position along the Italian–Austrian front, which stretched from the Dolomites to the plains of north-eastern Italy. But in late 1917 the Austrians, aided by the Germans, broke through the Italian lines at the village of Caporetto, north of Trieste. The Italians retreated from their mountain-top positions to form a last line of defence on the River Piave, north of Venice. The victorious Austrians abandoned the City of Ice to pursue the Italians south, and it was never used again.

Today the Italian authorities have ordered troops to start cleaning the honeycomb of tunnels surrounding the City of Ice for public visits. A museum has been opened at the second-stage station of the Marmolada cable car, so that young generations of Italians and Austrians can see the conditions in which their grandfathers and great-grandfathers fought in defence of their fatherlands.

of the lift. The total time for the descent from the summit to the lift is around 2 hours.

Additionally, if you don't want to climb the via ferrata but wish to climb to the Punta Penia summit of the Marmolada directly, you can do so via the glacier crossing and the crescent-shaped snow ridge. Your descent would return the same way, back down the glacier, without doing the west ridge. This alternative ascent can also be used if the via ferrata is not in condition, which is often the case. Guides can be arranged for either trip if required.

Don't forget, this is a committing, long route subject to the vagaries of high mountain weather, and as such should be tackled only by experienced or guided parties.

FASSA 14:
VF Eterna Brigata Cadore –
Punta Serauta

Grade:	5, Seriousness: C
Departure point:	Passo di Fedaia
Ascent:	1000m
Descent:	by cable car
Via ferrata:	1200m
Approximate time:	6 hours climbing, plus cable cars and road transport
Highest altitude:	2962m

Access to the start of the route is an easy 30 minute walk from the Passo Fedaia car park on the east end of Lago Fedaia. Follow signs and waymarks downhill on a gravel road at first and then on a rising path round the side of rock walls on your right. The start of the route is obvious, and is to the right of a large red F painted on the rock. There is also a plaque 'Ferrata Brigita Alpina Cadore Alla Zona Monumentale Di Punta Serauta – Classificata Molto Dificile Dislivello 800m Per Correnza Media Ore 6 Zendra 87'.

The route up the slab has continuous wire protection from start to finish. However, the wires are not tensioned between bolts, and this looseness, along with long runouts (mostly from 15–20m), means that climbing on the rock rather than the wires is a more secure option. The route up the large slabby face takes some drainage, and,

Panoramic view of the big slab of Punta Serauta and its ridge,
with Marmolada in the background

although at a fairly easy angle, is very committing and sustained. Once on the ridge, which has some broken rock, progress is made mostly on the north-facing side, so snow and ice can create additional problems in cold weather at any time of the year. All this means that good, stable weather is essential, along with a good climbing fitness and mental stamina. It is a committing route and has some of the best (!) exposure you can get on via ferrata routes.

From the bottom of the large slabby face to the crest takes around 2½–3 hours, generally on good rock, although there is an area of loose rock and scree about half-way up. Some stone-fall may be generated by movement of the wires, even if climbers are careful with foot placement in the area of unstable rock.

Once onto the Punta Serauta ridge, the route traverses, descends and ascends around a number of buttresses and pinnacles, mostly in very exposed positions. Again the looseness of the wire protection requires good climbing technique, and, in some of the descents, continued strength in down-climbing. Route timing from the top of the slab to the cable car is around 2–2½ hours, making 5–6 hours total climbing.

Descent can be made via the glacier directly back to Passo Fedaia in around 2 hours, but for this crampons and ice-axe are needed. The easier (recommended) way is to use the two-stage cable car back down to Malga Ciapella. The last descent leaves at 1625, so an early start is required on the route if the cable car descent is to be an option. From Malga Ciapella, there is a bus to Passo Fedaia at 1450 and 1650 (always check times and operating dates if considering this option). Whilst a further track is shown on some maps heading south from the cable car station and then eastwards down to the road above Malga Ciapella, this is not recommended.

FALZAREGO

Maps:
Tabacco Carta Topographica 1:25,000 Sheet 07 or
Kompass Wanderkarte 1:25,000 Sheet 616

Tourist Information Office:
APT Corvara – Colfosco, Via ColAlt 36, Cap 39033
Corvara, Italy. Tel: (0471) 836176, Fax: (0471) 836540

Tourist Information Office:
APT Cortina, Piazzetta S. Francesco, 32043 Cortina
D'Ampezzo (BL) Italy. Tel: (0436) 3231/2/3/4 or 2721,
Fax: (0436) 3235
Internet: www.dolomitisuperski.com/altabadia or
www.sunrise.it/dolomiti
E-mail:corvara@dnet.it or apt1@sunrise.it

Although Passo Falzarego is an important jumping-off
point for some of the finest and most rugged mountains
in the Dolomites, facilities and accommodation are very
limited here. However, there are several rifugios in the
mountains nearby, and the pass is an easy drive from
several other centres which we have included, notably
Pedraces, Arabba and Cortina. There is also a good bus
service from Cortina, taking about 35 minutes, although
the more limited services from centres to the west would
only be useful if you were planning an overnight stay in
a rifugio, since timetables do not lend themselves to a
return day-trip.

Access into the heart of the Lagazuoi mountains to
the north is provided by the cable car from the crest of
the pass, whilst the Cinque Torri chairlift, leading into the
Averau area, is about 3km down the road towards
Cortina.

The mountains around Passo Falzarego have everything for the ferratist: one of the hardest routes in the
Dolomites, a wet-weather option through wartime tunnels, and easy routes in splendid mountain scenery.

THE MOUNTAIN WAR

Passo Falzarego and the surrounding area was the scene of particularly intense activity during the so-called 'Mountain War' of 1915–1917. When Italy entered the war, in May 1915, Austria judged that the maintenance of its then border with Italy was unrealistic, and so chose to retreat to geographically defensible mountain tops and passes. Passo Falzarego, as the key to progress onwards to Val Badia and to Val Pusteria with its vital rail link, was a vital part of the defensive network created. In fact, anticipating conflict at some stage, the Austrians had constructed the Tre Sassi Fort on the adjoining Passo Valparole as early as 1901. At the outbreak of war the Austrians constructed a much more elaborate network of fortifications in the vicinity. Trenches and gun emplacements were erected to the front of the fort, on the adjoining peak of Sass di Stria, and on the face and summit of Lagazuoi.

The Italian forces rapidly occupied the abandoned areas, including the town of Cortina, and then advanced more cautiously towards the Austrian front line, where they proceeded to create their own opposing network of fortifications on Passo Falzarego, at Averau, and on Tofana di Rozes and its subsidiary peak, Il Castelletto. This replicated the stalemate situation seen throughout the various combat zones of Europe, and exploratory forays by both sides proved completely ineffective in this difficult terrain.

Consequently, in October 1915, in an attempt to break the stalemate, Italian Alpini troops advanced under cover of darkness up the gullies of the Lagazuoi face. Their objective was the occupation of the eastern end of the broad ledge which runs across the face. The initiative was successful, and was to shape the pattern of hostilities in this area for the remainder of the mountain war. This ledge, still named Cengia Martini ('Martini ledge') after the officer who led the assault, provided the Italians with a comparatively secure position overlooking the Austrian fortifications. In fact, dislodging the Italians effectively dictated all the subsequent efforts of the Austrians on this part of the front.

The Italian position was gradually consolidated, and a large number of buildings providing facilities such as stores and sleeping quarters were erected, subsequently supplied from the safety of a tunnel running up the inside of the face. Early assaults by Austrian troops involved men being lowered on ropes into positions from which they could hurl grenades onto the Italians below! A less risky strategy, employed for the first time in January 1916, involved the use of explosives. In the first instance, the Austrians inserted explosives in natural fissures in the rock face above the ledge, but the subsequent rock-fall made little impact on the Italian positions.

The Austrian initiative then gave rise to a quite astonishing campaign of tunnelling by the Italians which occupied the two sides for the remaining two years of the Mountain War. Some were tunnels leading to detonation chambers for huge mines, others included counter mine tunnels, tunnels leading to firing or observation positions, and access or escape tunnels. Needless to say, concealing these activities was difficult; equipment noise, the construction of windows, the disposal of spoil, all gave the opposing side a good idea of what was planned. Consequently, much effort went into concealment, including even the digging of decoy tunnels. Following the January 1916 explosion, four further detonations occurred during 1917. Three of these were by the Austrians (in January, May and September) and one by the Italian side (in June). Whilst the combined effect of these explosions had a massive impact on the appearance of Lagazuoi (including leaving huge debris cones, still raw-looking to this day), the military achievements were extremely limited.

Perhaps the most successful was

the Italian effort, which followed the construction of a tunnel upwards from the Martini ledge to a point under the Austrian emplacements on the eastern end of the crest of Lagazuoi. Whilst no Austrian lives were lost, because their position was evacuated shortly before the detonation, the emplacements were destroyed, enabling its capture by the Italian forces, thus creating a second strategically important position from which to bombard Austrian trenches.

The Mountain War came to an end in 1917 because of events elsewhere in Europe. The massive Austrian and German onslaught at Caporetto, many miles to the southeast, led to the Italians abandoning their Dolomite theatre in order to marshal their available forces to form a last line of defence for Venice. Two years of intense activity and much bitter fighting, with great heroism displayed on both sides, achieved nothing in military terms. What remains is an extraordinary legacy of caves, galleries and fortifications at Falzarego and many places like it. The Lagazuoi face is notable for the scale and complexity of the tangle of tunnels which survive, and for the effort which is being invested in excavation to enable the public to experience something of the conditions in which these brave mountain men lived and died; this can be best seen on route FALZ 2.

FALZ 1:
VF TOMASELLI – PUNTA SUD

This is a very good quality route, which is technically hard in places and fairly sustained. Some of the route is north facing and so can be prone to icing, especially if an early start is made.

Grade:	5, Seriousness: C
Departure point:	Passo Falzarego
Ascent:	450m
Descent:	1000m
Via ferrata:	600m (300m ascent, 300m descent)
Approximate time:	6–7 hours
Highest altitude:	2980m
Note:	torch required for optional diversion to Cima Scotoni

The approach to the route is by the Lagazuoi cable car, which operates from the end of May to the end of October. You then have the option of walking round either the east or the west side of the great bulk of Lagazuoi Grande in order to reach Bivacco della Chiesa, which marks the start of the route. The most satisfying method is to make a clockwise circuit, ending the day with a walk down to Passo Falzarego on path 402, which has recently been rerouted to a line closer to the cliffs and the adjoining wartime artefacts. This also obviates the need to buy a return ticket on the cable car (save your money for a beer at the end of the day at one of the bars back at Falzarego pass; you will certainly have earned it!). From the top station of the cable car, walk north on path 20, branching right onto 20b at the sign-posted junction. The route now hugs the bottom of the rock face, ascends a steep rake equipped with steps, and leads up to the bivouac, which sits on a levelled plateau, formerly the site of an Austrian artillery position. Allow about 1½ hours from the cable car to the start of the route, which is just above the bivouac; this is a good place to gear-up, have a break, and with a bit of luck enjoy the sun whilst you inspect the route.

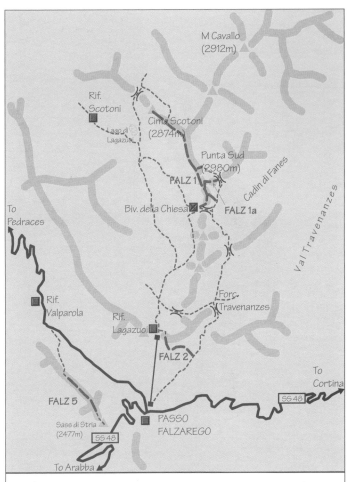

M Cavallo
(2912m)

Rif.
Scotoni

Cima Scotoni
(2874m)

Lago di
Lagazuoi

Punta Sud
(2980m)

FALZ 1

Cadin di Fanes

Biv. della Chiesa

FALZ 1a

Val Travenanzes

To
Pedraces

Rif.
Valparola

Rif.
Lagazuoi

Forc.
Travenanzes

FALZ 2

To
Cortina

SS 48

FALZ 5

PASSO
FALZAREGO

Sass di Stria
(2477m)

SS 48

To Arabba

ROUTE Nos: FALZ 1, 1a, 2 & 5

VFs Tomaselli, Sass di Stria
& Lagazuoi Tunnels

2 Kilometres

Climbers on 'the nose' of VF Tomaselli

The route is immediately strenuous and airy as it climbs and then traverses round an awkward bulge (The Nose) on fairly loose cables. The next section climbs steeply past some old wooden ladders, and then continues until the angle eases to become a broken scree slope. At about 2740m, an old route with rusted iron bolts is apparent off to the right (east); if the weather is deteriorating and you are looking for an escape route, it is best to ignore this and climb for another 30m or so, where a better option is available. The route, now unprotected, continues up a short, easy-angled and rather dirty gully, at the top of which is a line of old bolts (without cable) running up an area of broken slabs. An easy path zigzags up through the slabs and on up some quite exposed ledges on steep scree slopes towards the foot of a steep rock face (which turns out to be a huge, detached pillar). The escape route, should you need it, is along the track to the right at the foot of this face, at roughly 2770m. Walk to the obvious shoulder, a few metres away, where a couple of cairns indicate an easy way down into a gully and on down to the return track (20b) to Forcella Travenanzes.

The ascent continues to the left at the foot of the face. The cable resumes as the path narrows and the exposure increases. The ledge soon peters out, and the cable now leads up quite a steep wall, fairly broken and well provided with holds. The angle eases once more at a gap in the protection a little below the final steep passage of the climb. At this point, a choice of cabled routes presents itself, at about 2820m. The line to the left links with the Alta Via Fanis, an interesting diversion which is described in the note below. The cable to the right is the continuation of the Tomaselli route (confirmation of this choice is provided by a double arrow painted on the rock, with G pointing left, and T pointing right). The route continues up over more broken rock to the foot of the rock wall, then right to the point where the cable resumes at 2840m. The climb continues up a fairly easily angled broken buttress, which then steepens into quite a strenuous groove before the angle eases off again. A short but awkward corner, which is quite hard and rather strenuous, leads immediately into a pleasant, quite broken groove with a narrow crack in its angle. This is best climbed, more easily than it looks, by bridging, and leads up to an airy *à cheval* stance (if you don't speak French and you've not met this climbing term before, you'll understand it when you get there!). Now for a splendid, very exposed, steep airy slab, followed by a couple of final easy ledges which lead to the Punta Sud summit. Allow for about 1½ hours' climbing from the start of the ferrata, not including the diversion on the Alta Via Fanis.

The descent line (also see FALZ 1a below), which is cabled right from the summit platform, goes to the right (north-east). Whilst it is always well protected, it is a quite sustained climb, and at grade 3C is not to be taken lightly. The hardest passage is a short, slightly bulging square-cut chimney, the key to which is locating the small holds just below the platform at the top. Allow about 45 minutes for the descent to the bottom of the cable.

You now descend a series of loose scree gullies on a rather poorly defined path to Forcella Grande, which overlooks the bivouac. Here you join path 20b for the splendid walk to Forcella Travenanzes, and go onward by path 402 to Passo Falzarego.

Diversion to Cima Scotoni on the Alta Via Fanis (torch required for exploration of galleries)

If time permits, an interesting diversion can be made from the upper reaches of the via ferrata (see description above) to Cima Scotoni, a little over 1km to the north-west. At the point where a choice of cable presents itself, at about 2820m, walk left along a narrow boulder- and scree-strewn ledge on a gently ascending traverse line. After about 100m or so, you come to a dirty-looking gully, which steepens into a broken chimney just above you; an old timber ladder still clings to the rock face at this point. Your route, however, is across the face of the gully, rather precariously given its loose and sandy nature (the cable was also damaged and loose at the time of writing). Move up left to the obvious shoulder, where there are the remains of several old wartime structures. The path continues to the north-west on a shelf

along the foot of a fairly steep broken slab, with a steep
scree slope below, at times decidedly airy. In about 15 minutes, the shelf broadens out somewhat, and the entrance to
two adjoining tunnels can be seen, a little above the track
(easily missed, so watch out for some old rusted cable fes-
tooned across the rock at this point). The route will return to
the tunnels shortly, but for the moment it continues with the
diversion to Cima Scotoni.

Adjoining the tunnels, a metal sign indicates 'Alta Via
Fanis. Luigi Veronesi. 3. 8. 1969' (some maps refer to this as
Via Ferrata Veronesi). The track beyond the tunnels is not
immediately easy to spot, but persevere and waymarks
become apparent, traversing at the same level that you have
taken thus far. Whilst nowhere difficult, the route is frequently exposed, although cables are provided for the more
airy passages. The views alone make this diversion worthwhile; particularly impressive is the sight of Lago di
Lagazuoi and the adjoining Rif. Scotoni, almost 1000m
below. The traverse eventually ends at a col (about 2840m)
just to the south-east of the summit of Cima Scotoni
(2874m), which is a further 15 minutes' scramble away, with
care required since the rock is decidedly friable. The whole
diversion will take about an hour from the VF to this summit.

*The airy slab above
the 'à cheval' stance
on VF Tomaselli*

Return by the same route, but allow time to explore the tunnels you passed earlier. The lower tunnel is now completely blocked by debris, although the other, at a slightly higher level, is in perfect condition. It curves gently, on a slightly descending course, for a little over 100m before emerging on a ledge above the vestigial glacier of the Ciadin di Fanes, a wild and rugged cirque above Val Travenanzes. A track follows the ledge to the right (south-east) for about 100m, exposed and protected by cable as it narrows. The cable now leads down a 10m rock step to the floor of the cirque, from where access to Forcella dei Quaire (sometimes known as the Fanes saddle) is mapped but is not straightforward. Apart from the extremely friable nature of the rock at the foot of the wall, you will almost certainly have to contend with old snow at a steep angle. Consequently, it is strongly recommend that you return to the original route from this point. You should certainly not regard this as a potential escape route from the via ferrata in deteriorating weather; if conditions require a speedy exit from the mountain, you should return to the escape route referred to in the description above.

FALZ 1A:

ASCENT OF PUNTA SUD BY
TOMASELLI DESCENT ROUTE

Grade:	3, Seriousness: C
Departure point:	Passo Falzarego
Ascent:	450m
Descent:	1000m
Via ferrata:	600m (300m ascent, 300m descent)
Approximate time:	6–7 hours
Highest altitude:	2980m

The approach for the descent route is the same as for VF Tomaselli Route (FALZ 1 above) as far as the bivouac. Here, you continue to the east up to the obvious col (Forcella Grande) which overlooks the bivouac. Just over

the col, the path splits; the main route, waymarked 20b, heads south for Passo Falzarego (this is your return route for later in the day). To reach the via ferrata descent route, you turn left (north-east), negotiating rather unpleasant scree slopes, on a path which is not always easy to discern. The route eventually swings to the north to climb a series of loose scree gullies until you are confronted by a huge and desolate basin surrounded by impenetrable crags. You are now at Forcella dei Quaire, and the cable, marking the start of the route, is to be found on the left. Allow about 2½ hours to here.

View of Punta Sud (VF Tomaselli) from south east of Forcella Grande

You will see from the description of the route in FALZ 1 that its descent route is not without difficulties. Whilst always well protected, it is an airy route with some quite difficult passages. The square, blocky chimney described above is probably best tackled by bridging in ascent, but will prove quite strenuous no matter how you overcome this obstacle. It goes without saying that if you choose to use this route as an easier option to reach the summit of Punta Sud, then you will have to be confident of your ability to down-climb the route to make your escape! Allow about 1 hour for the ascent, and 45 minutes for the descent.

Return to Passo Falzarego by paths 20b and 402 as described in FALZ 1 above.

FALZ 2:
LAGAZUOI TUNNELS

A route which can be done on a bad weather day (not, of course, in thunder!).

Grade:	1, Seriousness: A
Departure point:	Passo Falzarego
Ascent:	0m
Descent:	650m
Via ferrata:	200m
Approximate time:	1 to 1½ hours
Highest altitude:	2752m
Note:	torch essential; gloves advisable

By taking the Lagazuoi cable car (summer operation: end of May till end of October) the route simply descends through the wartime tunnels to Passo Falzarego. Via ferrata kit is not essential, although a torch definitely is, and a helmet and gloves are strongly recommended to save your head from low tunnels and protect hands on the cold and damp wire, which you will tend to use as a handrail as you come downhill in the dark. An atmospheric alternative to a conventional battery torch is to purchase the flaming version from the rifugio to light your way.

The route starts from the top of the cable car station (Rif. Lagazuoi is a short walk up from here and is an excellent viewpoint) down a protected path, which leads down and then traverses to the tunnels. Work is being carried out to restore some trenches to their original state as an open-air museum, see note below. Descent takes around 1 to 1½ hours.

The route, can of course, be approached by walking up from Passo Falzarego on waymarked paths 402 and 20, but this is a tedious option when the cable car is available. Descent of the tunnels is recommended because most people do it this way, and to ascend the tunnel would involve a couple of hours going against the traffic instead of descending with it.

Note

The Little Lagazuoi (above Passo Falzarego) was the site of fierce combat during the First World War. For two years the Austrians defended the top of the mountain while the Italians attacked from their position on the Martini Ledge below. On June 20, 1917, after six months of tunnelling 1100m into the mountain, the Italians detonated 33,000 kg of blasting gelatin in order to dislodge the Austrians. However, the Austrians, hearing the constructions work, abandoned their position before the explosion, and all the efforts of the Italians were wasted.

FALZ 3:

AVERAU

Grade:	2, Seriousness: A
Departure point:	Cinque Torri chairlift
Ascent:	390m
Descent:	390m, from Cinque Torri chairlift
Via ferrata:	75m
Approximate time:	2½ hours
Highest altitude:	2649m

Whilst this is not a route to occupy a whole day, it makes a pleasant embellishment to a walk in this attractive area.

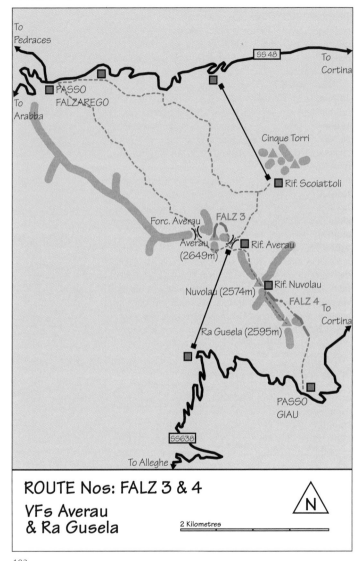

To Pedraces

To Cortina

SS 48

PASSO FALZAREGO

To Arabba

Cinque Torri

Rif. Scoiattoli

Forc. Averau

FALZ 3

Averau (2649m)

Rif. Averau

Nuvolau (2574m)

Rif. Nuvolau

FALZ 4

To Cortina

Ra Gusela (2595m)

PASSO GIAU

SS638

To Alleghe

ROUTE Nos: FALZ 3 & 4

VFs Averau & Ra Gusela

2 Kilometres

N

The views of the Tofane group to the north are outstanding on this route, and the historic training ground of generations of rock climbers, Cinque Torri, is just below the imposing bulk of Averau. The route is suitable for beginners, although not entirely free of difficulties.

The approaches from Passo Falzarego and Passo Giau are full of interest, and make for a splendid day's walk. However, the shortest and quickest route, which is suitable if only half a day is available, is on the Cinque Torri chairlift (operates from 0900 to 1730, from the beginning of July until mid-September, with a return trip being much better value than singles in either direction). This is reached from the Cortina to Passo Falzarego road and has a very large car park; buses from Cortina also stop close by on the main road. From Rif. Scoiattoli, which is at the top station of the chairlift, it is an easy 30 minute walk to Rif. Averau (2416m).

Whichever approach route you choose, details of the climb and descent of the ferrata are given below from Rif. Averau. Follow a waymarked track (Ferrata Averau) contouring around the east side of Averau. In about 5 minutes the path turns left and zigzags up the hill to the start of the ferrata (15 minutes from the rifugio). The route utilises the only significant line of weakness in the ring of cliffs which protect Averau to reach the broad summit plateau from its north side.

Although the ferrata is only 10–15 minutes long, it provides some pleasant climbing on very nice rock. It even offers a choice of route in its central portion. The main line climbs a short, slightly bulging wall, whilst a rather damp chimney to its left provides slightly easier climbing on stemples. Both options are well protected, and you might as well get the most out of this little route by going up the wall and coming back down the chimney.

The upper half of the route is straightforward and brings you to the end of the ferrata at the foot of a large, featureless scree-filled combe. A well-worn path (with some cairns but no waymarks) then zigzags up and

The short ferrata section on the ascent of Averau

through rough ground to the summit in about 20 minutes. As mentioned earlier, Averau summit is a wonderful viewpoint. It should be noted, however, that the area is largely devoid of landmarks, and is not a place to be caught out if clouds descend suddenly.

Descend by the same route, having made a note of the position of the cairn at the top of the ferrata; it takes about 30 minutes back to Rif. Averau.

FALZ 4:
NUVOLAU/RA GUSELA

Grade:	1, Seriousness: A
Departure point:	Cinque Torri chairlift
Ascent:	480m
Descent:	480m
Via ferrata:	25m
Approximate time:	3 hours
Highest altitude:	2595m

Nuvolau summit can be climbed in about 20 minutes from Rif. Averau on path 439 without using the ferrata. For approaches to Rif. Averau, see route FALZ 3 above.

The Nuvolau path, on the south side of Rif. Nuvolau, has a short ferrata section of about 25m of wire and a small ladder; for those with a good head for heights, it can be descended or ascended without equipment. The route is either a way to or from Passo Giau on path 438, or simply an extension of the day to climb to the summit of Ra Gusela (2595m, and with a small Madonna statuette) and return to Rif. Nuvolau; this takes about 20 minutes each way. On leaving the summit of Ra Gusela in mist beware of a decoy path and stay on the ascent route above a deep rock crevasse on the right to return to Rif. Nuvolau.

FALZ 5:

SASS DI STRIA

Grade:	1, Seriousness: A
Departure point:	Passo Valporola
Ascent:	300m
Descent:	300m
Via ferrata:	20m
Approximate time:	2 hours
Highest altitude:	2477m

This is not really a via ferrata at all, but is included in the guide for completeness, as most maps show ferrata crosses. However, it is a very nice short walk to Sass di Stria from the Passo Valporola (see map p.173), where there is plenty of parking. Ascent and descent of Sass di Stria takes about 2 hours on quite good paths most of the time. There are good views to the higher peaks around and a lot of interest in wartime trenches and tunnels. One trench has two short ladders to ascend and reverse, but these are not at all exposed and do not warrant the use of via ferrata equipment.

CORTINA

Maps:
Tabacco Carta Topographica 1:25,000 Sheet 03 or
Kompass Wanderkarte 1:25,000 Sheet 617

Tourist Information Office:
APT Cortina, Piazzetta S. Francesco, 32043 Cortina
D'Ampezzo (BL) Italy. Telephone: (0436) 3231/2/3/4 or
2721, Fax: (0436) 3235
Internet: www.sunrise.it/dolomiti
E-mail: apt1@sunrise.it

If chic is your thing, then Cortina is the place for you!
This deeply fashionable town is an extremely popular
holiday destination with well-heeled and trendy Italians;
in August it positively heaves! The skiing season sees just
as many visitors, this time a more cosmopolitan crowd,
since Cortina is internationally famous as a winter sports
venue, having hosted the Winter Olympics in 1956. It
also has a long history of independence, and today is
unique in the Dolomites in still having its own legislative
system, the Regole D'Ampezzo.

This rather sprawling town provides everything the
visitor could possibly want, with its cafes, pizzerias,
sports shops, hotels and supermarkets. Those familiar
with the rather grim shopping experience of British Co-
ops should check out the Italian equivalent on Cortina's
main drag! For a real Italian experience, visit Cortina
after a hard via ferrata day to enjoy the evening passeggiata, have a drink in one of the many outside bars, and
just people-watch.

Inevitably, this popularity comes at a price, with
accommodation in particular being much more costly
than in other, smaller, centres. There are, however, several camp sites if your budget does not run to Cortina's
prices. Unsurprisingly, parking can be difficult, especially

in August, and you should note that Cortina has a traffic-free centre, with an initially confusing one-way system around the town. Of all the potential bases in the Dolomites, Cortina is certainly the one best served by public transport. So if you do not have a car available, you can reach a greater number of routes from here than from any other centre.

There are several lift systems to make life easier for visitors to these mountains, four of which provide access to routes featured in this section. The Pomedes lift and the famous Sky Arrow serve the Tofane group; the two-stage Rio Gere lift takes you to the start of the Cristallo routes; and the Faloria lift is one of the access points for the Sorapiss group.

Because of the wide geographic distribution of the routes accessible from Cortina, walks in this section are arranged according to location. The Tofane group offers routes ranging from technically easy to very challenging, but with big days in big mountains the common factor. The Boite valley, north of Cortina, contains a couple of real gems in the middle grades, whilst the Cristallo group provides grand mountain days on big, but relatively easy, routes. Finally, the Sorapiss circuit is a classic Dolomite excursion.

Information on route conditions can be gleaned from Cortina Guides (tel. 0436 868505 or email info@guidecortina.com and web site www.guidecortina.com).

CORTINA – NORTH

There are four routes in this section, all of which are at relatively low levels and therefore maybe in condition when other high-level routes are not. Access to them all is gained from the SS51 Cortina to Dobaccio road, and they can be easily reached by public transport from Cortina.

CORT 1:
VF GIOVANNI BARBARA AND
VF LUCIO DALAITI

Grade:	1, Seriousness: A
Departure point:	Visitors' Centre car park, Valle di Fanes
Ascent:	200m
Descent:	200m
Via ferrata:	100m
Approximate time:	2 hours
Highest altitude:	circa 1400m

A good route for a short day out, which can even be done on a wet day; it has spectacular views around a large gorge and so is also worth doing in good weather for photo opportunities.

Reconstruction and realignment, to make the waterfalls more accessible to the public, have largely removed any limited difficulties this route might once have had, so only the most inexperienced of ferratists need bother to carry their climbing equipment.

Approach by the SS51 road north from Cortina, and about 1km past the Fiames Hotel a left turn onto a side road (just round a right-hand bend, so approach slowly) leads to a small car park and visitor centre. The local (orange-coloured) buses from Cortina run as far as the Fiames Hotel.

Take the metalled road (waymarked 10, and sign-posted Cascate Val di Fanes/Punto Outo) for about 20 minutes as far as a fork at Pian de Loa. Follow the signs indicating the way to the via ferrata by the main track to the left. Continue for a further 25 minutes to the Ponte Outo, where the start of the via ferrata is to be found at the back of a small clearing/picnic site, about 150m beyond the bridge on the right.

A metal plaque marks the start of the first cable, which leads down a sloping ledge to the higher cascade, which you walk behind without getting more than

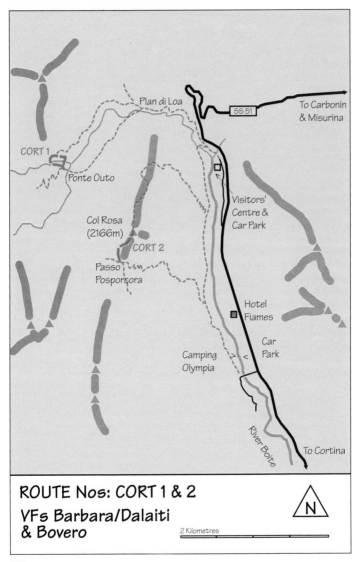

To Carbonin
& Misurina

SS 51

Plan di Loa

CORT 1

Ponte Outo

Visitors'
Centre &
Car Park

Col Rosa
(2166m)

CORT 2

Passo
Posporcora

Hotel
Fiames

Car
Park

Camping
Olympia

River Boite

To Cortina

ROUTE Nos: CORT 1 & 2

**VFs Barbara/Dalaiti
& Bovero**

N

2 Kilometres

slightly damp! The route continues easily to the valley floor with the aid of a sturdy ladder, and on to a metal bridge downstream from the main cascade. Note the track leading up to the top of the gorge on the left, which is an alternative return route. You should now climb up the to the top of the gorge on the south side by the VF Lucio Dalaiti. This is reached by crossing over the metal bridge and walking up the shale slope to the obvious ramp and the start of the cable with its metal plaque. This second via ferrata offers hardly any greater difficulties than the first one did on descent, with only a couple of somewhat steeper rock steps to surmount before the top is reached. The whole circuit can be completed in about 15 minutes, but you will undoubtedly spend longer in this charming spot. You can now return to your starting point by retracing your steps, or if you want to take a little longer and return by a more scenic, pleasant path then braving the higher cascade (VF Barbara) for a second time is recommended. Then once back in the gorge floor, take the signposted track, which leads up a steep gully (north) by means of an impressively constructed series of ramped steps. These lead to a fine viewpoint of the cascades. A most attractive track now leads through woodland and over small meadows to Pian de Loa and back eventually to your starting point.

CORT 2:
VF ETTORE BOVERO – COL ROSA

Grade:	3, Seriousness: B
Departure point:	Hotel Fiames
Ascent:	900m
Descent:	900m
Via ferrata:	300m
Approximate time:	6 hours
Highest altitude:	2166m

An excellent, albeit occasionally strenuous, route on good rock with some superb positions on steep solid limestone.

Cars can be parked in a car park adjoining the new National Park Office, about 0.5km north of the Olympia campsite entrance, just before Hotel Fiames. Alternatively the local (orange-coloured) buses from Cortina run as far as the Fiames Hotel. Take the path through the woods adjoining the river to the bridge over the River Boite and the entrance to the campsite (parking is not allowed in the vicinity of the campsite unless you are camping there). Approach the via ferrata on path 417 then 408, which zigzags steeply up to Passo Posporcora, which you will reach in about 1½ hours. Just over the pass, take the path signposted to the via ferrata off to the right (north). This climbs steeply uphill, negotiating a series of short ledges through scrubby bushes, taking a further 30 minutes to reach the start of the route, a little beyond the memorial plaque to Ettore Bovero.

The route starts with a section of wire that leads past some scrubby bushes clinging to the steep rock wall. It is followed by some good but airy climbing, with no protection, for about 10m. Protected again, ascend a superb arete, followed shortly by a splendid airy traverse to the left, until the main climb is complete and a path leads towards the final summit rocks. The ascent to Col Rosa summit goes up a gully on stemples. Allow around 1½–2 hours for the ascent from the pass. The summit offers excellent views of Cortina and the surrounding peaks, but closer exploration also reveals a network of wartime tunnels and chambers. The entrance is not obvious, but is to be found in the trench running across the summit plateau, about 25m from the cross.

The descent, which is straightforward (and also passes more wartime ruins), follows path 447 along the gradually descending north ridge of Col Rosa until it swings to the right (south-east) to drop through pleasant pine forests towards the valley. The final couple of hundred metres involve a somewhat laborious passage on recently constructed steps. This leads back to the attractive forest trail, waymarked 417, which follows the river back to the camp site. Allow about 2 hours for the descent.

CORT 3:
VF MICHIELLI STROBEL – PUNTA FIAMES

Grade:	3, Seriousness: B
Departure point:	Hotel Fiames
Ascent:	950m
Descent:	950m
Via ferrata:	600m
Approximate time:	5–6 hours
Highest altitude:	2240m

An excellent route with fine views and good airy situations.

The approach is opposite the Hotel Fiames, which has a large car park adjoining, and which can be reached by the local (orange-coloured) bus from Cortina. The via ferrata is some 45 minutes' steep climb up the scree slope to the east of the road on a route signposted opposite the hotel. Within 2 minutes of leaving the road, turn right (south) on a gravel track, which is followed for about 100m. A second signpost now takes you up to the left (east) through thin pines and then small pine shrubs, crossing the old railway line (now a footpath and cycle track) on the way. The route winds upwards over scree to an obvious deep corner in the rock face, at the back of which is a narrow cleft. To the right of the cleft a memorial plaque is reached. This seems to be the place for gearing up, although the route initially goes to the right following a path through scrubby bushes along a wide ledge for about 400m. The protection starts at the end of this ledge, although the wires seem fairly old and are not always taut between anchors. A good arete of steep rock is followed by some ledges and further short ascents until a short walk across a wide gully to the right leads to a ladder. This is not the best of ladders, but leads up to good rock with some stemples and more wires. When the wires end follow a clear path to the summit of Punta Fiames.

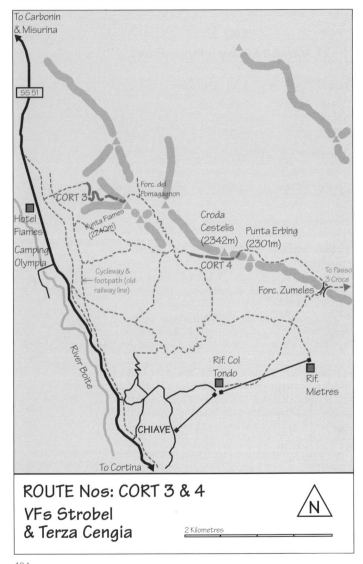

ROUTE Nos: CORT 3 & 4
VFs Strobel
& Terza Cengia

N

2 Kilometres

Descend by retracing your steps north for 100m and turn right (east) to follow a waymarked path to Forcella del Pomagagnon. Next comes a delightful 300m scree-run! Take the right-hand path at the end of the scree,

Climber on VF Michielli Strobel

path 202 towards Chiave. This is quite rough, but eventually leads down to the old railway track back towards Fiames. At the end of the scree-run, it is possible to follow waymarks on a traverse path north-west more directly back to Fiames. Descent from here through the rocks and scrub is fairly rough, but the route much shorter. Alternatively, if you wish to extend your day, then instead of descending you can pick up the path leading up to Terza Cengia (see route CORT 4, below). Total time up and down is around 5 hours.

CORT 4:
TERZA CENGIA – FORCELLA ZUMELES

This route presents no technical difficulties. However, it has only intermittent sections of cabled protection, together with long unprotected stretches on narrow ledges with extreme exposure.

Grade:	2, Seriousness: C
Departure point:	Col Tondo or Mietres
Ascent:	650m
Descent:	650m
Via ferrata:	250m
Approximate time:	5–6 hours
Highest altitude:	2301m

This is not a route for the faint hearted or anyone who does not have a head for heights. It is also not recommended as a down-climb (of almost 500 vertical metres) from Forcella Zumeles, as descending will seem more exposed than going uphill. Having said all this, you can enjoy quite spectacular views down to Cortina, 1000m below you as you climb the ledge.

It is possible to do this route either on its own or as an extension to CORT 3, VF Michielli Strobel, which is recommended. To make this approach, when you reach the foot of the scree-run described in the descent from the Strobel route, continue beneath the walls of Croda del Pomagagnon (at approximately 1850m) to pick up an ascending path on scree, which leads to the start of the Terza Cengia ledge.

However, should you choose to tackle the route as a stand-alone excursion, you are strongly advised to do this in a west to east direction, **not** east to west (that is, uphill, not downhill). Your choices of approach are:

- take the Mietres chairlift (1711m; this operates from mid-July to the beginning of September, from 0900 to 1645; it is signposted from the Cortina to Dobaccio road),
- drive to Col Tondo at 1435m (the middle station of the Mietres chairlift) or
- start from the hamlet of Chiave (1300m), reached by the Servico Urbano (orange coloured) bus from Cortina.

The timings and ascent statistics below assume a Col Tondo start point.

There are lots of paths in the area (best shown on Tabacco 1:25,000 Map 03). From the top of the chair at Mietres follow path 211, generally north-west, crossing path 204 (on which you will have ascended if starting from Col Tondo). Continue on path 211 until you meet path 202 (which is the way up from Chiave, and climbs steeply through forest, small pine shrubs and scree). Path 202 leads up towards Forcella Pomagagnon/Terza Cengia. Whichever approach you use the final steep scree slope becomes very laborious, but is perhaps slightly easier on the left side (uphill) until you arrive under the rock walls of Pomagagnon. Now ascend more loose scree by the side of the big wall until reaching some good rock where the ledge proper starts. This is a good spot to stop and have lunch, enjoy the view and put on your ferrata kit, which, even though you won't be able to use it very much, will be reassuring when you do!

The first cable lasts for only 10m, and then you climb along unprotected ledges for around 20 minutes, with some spectacular exposure, until a long section of cable is reached. At the end of the cable (about 10 minutes) a desperately 'chossy' 45 degree ramp is reached, with unpleasant and laborious climbing. At the top of the ramp continue along the ledge, with occasional protection, to arrive at a small col with views across to Cristallo; this is the top of the climb (1¼–1½ hours from the start of the ledge). The summit of Punta Erbing (2301m) is just above you with a small cross; this small peak can be climbed in 5 minutes, and it's worth it for the view.

Descend on the north side of Pomagagnon; it is steep at first, and the waymarks it follows are not always easy to see. Eventually the path becomes clearer, leads down a gully and then through trees, and arrives at Forcella de Zumeles (2075m) in about 45 minutes. From Forcella de Zumeles follow path 204 down well-constructed zigzags and then down an open gully to spot height 1724m, Pousa de Zumeles, in about 30 minutes. To return to Mietres follow path 211 from here, or for Col Tondo in a further 45 minutes (and Chiave beyond there) continue down on path 204.

An **alternative descent option** from Forcella Zumeles, if you are based in Cortina and have approached the route using public transport, would be to stay high and follow a pleasant path (205) to Passo Son Forca. You then join path 203 and zigzag down to Passo Tre Croce, from where you can catch a bus back to Cortina.

CORTINA – CRISTALLO

There are many permutations around the Cortina Cristallo routes CORT 5, 6 and 7. Which way you choose to spend your day (or days) tackling these routes will depend on the circumstances of your visit and perhaps your specific interests, whether it be climbing ferratas, mountain walking or the legacy of the First World War. Where you stay and transport logistics (car or public transport) will also influence you choice of itinerary.

You may prefer one or more day-trips from a Cortina base, or you might opt for an overnight stay in Rif. Lorenzi in order (if you are lucky) to enjoy a high-altitude sunset and sunrise. Four suggestions are given below.

1. A logistically simple day out maximising the via ferrata potential. Starting from Rio Gere take the two-stage lift to Rif. Lorenzi, climb CORT 5 (Marino Bianchi) and return to the rifugio for some refreshment. In the afternoon you then climb the first (and perhaps most spectacular) part of CORT 6 (VF Ivano Dibona) as far as the summit of Cristallino d'Ampezzo. Then return to the rifugio to take the lift back down to Rio Gere.

2. Another one-day option which requires more thought logistically, but offers a long, high-level mountain traverse, is VF Ivano Dibona CORT 6 in its entirety.

3. An excursion over two days, which requires some thoughts on transport logistics. Climb CORT 5 in the afternoon and stay overnight in Rif. Lorenzi. On day 2, complete CORT 6.

4. A further single day out completing a round-trip incorporating CORT 7, VF Renato de Pol.

The Cristallo routes can be easily approached using the two-stage Rio Gere chairlift system east of Cortina, which is open from the end of June until mid-September (first uplift 0845, and the last descent from Rif. Laurenzi at 1710). As with most lift approaches, there is always the option of saving the fare and approaching on foot. However, the climb up the Grava di Staunies on the steep scree slopes under the strange little yoghurt pots of the lift would be tedious in the extreme!

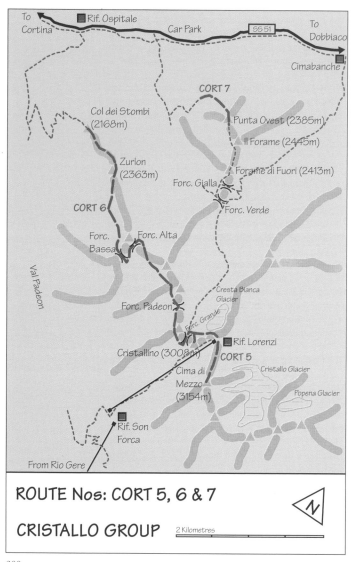

ROUTE Nos: CORT 5, 6 & 7

CRISTALLO GROUP

2 Kilometres

CORT 5:
VF Marino Bianchi – Cima di Mezzo

Grade:	2, Seriousness: B
Departure point:	Rif. Lorenzi
Ascent:	220m
Descent:	220m
Via ferrata:	200m
Approximate time:	3–4 hours
Highest altitude:	3154m

This route can be climbed on its own or, as suggested in the introductory remarks above, combined with VF Ivano Dibona (CORT 6). To climb it on its own in a short single day, use the chair and gondola lifts for the return trip from Rio Gere to Rif. Lorenzi. If you want to make the most of your investment in the lift ticket then follow suggestion 1 above and climb the first part of CORT 6 on the same day.

Starting immediately from the sun terrace of the rifugio the route ascends and descends the same way. Climbing is pleasant and well protected from rifugio to the summit of Cima di Mezzo. The ascent takes about 1 ½–2 hours, although, with the descent being by the same route, heavy traffic could extend this further. Descent could be completed in an hour, but of course this also has the same potential for delays whilst passing people coming up. Total time 3–4 hours.

Don't be put off by the mention of traffic; this is a really good route which, with the ride up to the rifugio, gives you an opportunity to climb in a high-level mountain environment without too much effort. If you choose suggestion 3 above, to stay at the rifugio (it's a wonderful place for a mountain sunset and sunrise!) overnight, be warned it can be quite cold at 3000m when you wake up in the morning.

CORT 6:

VF IVANO DIBONA

This is, rightly, a very popular route, and whilst there are no real technical difficulties, there are some exposed traverses along quite narrow ledges.

Grade:	2, Seriousness: B
Departure point:	Rif. Lorenzi
Ascent:	100m
Descent:	1600m
Via ferrata:	500m
Approximate time:	7–8 hours
Highest altitude:	3008m

It is quite a long route and, being an extended traverse of the main Cristallo ridge, the finishing point is some considerable distance from the start. As mentioned in the introductory section above, there are many ways to complete this route. The first three suggestions will give you a good idea of the choices that are available, and you may, of course, have your own ideas on what the ideal itinerary should be. One option not to be recommended is the long walk back to Rio Gere along Val Padeon. Whichever way you choose you will be guaranteed an excellent mountain day or days.

It is necessary to give some thought to transport logistics at the outset. Uplift using the Rio Gere system gives speedy access to the start of the route. How you get to Rio Gere for the start and back from Ospitale at the end will depend on factors such as where you are staying, and whether you are using your own or public transport. If the latter, then we suggest you take the bus from Cortina to the Rio Gere lift, complete the route, and pick up the bus from Ospitale back to Cortina. Bus times vary only slightly from season to season (but do check), with the first bus from Cortina in the morning being at 0835, and buses back from Ospitale at 1610 and 1840. The route as described from Rif. Lorenzi to Ospitale assumes use of the Rio Gere uplift system.

Start immediately from the top gondola station via ladders, wires and a short tunnel. Then cross the longest suspension bridge in the Dolomites (spectacular) and ascend a ladder onto an airy ridge. An optional diversion can be taken to ascend Cristallino d'Ampezzo, a 3008m summit which is clearly waymarked at the end of the ridge (this will add 30 minutes to your day, and will be the point from which you return if following the first suggestion for a ferrata day out). The main route continues down a ladder and a series of down-climbs to the Forcella Grande (be aware of possible icing at any time due to altitude). VF Renato de Pol (see CORT 7 below) heads north-west at this point and VF Ivano Dibona begins; there is a sign saying 'Ospitale 5 to 7 hours' at this point – a good indication of the overall length of day.

The route is mainly well waymarked, with Forcella Alta (at 2889m, about 2 hours beyond Forcella Grande) being perhaps the only place where the route could be missed. At this point, it is necessary to descend the

The longest ferrata bridge in the Dolomites, at the start of Ivano Dibona

In a fatal accident on 21st July 2003 three climbers were engulfed by an avalanche of mud and rocks when trying to escape from the route by descending from Forcella Alta in a storm.

obvious reddish-coloured scree gully to the left (south) for about 200m as far as a large notice which warns of the dangers of attempting to descend further (despite a route being indicated on most maps). At this point, turn right (north-west) towards Forcella Bassa and continue the waymarked route up along the ridge leading to Zurlon and eventually Col di Stombi. Note that this is not a col in the English sense of the word, but a small summit at the end of the ridge and a good viewpoint. Descent from here is on a good zigzag path, which leads down to path 203 and the walk out down a gravel road to Ospitale. Allow an overall time, from Rif. Lorenzi to Ospitale (including the diversion to Cristallino d'Ampezzo), of around 7–8 hours.

CORT 7:
VF RENATO DE POL – PUNTA OVEST DEL FORAME

Grade:	2, Seriousness: B
Departure point:	SS51, north of Ospitale
Ascent:	1000m
Descent:	1000m
Via ferrata:	300m
Approximate time:	6 hours
Highest altitude:	2413m

You could approach this route from Rif. Lorenzi in a similar way to VF Ivano Dibona as far as Forcella Grande – the logistics would be the same (i.e. use of two-stage uplift from Rio Gere plus public transport and/or car), see route CORT 6 above. However, the ferrata section of VF Renato de Pol is on the north side of Punta Ovest del Forame (2385m), with direct access from the Cortina to Dobaccio road (SS51), and climbing this route in a single day from that point is recommended.

Although this route will never be a classic (technically the climbing is easy), there are a lot of wartime remains adding interest to the day. Approach from the SS51 road (Cortina to Dobaccio) where you have a choice of departure points between Ospitale and Cimabanche; this is because the valley part of the round, on path 208, can be done either at the start or end of the day depending on your preference. There is a parking area on the north side of the road just after crossing Rio Gotres in the entrance to a military zone at kilometre marker 115.8. From here cross the road to path 208, and in around 200m west, after crossing a wooden bridge, Ferrata Renato De Pol is signposted *(or start from the large car park at Cimabanche and walk south-west to here on path 208)*.

Initially the path goes steeply uphill through a pine forest, passing a sign 'Pian del Forame' in about 20 minutes. Eventually the path zigzags through small pine bushes to a signpost and a branch in the path (around 1800m, and about 45 minutes from the road). Forcella Verde and Ospitale are to the right, with Renato de Pol continuing on a traverse to the left. After crossing a wide gully follow red waymarks, including Alta Via 3 (red triangle signs). The path continues uphill and then traverses past wartime caves and trenches to the start of the via ferrata; this takes around 1½ hours from the road. Just prior to reaching the start of the wire protection the route book can be found in a green metal box kept in a cave.

The route goes round a corner to the right, ascending a gully (a lot of loose stones here) and then a short ladder onto a ledge. The wire ends here, and throughout the route there are short protected sections alternating with unprotected climbing on steep scree slopes and exposed ledges. However, waymarking is good throughout, and interest is maintained as the route works it way up past trenches, caves and old wooden ladders. Quite near the top of the ferrata the remains of an amazing old walkway are seen crossing a vertical wall to the right, and in a few minutes a climb up a gully emerges on open ground; this is the end of the ferrata (about one hour) and a good place for lunch, with views to the

Tofanas and also the north side of the Ivano Dibona route with its long suspension bridge to Cresta Bianca. A further 15 minutes leads to the summit of Punta Ovest del Forame (2385m). From here the path descends on the west side of Il Forame, dropping to around 2200m before ascending to the summit of Forame di Fuori (2413m), with more wartime fortifications continuing along the ridge.

Descend to Forcella Gialla and, if feeling adventurous, you can head down a steep track (which is not shown on maps) from here to the east, passing more remains of wooden buildings, and then descending steep scree to join path 233 coming down from Forcella Verde. If you prefer an easier descent continue on the main path from Forcella Gialla to Forcella Verde and pick up the path down to the east from there as shown on the map. Path 233 leads down through a spectacular gully (mostly on a good path) all the way to the road at Cimabanche. The total descent time is around 2 hours. Now return along path 208 to your start point. Allow a total time for the round excursion of about 5½ to 6 hours.

CORTINA – TOFANE

These are some of the highest mountains in the Dolomites and consequently need to be taken seriously, notwithstanding the relatively easy technical standard of some of the routes. In addition to some excellent via ferrata days, these mountains offer wonderful rugged walking. You will notice that the maps of this group show several sections of paths with via ferrata notation which are not included in this guide, since they hardly provide an adequate focus for a day's outing. They are, however, useful links which can be incorporated in grand mountain days, with the need for protection underlining the serious nature of the terrain. (One such link, VF Scala del Menighel, is described in Gillian Price's book *Walking in the Dolomites*, also published by Cicerone Press.)

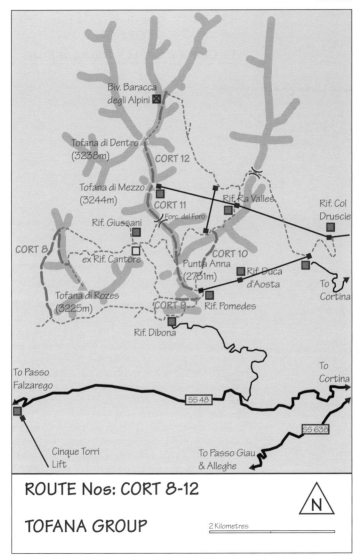

ROUTE Nos: CORT 8-12

TOFANA GROUP

2 Kilometres

N

CORT 8:
VF GIOVANNI LIPELLA – TOFANA DE ROZES

A sustained and demanding ferrata which is not at the hardest technical grade but goes on for a long time on a serious mountain.

Grade:	4, Seriousness: C
Departure point:	Rif. Dibona (2050m)
Ascent:	1250m
Descent:	1250m
Via ferrata:	600m
Approximate time:	8 hours
Highest altitude:	3225m
Note:	torch essential

It climbs the northern side of Tofana di Rozes, and this, coupled with its height, means that icing and snow are possibilities at any time of year. A torch is required on the tunnel section.

About 8km (5.5 miles) from Passo Falzarego on the SS48 road towards Cortina, turn left on a small road at kilometre mark 113.6 to Rif. Dibona. This road is narrow and windy, so be ready to give way and make use of passing places; it is uphill all the way for about 4km (2.5 miles) (metalled for the first half and then a gravelled track with some potholes for the last mile or so). There is a good deal of space at the roadhead, beyond the rifugio, but this could be congested in peak season.

From the car park go uphill on path 442, which leads to path 404 and a fine traverse under the Tofana rock walls. In about an hour the entrance to the tunnels and the start of the ferrata is reached. Ascent through the tunnel (where there are well-preserved remains of barracks) is quite steep and wet underfoot, and a head torch is essential. At the end of the tunnel follow the wire until it descends to a path. Now walk, unprotected, along a ledge on the scree slopes and look out for the start of the wire in about 10–15 minutes.

The route now continues with intermittent wire protection along a series of ledges, climbs and horizontal traverses – going up, down and along; it keeps on coming! Eventually, after some fairly steep sections a large ledge is reached with a black arrow to the left; this is the route to Rif. Giussani. To this point will have taken you around 2½ hours from starting the via ferrata in the tunnels. As well as being an escape point, this is a good place for lunch if you are tired or the weather is deteriorating. Round the corner to the left is a spectacular view of the Tre Dita ('Three fingers'). The route continues to the right, ascending a wide ledge passing the word 'Cima' on the rock and another arrow. This final ferrata section takes some drainage in places and so can be iced up even in dry weather; it has some short, hard pitches and lots of up and across moves as it ascends 300m to the shoulder of Tofana di Rozes, where there is a memorial tablet to Giovanni Lipella. At this point you have finished the ferrata and you join the walking route (used later for your descent) from Rif. Giussani, but you are still 200m (vertically) from the summit. Again this is an escape point if you want to avoid the return trip to the summit. The walk zigzags up to the summit on steep scree slopes and ledges; it is waymarked with small cairns but is not easy in mist, and it is worth noting landmarks for the descent as you go uphill. The summit is a commanding viewpoint. The total time for ascent from Rif. Dibona around 6 hours.

Descend by retracing your steps to the memorial tablet, and then go down north-east turning east following painted markers and an occasional cairn through ledges and steep scree; this route is not easy and holds snow in the north-facing bowl in early season. The path leads to Rif. Cantore (now closed), which is just south of the Rif. Guissani, where you can get refreshments. However, it is quite a detour to Rif. Guissani, and you may choose to continue east then south-east on a waymarked track through the ruins of Rif. Cantore directly onto the descent roadway, which (as path 403) leads back down to Rif. Dibona. The descent takes around 2 hours, giving a total time of about 8 hours; this assumes fairly sustained movement and includes only short break stops.

CORT 9:
SENTIERIO ASTALDI

This is a delightfully airy walk through terrain of considerable geological interest.

Grade:	1, Seriousness: A
Departure point:	Rif. Dibona
Ascent:	300m
Descent:	300m (back to Rif. Dibona)
Via ferrata:	400m
Approximate time:	2 hours
Highest altitude:	2303m

On the face of it, this is simply a convenient link from the Vallon de Tofana (which has Rif. Giussani at its head and Rif. Dibona at its foot) and Rif. Pomedes, which lies at the base of the superb south ridge of Tofana di Mezzo/Punta Anna. It could be used as a more interesting alternative to track 421, which is the quickest way of approaching VF Punta Anna (CORT 11 below) from this direction. However, do try to include this splendid little path in your itinerary, even if your ambitions fall short of that rather demanding route.

From Rif. Dibona, walk uphill on path 403, which follows the dirt access road to Rif. Giussani, cutting out some of the zigzags along the way. When level with the top of the steep rock band which runs directly above Rif. Dibona, take a less well-defined path running off to the right (east) up to the crest of a grassy ridge. Sentiero Astaldi begins at the point where this ridge meets the rock wall above. It is the nature of this rock wall, and the steep slope falling away below, which provides much of the interest on this route. The limestone strata is interleaved with layers of pale green and reddish clay-like

Fantastic rock strata on Sentiero Astaldi (photo: Meg Fletcher)

material of the 'Raibler' series, which glow startlingly in sunlight.

The route is an undulating traverse, the more airy passages of which are protected by cable, although only the most inexperienced via ferratist would feel inclined to gear-up for the outing. Towards the end of the ledge, a couple of hundred metres before the junction with path 421 (which you can see zigzagging up from Rif. Dibona), you follow the route indicated by the rather faded red lettering to Rif. Pomedes; this goes up the left side of a shallow, broken gully. Within a few metres, the way-marking takes you back to the right (north-east). At this point, if you look back and above, you will perhaps spot climbers on the impressive ridge, which is the line of VF Punta Anna. In a few minutes, you arrive at the beauti-fully located Rif. Pomedes, which is the end of the sen-tiero and the point of departure for the altogether more serious via ferrata you have just been admiring. You can, alternatively, return to Rif. Dibona by descending the clearly marked path 421.

CORT 10:
SENTIERO GUISEPPE OLIVIERI

Grade:	1, Seriousness: B
Departure point:	south ridge of Tofana de Mezzo, about 75m above summit of Punta Anna
Ascent:	none
Descent:	500m
Via ferrata:	300m
Approximate time:	2 hours (from ridge to Rif. Pomedes)
Highest altitude:	2800m

This route is frequently used by via ferratists who have climbed VF Punta Anna (CORT 11), the most interesting and demanding part of the south ridge of Tofana di Mezzo, and who choose to return to the valley rather than continue to the Torri Gianni wind-gap, the Bus di Tofana, or the summit. Consequently, this is how the route is described here. However, examination of the map will reveal that it could be climbed as part of a less ambitious itinerary from Rif. Pomedes to Ra Valles.

Whilst the officially designated line of Sentiero Olivieri begins some distance below, the track which makes the link from the via ferrata leaves VF Punta Anna some 75m above the summit of Punta Anna, at an altitude of about 2800m. The continuing line of VF Punta Anna is indicated by the word 'Cima' painted on a rock, whilst the route to this sentiero is marked by the rather faded inscriptions 'Sent. Olivieri' and 'Pomedes'. After the rigours of the via ferrata, the gently descending track comes as a pleasant relief. The route, indicated by waymarks and cairns, initially follows a broad scree-covered shelf in a north-easterly direction. This leads to the top of an easily angled and shallow scree-filled gully, at the foot of which is a large bowl containing the top station of a chairlift (open only in winter). This is your target for the start of the sentiero. Make your way down the scree, now heading in an easterly direction, to the chair-lift station, and continue down on the right-hand side of the line of the lift as far as pylon number 9 (the supporting pylons of most lifts are numbered for identification purposes). Whilst it is very easily missed, the memorial plaque which marks the start of the sentiero is to your right, immediately adjoining this pylon (if your attention wanders at this point, you will find yourself continuing the descent to Rif. Ra Valles, some 130m below). You are now at an altitude of about 2600m, and should have taken about 30 minutes to reach this point after leaving VF Punta Anna.

The first few metres of the route involve a traverse through very broken terrain, with a deep gully plunging down to the left. Splendid views over Cortina are now opening up; make the most of the photo opportunity, because the route will soon demand your full attention. The route now begins its gradual descent to Rif. Pomedes, with cable protection safeguarding the more exposed sections. Two of the steeper steps are descended with the aid of ladders; the move down onto the lower ladder is somewhat awkward and requires particular care. The sentiero now leads into the back of a steep, rather gloomy gully, which usually holds old snow for much of the year. An airy traverse with intermittent protection follows, leading to a large scree-filled bowl, at the other side of which is Rif. Pomedes. This final section of the route offers fine views of the Punta Anna ridge and the line of the VF above. The sentiero ends at the rifugio, some 300m below the memorial plaque which marks its beginning, and about 500m below the point where you left the line of the via ferrata on the ridge.

CORT 11:

VF PUNTA ANNA AND
VF GIANNI AGLIO – TOFANA DE MEZZO

This is a very sustained and demanding via ferrata, which is both technically hard and also committing. The climbing and exposure go on for a long time on a high, serious mountain.

Grade:	5, Seriousness: C
Departure point:	Rif. Dibona or Rif. Pomedes
Ascent:	1200m
Descent:	1200m
Via ferrata:	800m
Approximate time:	8–9 hours (less from Rif. Pomedes)
Highest altitude:	3244m

The route traverses the summit of Punta Anna and ends on the summit of Tofana di Mezzo (3244m), the highest of the Tofana group. The length and airiness of the route, and the committing and technical nature of the climbing, require stamina and a head for heights. This is a route for experienced, fit climbers only. The height of the summit means that icing and snow on the route are possibilities even in the middle of summer.

There are two good approaches to this route.
1. Turn left on a small road at kilometre mark 113.6, on the SS48 from Cortina to Passo Falzarego, and drive up to **Rif. Dibona** (2083m). **Note**: from Passo Falzarego the turn-off is about 8km (5.5 miles). The road is narrow and windy and can be quite busy, so be ready to give way and make use of passing places. It is uphill all the way for about 4km (2.5 miles); the road is metalled for the first half, and then becomes a gravelled track with some potholes for the last mile or so. There is a good deal of space at the roadhead beyond the rifugio, but parking may be congested in peak season. From the car park head north-east and then zigzag uphill on path 421; this leads to Rif. Pomedes (2303m) in about 30 minutes.

2. Use the chairlifts from Rumerio to Duca d'Aosta and on to **Rif. Pomedes**; these operate between early July and early September from 0830 to 1700. They are easy to locate from just outside Cortina, and good parking is available next to Rif. Pietofana.

There is some confusion about the names of the routes up this ridge. The name Via Ferrata Guiseppe Olivieri is used by some maps and guidebooks – sometimes applied to the whole length of the ridge, and sometimes only to its lower portion. Via Ferrata Tofana di Mezzo is also encountered in relation to the upper stretch. However, the most commonly used names now appear to be Via Ferrata Punta Anna for the lower portion of the ridge and Via Ferrata Gianni Aglio for the upper portion. In any event, the name 'Punta Anna' is clearly signpost-ed just above Rif. Pomedes. It is also worth noting that Senterio Guiseppe Olivieri (see CORT 10) is also signposted at this point, leading off to the right (north).

For the route, follow a zigzag path uphill past the top of the Pomedes chairlift and continue by following waymarking to the start of the ferrata in about 15 minutes (2450m). The route goes up to the left, and then an airy traverse leads to a steep ridge giving an immediate feel-ing of exposure. The technical difficulties increase as the ridge is followed, with some good climbing in excellent positions; however, the wire is not continuous, so unpro-tected movement across exposed narrow ledges is some-times required. The summit of Punta Anna (2731m) is reached in about 1½ hours from the start; this is the first real chance of a rest point (although there is also a wide ledge in an open gully just before the summit).

From the summit of Punta Anna a waymarked (and cairned) narrow path leads, mostly unprotected, along the crest of the ridge to a wind-gap. Note that in bad weather care must be taken to follow the waymarks and the ridge, as false tracks appear to lead down ledges, especially on the western side. About 15–20 minutes after the summit of Punta Anna, the word 'Cima' appears painted on the rock. At this point there is also a

Approaching the serious climbing on VF Punta Anna

waymarked route to Rif. Giussani down to the left; this is the first escape point, and leads down ledges and steep ground (some wires) past the ruined Rif. Cantore. However the route continues, following the waymarks up to the right, where a sloping ledge is reached, again leading off to the right. In about a further 15 minutes, after an exposed rightward-leading ledge traverse, the angle of the slope eases off and the next junction is reached. A painted rock indicates 'Cima', up diagonally to the left, for the continuation of the via ferrata. A separate rock on the other side of the track indicates 'Pomedes' and 'Sent. Olivieri' straight ahead to the north-east. This is another escape route, and is described as CORT 10 above. Following the direction indicated by 'Cima', the route continues uphill to the left on a way-marked path through scree-covered slopes. Once on the next ridge there is some protection (not continuous) before a ladder aids progress in ascending a short, steep wall of rock. Following waymarks, the path continues along the ridge, eventually leading to a descending, exposed ledge on the west side of the ridge to the Torri Gianni wind-gap.

The Torri Gianni wind-gap is an exposed crossing on dirty rock and loose earth, with gullies falling away on both sides, after which a strenuous pitch leads from the gap onto the base of the tower above. The protection branches uphill for an optional ascent of the tower (which has to be reversed back to this point as there is no way off its steep north side). However, the route continues to the right along a ledge to a strenuous, exposed move round a corner; the protection is good, but the drop below is quite spectacular. Now pass a gap behind a rock pillar to arrive at the Bus de Tofana (to underline the scale of this route, you will have spent anything up to 4 hours on the route to this point, and still have at least a further 1½ hours to go to reach the summit).

Before continuing the route to the summit it is worth following the wire which leads downhill on the right to the giant rock window of the Forcella del Foro (2910m). Through the rock archway a track leads down steep scree to the west; this is the return route to Rif. Dibona. The route to the summit continues straight on (north) from the Bus de Tofana across broken ground on a path which leads up to a series of avalanche fences. Early in the season (or after fresh summer snowfall, which is not uncommon at this altitude) there may be a snow-field to cross at this point. waymarks lead through the avalanche fences, with some intermittent sections of wire protection. Above the fences the corner of a wall is climbed on two connected ladders which lead onto more exposed ledges, continuing to make upward progress (including some rock scrambling) again following waymarks. A final short ladder is ascended; this is the end of the protection. Waymarks now lead to the summit, but this is serious terrain with big drops around, so it is important to keep to the marked path, particularly if the weather is bad and visibility is poor. In clear weather the views from the summit are outstanding, and just reward for the 5½–6 hours of ascent from Rif. Dibona (less if starting from Rif. Pomedes). Marmolada, Civetta, Sella and Catinaccio – in fact, it almost seems like the whole of the Dolomites – form part of the panorama, in addition to the Stubai, Zillertal and Glockner ranges in Austria.

The descent can be made most easily by using the Tofana cable car back down to Col Druscie (the second stop on the way down) and following a track back to the car park at the bottom of the Rumerio chairlift, at Rif. Pietofana, about 5–10 minutes from the cable car.

However, if you have started from Rif. Dibona and wish to return to collect your car, your descent is made by reversing the ascent route (VF Gianni Aglio) to Bus de Tofana (allow about 1¼–1½ hours), although care will be required in following the waymarked ledges and down-climbing between them. Once at Forcella del Foro, go through the window to the west side and follow a path down through the scree to join path 403 below Rif. Giussani to return to Rif. Dibona. Allow around 2½ hours for the descent from the summit to Rif. Dibona.

Overall a first-class day, but definitely at the top of its grading as one of the most difficult via ferrata routes in the Dolomites.

CORT 12:
VF LAMON AND VF FORMENTON –
TOFANA DI DENTRO

Grade:	2, Seriousness: B
Departure point:	Tofana di Mezzo (top of cable car)
Ascent:	200m
Descent:	950m
Via ferrata:	200m
Approximate time:	4 hours
Highest altitude:	3244m

VF Lamon is best combined with VF Formenton, but can be completed on its own simply to visit the summit of Tofana di Dentro and return by the same way to the cable car and back down to Cortina.

The Tofana cable car (Freccia nel Cielo, 'Arrow in the sky') is the simplest approach; this operates from mid-July to early September, and can be accessed either by using all three stages, or by driving up to Rif. Pietofana, walking to the Col Druscie station (15 minutes), and using the top two stages only. Operating times are 0900 to 1625, on a half-hourly basis staggered between stages, with the last cars down being at 1610 from the top station, 1625 from Ra Valles, and 1640 from Col Druscie.

From the top cable car there is a short walk to the summit of Tofana di Mezzo (3244m). Return from here towards the cable car station and follow red waymarks down a ramp on the left (west) side of the ridge, utilising a steep rake, which is mostly protected by somewhat loose cables. Shortly before the col, a path descends to the left (west) with painted directions indicating Cantore. This should not be regarded as an escape route; it would be easier and safer to return to the top station of the cable car if deteriorating conditions make completion of the route unwise. Descend to the col between Tofana di Mezzo and Tofana di Dentro and then ascend the ridge, which leads up to Tofana di Dentro. Protection on this

From the summit of Tofana di Dentro looking towards Tofana di Mezzo and extraordinary rock folding

ascent is acceptable rather than good as the route works its way up the ridge, passing a number of First World War fortifications. Time from summit to summit (which involves a descent and ascent of 140m) is around 1–1½ hours, depending on traffic and weather conditions. Whilst this is a technically easy route, note that it is on a high mountain and can be subject to snow and icing even in the middle of the summer. From the top of Tofana di Dentro, either return by the same route (return trip 2–3 hours) or descend VF Formenton (see below). (The combined trip for VF Lamon and descent of VF Formenton is around 4 hours.)

To descend VF Formenton go north-east down the wide ridge passing a wartime fortification and following a waymarked path until reaching a very broken ridge with some unstable rock. After passing Biv. Baracca degli Alpini (2922m, a comfortable bivouac hut built into the east side of the ridge), the ridge descends on more discontinuous wires and drops down broken ground to the right. After an exposed traverse along a ledge to the right the route zigzags down a broken gully with some exposed, unprotected scrambling before passing through a window in the rock and out onto an open path below some more wartime buildings. The junction with path 407 is reached as the route continues south-east. The path descends into a rocky gully, and there is a traverse path which leads round the left-hand wall of some rocks and avoids some unnecessary descent. Finally the path ascends back to Rif. Ra Vales and the second intermediate station of the Tofana cable car system for your return back to Cortina.

Alternative route

You could start the route from Ra Valles, ascend VF Formenton to Tofana di Dentro, complete VF Lamon to Tofana di Mezzo, and return to Cortina by the cable car. This would, of course, require more expenditure of energy to cover the height gained rather than descended.

CORTINA – SORAPISS:
THE SORAPISS CIRCUIT

This section describes the Sorapis circuit ('Giro del Sorapiss') in three sections (CORT 13, 14, 15). The Sorapis circuit is a classic mountain round, which can be completed in either direction, although the anti-clockwise option (starting from Rif. Vandelli) seems to be the most popular way of attack, and this route is described below. To complete the whole circuit in a day would require high levels of fitness and stamina (mental as well as physical), along with the ability to cope with considerable exposure over a long period of time. Such an undertaking should only be attempted in stable weather, and even with good fitness you should allow over 12 hours.

The Sorapis circuit breaks down into three distinct sections enabled by the three via ferratas connected with long, often exposed, unprotected paths. En route accommodation is available at Rif. Vandelli (to the north) and two basic bivuoac huts (Slataper and Comici, to the south and east respectively). There is another rifugio to the south, Rif. San Marco, but use of this would involve an additional 430m of descent and re-ascent via Forcella Grande. If using the bivuoac huts you will, of course, have to carry food, water and a light-weight sleeping bag, and allow for the possibility that you may be sharing the very limited space with other people.

Following an approach from Passo Tre Croce (8km east of Cortina on the SS48) to Rifugio Vandelli, the three sections of the anti-clockwise circuit are:

- from Rifugio Vandelli to Bivouac S and G Slataper, Via Ferrata Francesco Berti (CORT 13); allow 5–6 hours
- from Bivouac S and G Slataper to Bivacco Comici, Sentiero Carlo Minazio (CORT 14); allow 3–4 hours,
- from Bivacco Comici, back to Rifugio Vandelli, Via Ferrata Alfonso Vandelli (CORT 15); allow 3–4 hours.

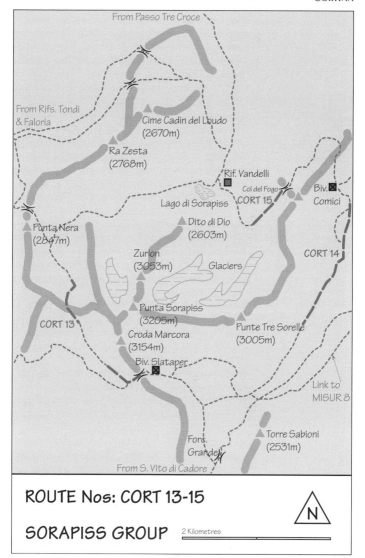

From Passo Tre Croce

From Rifs. Tondi
& Faloria

Cime Cadin del Loudo
(2670m)

Ra Zesta
(2768m)

Rif. Vandelli

Col del Fogo

Biv.
Comici

Lago di Sorapiss

CORT 15

Punta Nera
(2847m)

Dito di Dio
(2603m)

Zurlon
(3053m)

Glaciers

CORT 14

Punta Sorapiss
(3205m)

CORT 13

Punte Tre Sorelle
(3005m)

Croda Marcora
(3154m)

Biv. Slataper

Link to
MISUR 8

Torre Sabioni
(2531m)

Forc.
Grande

From S. Vito di Cadore

ROUTE Nos: CORT 13-15

SORAPISS GROUP

2 Kilometres

N

With the different possibilities for bases and approach routes there are many options available for completing the Sorapiss circuit and its via ferratas. Once you study the map and familiarise yourself with the area, you may choose to structure your own circuit or devise ways of climbing the three routes on different days (although Sentiero Minazio has merit only as a link in enabling the completion of the full circuit). So if a comfortable bed in the valley proves just too alluring, then you can consider breaking into the circuit from the SS51 Cortina–San Vito road, or even from the SS48 Misurina–Auronzo road. However, be warned, these alternative approaches are unremittingly steep and tiring!

Described below is the favoured (and recommended) approach route to Rifugio Vandelli, an alternative approach from Cortina, and the option of an ascent from San Vito di Cadore. The anti-clockwise circuit of the three via ferrata routes Berti, Minazio and Vandelli are then described (CORT 13, 14, 15), including suggestions for single-day outings on VF Berti and VF Vandelli.

Recommended approach: from Passo Tre Croce to Rifugio Vandelli

Drive or take the bus from Cortina to Passo Tre Croce; there is some roadside parking, but beware of the restricted tow-away areas. From the Hotel Tre Croce walk east down the road for 300m to the point where track 215 turns off to the south-east. The track initially contours easily before crossing a stream flowing down from the flanks of Cima di Marcoira above and to the south. After contouring (slightly descending) for a little while longer, the track begins to climb gradually before steepening on more broken terrain. However, this is a well-constructed, well-used track, and the rocky obstacles are easily surmounted with the aid of a series of timber or metal ladders and a few metal footholds in the rock faces. The rifugio, with its magnificent backdrop of the north wall of the Sorapiss mountains, is reached in 1¼–2 hours from Passo Tre Croce. Whether staying at the rifugio or just passing by, you will be unable to resist lingering on the terrace,

enjoying a drink and taking in the outstanding situation. On the rock wall of Torri de Busa to the east you can see the line of VF Vandelli, which climbs diagonally across its face from bottom right to top left.

View from San Vito di Cadore looking up to the VF Berti route

Alternative approach: direct to VF Berti from Cortina, via Rifugio Faloria

Take the cable car to Rif. Faloria (2123m; operating times late June to mid-September; first car up 0900 hrs last car down 1730 hrs. Note that a return ticket is much better value than a one-way ride). The second stage of the lift system, on to Rif. Tondi (2327m), is a winter-only operation, so you now face a short but steep slog up an unpleasant piste. Beyond Rif. Tondi path 213 becomes a pleasant, airy traverse eastwards as far as Forcella Faloria (2309m). At this point, branch off to the south on path 215, which hugs the foot of the cliffs of the north ridge of Punta Nera. You will eventually arrive at a splendidly situated col between Punta Nera and its smaller neighbour, Sella di Punta Nera. If you have time, make the short diversion to visit the latter, which is a magnificent viewpoint. Descend some slightly precarious slabs protected by cables and metal rungs; these provide security in icy conditions as the slabs take a good deal of drainage. From the foot of the slabs continue south-east, now below the eastern wall of Punta Nera, to arrive at the junction of paths 215 and 242. Path 215 heads north-east towards Rif. Vandelli, but to pick up the route towards VF Berti follow path 242 as it heads south then south-east to climb to the start of the Cengia del Banco ledge. For the continuation of the approach, refer to CORT 13 below.

Optional approach: from San Vito di Cadore to Rif. San Marco

Either walk or drive to the San Marco chairlift, just over 1km east of, and 200m vertically above, the village. Take the chairlift to Rif. Scotter and follow path 228 up to Rif. San Marco (see CORT 13 optional descent from Forcella Grande for chairlift and Rif. San Marco details). Allow at least an hour for the ascent to Rif. San Marco from the top of the chairlift. From the rifugio there are two possible single-day options which would take you to Rif. Vandelli, both climbing initially to Forcella Grande – firstly, a south to north traverse of VF Berti and, secondly, a south to north ascent of Sentiero Minazio and descent of VF Vandelli.

CORT 13:
VF FRANCESCO BERTI

Grade:	3, Seriousness: C
Departure point:	Rifugio Vandelli
Ascent:	800m
Descent:	200m
Via ferrata:	200m
Approximate time:	5 to 5½ hours (to Bivacco Slataper)
Highest altitude:	2670m

Take path 215 from Passo Tre Croce to Rif. Vandelli (1¾–2 hours), fully described in the introduction to the Sorapiss Circuit. From Rif. Vandelli follow path 215, signposted VF Berti, to arrive at Lago di Sorapiss in just a few minutes. Go around the lake on its northern side and then stay on the right-hand side of the steep glacial moraine, climbing steadily west up the rough, stony scree slope. As you climb you will see the walls of Zurlon rising above on your left, along with the impressive Dito di Dio (or 'Finger of god') towering above Lago di Sorapiss. After an hour or so the ground eases as you pass through an area of large boulders and into Tondi di Sorapiss; this is a most scenic glacial valley turning south between Punta Nera, ahead to the right (west), and the Sorapiss massif to the left (east). Continue through the valley as the path rises steadily to the junction of paths 215 and 242 at around 2400m, with the gap of Forcella Sora la Cengia del Banco ahead of you to the south (1¾–2 hours from Rif. Vandelli).

Follow the waymarks of path 242 uphill on faint tracks in the scree to the start of the Cengia del Banco ledge. The ledge starts with a fairly steep free climb following waymarks up a short rock wall; this sets the scene for the unprotected exposure you will then experience for at least an hour until reaching the first cables. Cengia del Banco heads generally south as you traverse, descend and ascend in very exposed and unprotected positions with stunning views plunging down to the Cadore valley 1300m below. The rock on the ledge is very broken, so, in addition to the exposure, you must be fully aware at all times of falling rocks from above and unstable rock rubble underfoot – go carefully!

After 45 minutes along the ledge a sign '242 Ferrata Berti' indicates that you will perhaps find some protection eventually, but it is still 20–30 minutes away. (**Note:** it is around this point that path 241 comes up very steeply from Dogana Vechia in Cadore; it is poorly waymarked, extremely laborious and is not to be recommended.) Around 3½ hours after leaving Rif. Vandelli you reach the first cables (what a relief!), but even now the

*Descending the ladder
pitch on VF Berti*

protection is not continuous. Continue following the ledge and cables up, then on a descending traverse, until you reach a corner where the rock looks very unstable.

Here you go down steeply on a series of four ladders reaching a sign '241 Ferrata Berti, Biv. Slataper' to the right, and '242 Cengia del Pis' (no comment) on the left. The route continues with a walk towards a gully up ahead on the left, and in 15–20 minutes climbs up again on cables to three more ladders. Now a short ladder and two stemples lead to a traverse along a ledge going rightwards to arrive at Forcella delle Bivacco (2670m). Allow at least 5 hours from Rif. Vandelli.

At the forcella Ferrata Berti is now over, and Bivacco Scipio and Giuliano Slataper is less than 15 minutes away, perched on a large limestone slab at 2600m. If visibility is bad be careful not to descend too far to the right from the forcella, but cross a deep gash in the limestone and then climb slightly leftwards, following the faint waymarks to the bivacco.

Continuation of Sorapiss Circuit
For details of the continuation of the Sorapiss circuit from Bivacco Slataper to Bivacco Comici see CORT 14, below.

A single-day option for VF Berti, or completion of the Sorapiss circuit with an overnight stay at Rif. San Marco
The introduction to the Sorapiss Circuit noted the possibility of descending from Bivacco Slataper in order to spend a more comfortable night at Rif. San Marco. A further option would be to continue your descent from Rif. San Marco all the way down to San Vito di Cadore. A night at the rifugio enables you to climb back into the circuit the next day, whilst a descent to San Vito would be appropriate if you wanted to tackle VF Berti as a single-day through trip from Rif. Vandelli. If the latter is your choice, you can catch a bus back to Cortina from San Vito, and if you have left your car at Passo Tre Croce catch the bus to there from Cortina. However, check all bus times first and make an early start from Rif. Vandelli, as connections are limited and buses do not run late in the day. Consequently, it is probably logistically better to bus up to Passo Tre Croce on your approach day if choosing this option.

Optional descent to Rif. San Marco and San Vito di Cadore

To descend from Biv. Slataper to Forcella Grande (and then on to Rif. San Marco) follow waymarks for path 246 descending to the right. The path is quite well defined, but the markers are faint and some have even been painted over in grey, which is not easy to see! However, the path is easy to follow as it goes downhill quite steeply before traversing around a grassy hillside towards Forcella Grande (2255m). A thin rock fin, Torre Sabbioni, is across the valley to the east, with the path (226) ascending from Valle di San Vito in the foreground and Monte Antelau rising up to the south-east. Forcella Grande is reached in around an hour from the bivacco, and from here path 226 descends steeply to Rif. San Marco, 430m below, in a further 45 minutes. Rif. San Marco (1823m), tel. 0436 944, has 40 beds if you want to stay there and re-ascend to Forcella Grande (allow 1–1½ hours) to continue the circuit on Ferrata Minazio and Vandelli the next day.

To descend to San Vito di Cadore follow path 228 down to Rif. Scotter (30 minutes). From here you can continue walking all the way down to San Vito (around an hour) or use the San Marco chairlift (350m height loss) and then walk from the bottom of the chair in under 30 minutes. The chairlift operates from late June to mid-September, 0800 to 1700.

This is not really a climbing via ferrata, but more of an enabling link, with some protection, in the completion of the Sorapiss circuit. Although little climbing is involved there is a lot of unprotected exposure on the route.

CORT 14:
SENTIERO CARLO MINAZIO

Grade:	1, Seriousness: C
Departure point:	Bivacco S and G Slataper
Ascent:	200m
Descent:	450m
Via ferrata:	200m
Approximate time:	3–4 hours (to Bivacco Comici)
Highest altitude:	2321m

Bivacco Slataper between VF Berti
and Sentiero Minazio

It is a remote route to do on its own, and although it could be approached from the SS48 Misurina–Auronzo road (even being combined with MISUR 8 Cengia del Doge), this is not recommended, particularly as descent path 227, shown on the map from Bivacco Comici, involves some very steep descent with unprotected (even quite dangerous) climbing on loose rocky ground. Consequently, undertaking Sentiero Minazio is recommended only as part of the Sorapiss circuit. The route is described, continuing the anti-clockwise circuit, from Bivacco Slataper to Bivacco Comici (see CORT 13 above); but, as indicated in the introductory remarks, the choice of how much of the circuit to do in a day and where to stay is your own.

To continue the Sorapiss circuit from Bivacco S and G Slataper (2600m) follow a faint and poorly marked path (247) that crosses the large scree bowl of Fond di Russecco, starting 200m below and east of the bivacco; this descends across the scree towards the buttress coming down from the first 'sister' of Punte Tre Sorelle ('Three sisters'). The path continues on stony ledges and grass slopes descending to meet the path 226/243 coming up from Valle di San Vito at a low point just below 2100m.

Note that from Bivacco Slataper there is an alternative approach to the start of the Minazio route, which is not shown on either Kompass or Tabacco maps except as a black dotted line. Descend path 246 from Bivacco Slataper to around 2300m, where a signpost indicates path '243 Biv. Comici', this descends north-east to join path 247, then 243 mentioned above. Either way, the descent to the low point at the path junction takes about 1 hour.

You are now at the start of Sentiero Carlo Minazio, which follows path 243 from the path junction as it traverses north-east leading easily up to Cengia inferiore dei Colli Neri. The ledge is followed, still generally northwards, with occasional protection, in quite spectacular surroundings, and offers good views across Valle di San Vito to Corno del Doge. After 1–1½ hours on the ledge you come to a large scree bowl where you have two options, both of which are waymarked. The easier route (taking slightly longer) climbs up to the left to Forcella Alta del Banco (2321m) and then descends to Forcella Bassa del Banco (2128m). The harder option, taking 30 minutes less, continues at the same height on an exposed traverse across an exposed slope covered in small pines to arrive at Forcella Bassa del Banco. The descent from Forcella Bassa, on an easy path, to Bivacco Comici, set among trees and small pines, takes 15 minutes.

CORT 15:
VF Alfonso Vandelli

Grade:	3, Seriousness: B
Departure point:	Bivacco Comici (2050m)
Ascent:	310m
Descent:	440m
Via ferrata:	300m
Approximate time:	3–4 hours (to Rif. Vandelli)
Highest altitude:	2360m

To complete the anti-clockwise circuit of Sorapiss from Bivacco Comici, follow path 243 (old waymarks 280) generally north across Busa del Banco. After a short climb you reach a ledge, which soon turns west, and then (after descending slightly) you climb steadily to Col del Fogo (2360m), a superb viewpoint, about 1½ hours from the bivacco. It is interesting to note here that Col del Fogo is shown on some maps as Col del Fuoco – Fuoco being Italian for fire. Of the two names, Col del Fogo seems to be the one most commonly used, and the guidebook follows this convention.

From Col del Fogo, the route descends west/south-west to traverse ledges and cross some steep gullies, with intermittent protection and some exposure, for around 1

*Action on VF Vandelli,
looking back to Lago
di Sorapiss and
Rifugio Vandelli*

hour of down-climbing. This route faces north, and snow-pack in the gullies may be a problem in the early part of the summer (check this out at either Rif. Vandelli or the Cortina guides office before you set off). Pass a sign for 'Alta Via 4 280 LUCIANO' painted on a rock in large letters, and continue to follow waymarks and intermittent cables that eventually lead to more continuous protection as you climb down the western flank of Croda del Fogo. The lower half of Ferrata Vandelli is better protected with cables and ends down a gully with a series of ladders.

From the bottom of the ferrata follow waymarks of footpath 243/Alta Via 4 (sometimes faded) as they lead you generally westwards across a vast glaciated limestone pavement to Rif. Vandelli in about 30 minutes.

Alternatively, this route can be done on its own as a

single-day excursion, climbed (as far as Col del Fogo) and reversed back to Rif. Vandelli in 3½–4 hours (or as a 7–8 hour return trip from Passo Tre Croce, if not staying at the rifugio). This route is described below.

Single-day outing on VF Vandelli

Grade:	3, Seriousness: B
Departure point:	Passo Tre Croce (1805m)
Ascent:	550m
Descent:	550m
Via ferrata:	300m
Approximate time:	7–8 hours (from Passo Tre Croce)
Highest altitude:	2360m

Take path 215 from Passo Tre Croce to Rif. Vandelli in 1¾ to 2 hours, fully described in the introduction to the Sorapiss Circuit. From Rif. Vandelli, follow marked footpath 243 (Alta Via 4, faded paint) signposted Ferrata Vandelli. At first the path leads uphill, then turns east to cross a vast glaciated limestone pavement to the start of the route in 30–40 minutes. The ferrata starts with a series of ladders to ascend a gully, and then follows good cables as it climbs the western flank of Croda del Fogo. After 20 minutes there is a break in the protection, but a short walk along a ledge leads to another good continuous section of cable for another 20 minutes. The cables now become more intermittent, and after 60–70 minutes climbing on the ferrata, you will pass a sign for 'Alta Via 4 280 LUCIANO' painted on a rock in large letters. From this point to the high point (Col del Fogo, 2360m), the route climbs and traverses ledges, with protection now more intermittent, for another hour or so. Col del Fogo is a superb viewpoint; it is about 2½ hours from Rif. Vandelli.

To complete the single-day trip retrace your steps to return back down the ferrata from Col del Fogo to Rif. Vandelli in 1½ hours, and then return to Passo Tre Croce in a further 1–1½ hours.

MISURINA

Maps:
Tabacco Carta Topographica 1:25,000 Sheet 07 or
Kompass Wanderkarte 1:25,000 Sheet 616

Tourist Information Office:
APT Misurina. Telephone: (0435) 39016, Fax: (0435)
39016
Internet: www.misurina.com
E-mail: mito@misurina.com

The view southwards across Lago di Misurina to the
Sorapiss group beyond must be one of the most pho-
tographed in the Dolomites. No surprise, then, that the
rather straggly little village of Misurina is much visited
during the day – although, at nearly 1800m above sea
level, this is no place for an evening passeggiata. Indeed,
the village goes to sleep at sundown. It does, however,
make a very good base, not just for the via ferratist, but
also for walkers wishing to explore the Tre Cime area.
The village is fairly small, so facilities are limited. There
is no bank, for example, but there are quite a few small
hotels in or adjoining the village, together with a large
campsite. There are also several restaurants, a few shops,
including a sports shop and a supermarket, together with
a small tourist office, where German is the first language.

The village is well served by public transport, with
services from Cortina and from the large towns in Val
Pusteria (Pustertal) to the north. Access to the mountains
is good from here, with the Col de Varda lift into the
Cadini group, the jeep taxi to Monte Piana and the bus
to Rif. Auronzo, the gateway to the Tre Cime area. This
area is particularly rich in wartime history. In this con-
text, the Monte Piana plateau offers a splendid and
instructive day in the mountains. The rest of the routes
included here are fine via ferratas in the middle grades.

MISUR 1:
MONTE PIANA

Grade:	1, Seriousness: A
Departure point:	Rif. Antorno
Ascent:	460m
Descent:	460m
Via ferrata:	N/A
Approximate time:	8 hours for thorough explo-ration (Note: use of jeep taxi to/from Rif. Bosi saves 240m of ascent/descent and 2¼ hours)
Highest altitude:	2324m
Note:	**torch required for the galleries**

Whilst there are several protected passages around the edges of the twin summits of Monte Piana, there is little to occupy the climbing-oriented ferratist who has no interest in the history of the Mountain War of 1915–17.

A visit to Monte Piana is recommended for a better appreciation of the circumstances in which the unfortunate protagonists of the Mountain War (see also Falzarego section) lived and died. The whole of the twin summits of Monte Piana, an area of particularly intense conflict, constitutes a vast open-air war museum, with a (limited) programme of excavation and restoration underway. A display of contemporary photographs and artefacts has been assembled at Rif. Bosi, where interpretation material (in Italian and German) is also available. Anyone wishing to research more deeply into this sad episode of the history of the region can find a wealth of material in local bookshops – although, again, little can be found in English.

The road to Rif. Bosi is no longer open to private vehicles, but there are a couple of pleasant paths leading from the Rif. Auronzo road, just north of Rif. Antorno, a little before the toll booth. The northernmost path is way-marked 119, whilst the other, more direct path is not given a number, and is shown on maps with a thin black dotted line. Whichever of the two you choose, allow

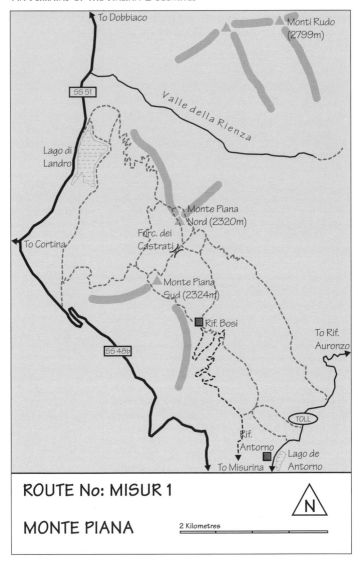

To Dobbiaco

Monti Rudo
(2799m)

Valle della Rienza

SS 51

Lago di
Landro

Monte Piana
Nord (2320m)

Forc. dei
Castrati

To Cortina

Monte Piana
Sud (2324m)

Rif. Bosi

SS 48b

To Rif.
Auronzo

TOLL

Rif.
Antorno

To Misurina

Lago de
Antorno

ROUTE No: MISUR 1

MONTE PIANA

N

2 Kilometres

roughly 1¼ hours to Rif. Bosi. If you feel like a more relaxed day, you can avoid the 240m climb by using the inexpensive jeep taxi service which operates during the summer months between 0900 and 1700 from outside the Restaurant Genzianella, just on the edge of Misurina.

From Rif. Bosi follow the yellow signposts indicating the 'Sentiero Storico'. This winds its way round the most historically interesting areas of the two summits of Monte Piana, visiting the remains of many fortifications, galleries and dugouts, as well as a number of memorials. Some of the major galleries are several hundred metres long, so a torch is essential for a thorough exploration.

MISUR 2:
VF DELLE SCALETTE – TORRE TOBLINO

Grade:	3, Seriousness: B
Departure point:	Rif. Auronzo
Ascent:	300m
Descent:	300m
Via ferrata:	150m
Approximate time:	5 hours
Highest altitude:	2617m

In addition to its historic resonance, this is a fine route, and it should find a place in the itinerary of any ferratist in the area.

Many via ferratas owe their existence, in some part, to the Mountain War of 1915–17 (see Falzarego section), and this route particularly so. The summit of Torre Toblino was an important Austrian observation post, but could only be reached under cover of darkness, since the wartime access route (your line of descent today, see MISUR 3, Sentiero del Curato Militare Hosp, below) was exposed to Italian fire. The rather forbidding looking north chimney, out of sight of the Italians, was therefore equipped as an alternative approach. When the via ferrata was created in the late 1970s the four surviving wooden ladders were retained, although their present condition suggests that the historic links will soon be broken!

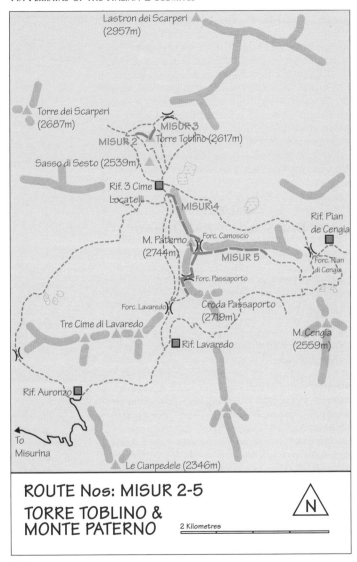

Lastron dei Scarperi
(2957m)

Torre dei Scarperi
(2687m)

MISUR 3

MISUR 2

Torre Toblino (2617m)

Sasso di Sesto (2539m)

Rif. 3 Cime
Locatelli

MISUR 4

Rif. Pian
de Cengia

M. Paterno
(2744m)

Forc. Camoscio

MISUR 5

Forc. Pian
di Cengia

Forc. Passaporto

Forc. Lavaredo

Croda Passaporto
(2719m)

Tre Cime di Lavaredo

Rif. Lavaredo

M. Cengia
(2559m)

Rif. Auronzo

To
Misurina

Le Cianpedele (2346m)

ROUTE Nos: MISUR 2-5

TORRE TOBLINO &
MONTE PATERNO

2 Kilometres

N

There are two other worthwhile via ferratas in the immediate vicinity (MISUR 4 and 5), and whilst climbing all three
in a single day would just about be possible, this would be
a waste unless time is really at a premium. Most climbers
will therefore create their own permutations of routes over
two days before moving on. This area is extremely accessible, being only about an hour's walk from the roadhead at
Rif. Auronzo, and is a magnet for walkers and ferratists. The
size of the car park at the rifugio tells its own story.
Weekends should therefore be avoided!

Rif. Auronzo is reached on a private road from Misurina.
Since there is a hefty toll charge for using this road, you
might prefer to use the bus service, which runs until mid-
September. The first bus from Misurina is at 0840 (arriving at 0905), and from Cortina at 0835 (arriving at 0935).
Note, however, that the last bus down leaves quite early,
at 1650. From the rifugio, follow the crowds heading
north-east on the well-made path towards Rif. Lavaredo,
where you turn north to Forcella Lavaredo, then continue on one of the two parallel paths to Rif. Tre Cime-
Locatelli. The higher, easternmost path is the better
choice, being quieter and more attractive.

The route is waymarked from the rifugio on the path
which heads north from the adjoining chapel and swings
north-west behind the rounded bulk of Sasso di Sesto,
which has partly hidden your objective from view up to
now. Continue round under the west wall of Torre
Toblino to its north side, where the start of the via ferrata is marked by a plaque. Allow 1½ hours from Rif.
Auronzo to here.

The route, which is well protected by cables
throughout, climbs steeply up the back of the pronounced corner, on good but small holds, until the first
ladder is reached. The first of the historic wooden ladders now comes into view. Further ladder pitches lead to
a leftward traverse into the foot of the chimney, which is
the exciting crux of the route and is surmounted by
bridging up to the ladder leading up on the left. The
climb continues airily for a time until the route returns to

the chimney, where the remains of a machine gun position are visible. More ladders, some quite exposed, lead to the splendid summit with views that befit this former observation post. This is not the easiest route on which to overtake slower parties, so allow about 1 hour for the climb, although this can be reduced significantly on a quiet day.

The descent utilizes the original means of access to the old observation post, often referred to as the normal route, but, more properly, is the Sentiero del Curato Militare Hosp (see MISUR 3). The protective cables begin a few metres east of the line of ascent. Allow about 1½ hours for the ascent and descent combined.

MISUR 3:
SENTIERO DEL CURATO MILITARE HOSP –
TORRE TOBLINO

Grade:	2, Seriousness: A
Departure point:	Rif. Auronzo
Ascent:	300m
Descent:	300m
Via ferrata:	100m
Approximate time:	4½ hours
Highest altitude:	2617m

This, the original route to the summit during the Mountain War (see Falzarego section), is now usually tackled as the means of descent from the summit of Torre Toblino by via ferratists who have climbed the VF Delle Scalette (MISUR 2, above). A separate description is included for this route, however, for those keen to visit this splendid summit, but for whom the previous route might seem somewhat intimidating.

The approach is the same as for MISUR 2 as far as Rif. Tre Cime-Locatelli. At the chapel adjoining the rifugio, where the previous route is signposted to the north-west, continue instead along the path waymarked 102 heading north-east. Within a couple of hundred metres a less pronounced path turns off to the left (north). This path leads, in about 20 minutes, to the easy-angled rocks of the north-east flank of the mountain, up which the route climbs. The rock is much less steep than on the northern face of the mountain, and there are no real difficulties to overcome. Consequently, the protective cabling is not continuous, but extends to any passages which involve any degree of exposure. Allow about 45 minutes for the ascent, and slightly less for the descent by the same route.

MISUR 4: SENTIERO DE LUCA/INNERKOFLER – MONTE PATERNO

This route provides an opportunity to explore a system of tunnels dating from the Mountain War and to ascend a shapely peak offering unparalleled views of the surrounding mountains, notably Tre Cime di Lavaredo.

Grade:	2, Seriousness: B
Departure point:	Rif. Auronzo
Ascent:	420m
Descent:	420m
Via ferrata:	1000m
Approximate time:	5 hours
Highest altitude:	2744m
Note:	torch essential

The route is dedicated to two of the most famous protagonists of the Mountain War, Piero de Luca and Sepp Innerkofler, both accomplished mountaineers whose skills and local knowledge were vital to the military campaign. Innerkofler fell to his death during a skirmish on this mountain.

Your starting point is Rif. Tre Cime-Locatelli, the approach to which from Rif. Auronzo is described above (see MISUR 2). The via ferrata is no more than a 10 minute walk to the south-east of Rif. Locatelli, a little beyond the famous rock feature the Salsiccia or, more commonly, Frankfurter Wurstel.

The route begins with a 600m long tunnel complex, which climbs increasingly steeply (and becomes increasingly damp!). Whilst a number of windows provide some limited lighting, a torch is essential. The end of the tunnel provides access onto a spacious shelf beneath a fairly steep wall, up which the route continues, now protected by cables. The steepness eases and the difficulties quickly diminish until a pronounced col is reached beyond a scree-filled groove. This is Forcella del Camoscio, roughly the half-way point, and the junction with the next route (MISUR 5). It is also the point at which the optional ascent to the summit of Monte Paterno begins.

The tunnel windows of Sentiero De Luca/Innerkofler offer superb views of Tre Cime

Ascent of Monte Paterno

Whilst the first 15m of the climb to the summit are quite steep, the difficulties are less than might appear, so don't be deterred. This steep pitch leads to a series of scree-covered shelves, unprotected but without difficulties, and on to the summit. This detour should take about 20 minutes, plus however long you are detained by the splendid view. Return to the col the same way, taking care not to dislodge loose rock since the continuation of the route is immediately below you and there may well be other climbers in the line of fire.

Once back at the col, you are ready to tackle the second half of the route in the knowledge that the main difficulties are now behind you. Turn south and descend an unpleasantly eroded gully for about 100m as far as the start of a system of ledges which traverse below the east side of the ridge. These climb gradually, with intermittent wire protection but without difficulty, to a second col, Forcella Passaporto. The system of ledges continues,

A vestigial path, to the left when facing outwards, makes the descent of the gully somewhat easier.

again with intermittent protection but no difficulties, now on the west side of the ridge. A final short tunnel leads to the end of the route above Forcella Lavaredo. Allow about 3 hours for the whole route.

MISUR 5:
SENTIERO DELLE FORCELLA –
MONTE PATERNO

As a traverse, this route can be tackled either east to west or west to east, but as the former is much more common, it is perhaps better to go with the flow rather than spend all your time having to cross other climbers.

Grade:	1, Seriousness: B
Departure point:	Rif. Auronzo
Ascent:	500m
Descent:	500m
Via ferrata:	800m
Approximate time:	6 hours
Highest altitude:	2744m

This via ferrata ends at Forcella del Camoscio, the mid-point of the De Luca/Innerkofler route (MISUR 4), and it is usually climbed (traversed would be better) in conjunction with that route. If, like most people, you are returning to Rif. Auronzo at the end of your day, it is most convenient to turn south at Forcella del Camoscio and finish the day with the second half of the De Luca/Innerkofler route. Do note, however, that you will need a torch to do so, but the grade is not affected, since this is the easier half of that route.

The most convenient point of access is Rif. Auronzo, described under route MISUR 2. Follow the walk-in as far as Rif. Lavaredo, but from there you should continue round the southern flank of Croda Passaporto on the splendid path (waymarked 104) to Forcella Pian di Cengia. The via ferrata is signposted at the forcella, and is approached on the path which winds gently along, first south then west, below the ridge of the Crode dei Piani.

A little past some old wartime dugouts, you encounter the first obstacle, a 10m deep trench equipped with a short ladder and protected by cables. This leads to a fairly steep 100m pull up a scree slope before the via ferrata starts in earnest at a rather cramped little col. You should allow 2¼ hours from Rif. Auronzo to here.

Protective cables lead down to the start of a series of broad ledges on which the route traverses, losing some 40m along the way, to Forcella del Camoscio, which is reached in about 30 minutes. Whilst there are no technical difficulties to speak of, cabling is only intermittently provided, and some of the unprotected ledges are quite airy. Before embarking on the second half of the De Luca/Innerkofler route in order to return to Rif. Auronzo, you should not miss the opportunity of visiting the summit of Monte Paterno (see MISUR 4 for description), but do note that this pushes up the grade for the walk from 1 to 2.

MISUR 6:
SENTIERO BONACOSSA

Grade:	1, Seriousness: A
Departure point:	Col de Varda
Ascent:	400m
Descent:	200m
Via ferrata:	400m
Approximate time:	5 hours
Highest altitude:	2475m

This is an extremely pleasant mountain traverse which is well protected on those relatively few stretches which negotiate difficult ground.

This route is more a protected walk than a full-blooded via ferrata, but it has the great merit of taking you through dramatic and dramatically contrasting scenery, the final stretch being dominated by outstanding views of Tre Cime.

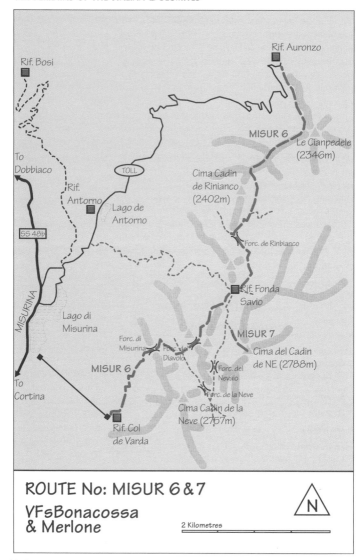

Rif. Auronzo

Rif. Bosi

MISUR 6

Le Cianpedele
(2346m)

To
Dobbiaco

TOLL

Rif.
Antorno

Lago de
Antorno

Cima Cadin
de Rinianco
(2402m)

SS 48b

Forc. de Rinbianco

Rif. Fonda
Savio

Lago di
Misurina

MISUR 7

Forc. di
Misurina

Forc. del
Diavolo

Cima del Cadin
de NE (2788m)

MISUR 6

Forc. del
Nevaio

To
Cortina

Forc. de la Neve

Cima Cadin de la
Neve (2767m)

Rif. Col
de Varda

MISURINA

ROUTE No: MISUR 6 & 7

VFsBonacossa
& Merlone

2 Kilometres

N

Take the chairlift from Lago di Misurina (on the SS48b) to Col de Varda (2115m, open July to mid-September, from 0900 to 1745). From the chairlift station, follow the waymarked route (number 117) northwards, although the first 100m or so, through an area of large boulders, could be clearer. The path ahead, however, is easy to pick out as it climbs diagonally up the scree-covered hillside beneath the impressive west wall of Cima Cadin di Misurina, the north-west ridge of which provides the first obstacle. You will reach this rather impressive look-ing band of rock after about 30 minutes of steady climb-ing from the chairlift. A via ferratist with a number of routes under his belt would probably not feel the need to carry any self-belay equipment on this route, but for the novice this would be the point to gear-up.

After the scramble up to the Forcella di Misurina (2375m) descend into a rather impressive broad gully and cross a path (waymarked 118) which descends from a wind-gap in the ridge high above to the right (south-east). Now climb in a series of zigzags to the north-east, head-ing for the next ridge to be crossed, this time by the Forcella del Diavolo (2475m), the high point of the route, another protected stretch presenting a similar level of dif-ficulty to the last. A gently descending traverse now leads to the splendidly situated Rif. Fonda Savio, which should take 2 hours from the chairlift.

Your path, still well waymarked, now drops to the north-east before swinging round towards Forcella de Rinbianco. Care is needed in this area to ensure that you do not stray onto the path heading north-west down to Lago de Antorno or, a little further on, onto the route into Val de Cianpedele. Your route hugs the east wall of Cima de Rinbianco, and then climbs to the last protected stretch, again without real difficulty. This brings you onto the home straight, with its superb views of Tre Cime straight ahead. Rif. Auronzo, your destination, is now clearly in view, and you can look forward to a well-earned drink (if you have enough time before the last bus leaves for Misurina at 1650). Allow about 5 hours for the whole route.

MISUR 7:
VF MERLONE – CIMA DEL CADIN DE NE

This is a strange one! Without the 100m or so of ladders, it would be an outstanding, hard via ferrata on mainly sound, often very steep rock, but with an abundance of handholds. The existence of the ladders, however, removes most of the technical difficulties on the steep face which the route negotiates.

Grade:	3, Seriousness: B
Departure point:	Lago de Antorno
Ascent:	920m
Descent:	920m
Via ferrata:	300m
Approximate time:	5 hours. Note: For alternative approaches 2 and 3 below, allow up to 3 hrs longer, although no additional ascent is involved
Highest altitude:	2788m

This is often described as a suitable route for beginners; in terms of the technical problems presented this is a fair description, but it is not a route on which to discover that one's novice partner suffers from vertigo!

The route is on the east wall of the impressive valley running south from Rif. Fonda-Savio (2367m), and can be reached in about 20 minutes from the rifugio. There are several options for the approach; here are just three for you to consider.

1. The normal, and probably the easiest, but certainly the least imaginative route is to follow the path signposted for Rif. Fonda-Savio (waymarked 115) from the small car park just off the private road to Rif. Auronzo, a few hundred metres south-west of Lago de Antorno. Allow 1½ hours.

2. Since this is a route which can be climbed relatively quickly, but also one which enjoys a particularly spectacular setting, make the most of the opportunity to explore this group of mountains, quite unlike any other in the Dolomites, with its gnarled pinnacles thrusting up into the sky. Take the chairlift from

Lago di Misurina to Col de Varda (for details of operating times see MISUR 6 above). Follow the southern section of the Sentiero Bonacossa, waymarked 117 (see MISUR 6), which traverses below the west face of the Cadini to the Rif. Fonda-Savio. Allow 2 hours.

3. An even more impressive approach is to follow approach 2 as far as the gully just beyond the Forcella di Misurina, and then take the route (waymarked 118) to the south-east up to Forcella della Neve (2471m). Scramble down the other side for about 70m until it is possible to turn back north, up through a jumble of huge boulders, on a route (waymarked 116) which is intermittently protected by cables and equipped with several ladders. This ascends some 250m to Forcella del Nevaio (about 2650m), which looks down on the desolate valley which contains your objective. The descent from here is steep and precarious, but you have the consolation of having travelled through some of the grandest scenery in the Dolomites! Allow 3½ hours.

Whichever approach you choose, the via ferrata begins at about 2480m at the foot of the impressive west wall of Cima del Cadin. It starts with about 15m of straightforward, unprotected scrambling over easy-angled rocks before the first short cabled section, where the difficulties increase somewhat. As the rock steepens you come to the first of the ladders which are the dominant feature of this route. These lead up without difficulty, but with a considerable degree of exposure, with a brief and exciting interlude provided by an extremely airy traverse leftwards on cable. Yet more ladders lead to a steeply sloping scree shelf, followed by some easy, unprotected scrambling to the summit of Cima del Cadin de NE.

The descent involves reversing the route in its entirety, so in times of heavy traffic care needs to be exercised when crossing other parties, particularly on ladder pitches. Parts of the route are also littered with rock debris, so always remember that there are likely to be other

Climbers on the lower part of the face of VF Merlone

climbers directly above and below you. The route can be climbed and descended in about 1½ hours in total, but allow longer for passing traffic and to enjoy the airy situations.

MISUR 8:
CENGIA DEL DOGE – MARMAROLE

Grade:	1, Seriousness: C
Departure point:	SS48, Punta degli Alberi (Somadida Forest Nature Reserve)
Ascent:	980m
Descent:	980m
Via ferrata:	150m
Approximate time:	7½–8 hours
Highest altitude:	2047m

This route is a long mountain day with about 1000m of ascent and descent and only short, fairly easy sections of ferrata protection. There is, however, considerable and unprotected exposure along the narrow ledge of Cengia del Doge, and so a good head for heights is a definite requirement.

Just off the SS48 at kilometre mark 141.5 (7km from Misurina, 12km from Auronzo), on the south side of the road, there is a small car park (1135m) with a barrier preventing further vehicular progress. Follow the road as it heads west then south-west through the forest. There are no footpath markings or numbers at first, but in a few minutes take the left branch in the road signposted 'Bivacco Comici 277' (even though mapped as 226/ 227), soon arriving at Rif. Tre Sorelle (1148m). You will not get a morning coffee here as this is not actually a 'rifugio' at all, but an open exhibition centre for the Somadida Forest Nature Reserve. Continue past here, on the main track, again following a left branch signed 277. Some 30 minutes after setting off you reach a large open flood plain with two dams. At the first dam, path 226 heads roughly south uphill through the trees, while 200m further on path 227 (note that it now matches the map) goes over the second dam and up to Bivaccco Comici; this path is not recommended, but see route CORT 14 for more detail.

You ascend path 226 on the east side of Valle di San Vito; it is a very pleasant path, which winds up through the forest giving good shelter if it is a sunny day. After an hour or so of ascent, a short descent leads into a large

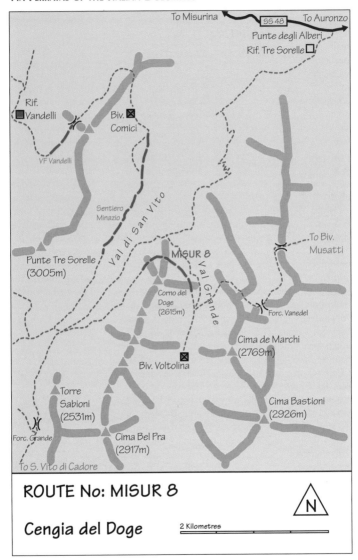

To Misurina   SS 48   To Auronzo

Punte degli Alberi

Rif. Tre Sorelle ☐

Rif.
☐ Vandelli ▓

Biv. ☒
Comici

VF Vandelli

Sentiero
Minazio

Val di San Vito

To Biv.
Musatti

Punte Tre Sorelle
(3005m)

MISUR 8

Val Grande

Corno del
Doge
(2615m)

Forc. Vanedel

Cima de Marchi
(2769m)

Biv. Voltolina ☒

Torre
Sabioni
(2531m)

Cima Bastioni
(2926m)

Forc. Grande

Cima Bel Pra
(2917m)

To S. Vito di Cadore

ROUTE No: MISUR 8

Cengia del Doge

2 Kilometres

Ⓝ

ampitheatre with the impressive sight of Corno del Doge (2615m) straight ahead and (after rain or snow melt) a really spectacular 100m waterfall. The ascent now becomes more tedious on scree slopes until the junction with path 278 marked on a rock wall circa 1650m. Now follow path 278 along a short traverse and ascent, and in a few minutes you reach an easy ferrata climb of about 30m. Further tedious ascent follows up more scree slopes, and eventually the path leads into Val Grande, a wonderful high-level glacial valley. After 1¼–1½ hours on path 278, a junction with Alta Via 5 is reached and you pass a sign for Biv. Musatti. Some 100m further on from here, you join path 280 and can see Bivacco Voltolina ahead, a red box perched high among the rocks.

A faded sign painted on a large rock indicates 'Val di S Vito/Forc Grande' to the right (north). Take this path heading uphill; it is quite indistinct at first as it winds through boulders and small pine bushes, and then becomes very narrow and exposed. In 10–15 minutes (circa 2000m) the first wire protection of Cengia del Doge is reached. The ledge is fairly narrow, with intermittent protection and a lot of broken rock to contend with as well as the exposure. In 20–25 minutes progress becomes easier and continues to spot height 2047m, joining path 226 (the main path up Valle di San Vito) and path 243 (which leads to Bivacco Comici, see route CORT 14). To the south-west path 226 climbs steadily to Forcella Grande, before descending to San Vito di Cadore, but you complete the day's circuit, back down Valle di San Vito, by descending path 226 north-east to the car park; this takes 2½–3 hours.

SESTO

Maps:
Tabacco Carta Topografica 1:25,000 Sheet 010 or
017, or Kompass Wanderkarte 1:25,000 Sheet 617

Tourist Information Office:
APT Sesto I-39030 Sesto-Dolomiti, via Dolomiti, Alto
Adige. Telephone: 0474-710310, Fax: 0474-710318
Internet: www.sesto.it.
E-mail: sexten@rolmail.net

The culture of the twin villages of Sesto/Sexten and
Moso/Moos is emphatically Austrian. You may even
come across people who claim (implausibly, perhaps)
not to be able to speak Italian. You will probably see
more cars with German and Austrian registration plates
than Italian.

This attractive valley forms the north-eastern boundary of the Dolomites, but it is a base which offers splendid opportunities for via ferratas of a wide range of difficulty, as well as rugged mountain walking. The villages
are different in character, and each has its own nucleus.
However, a straggle of ribbon development along the
road now links the two with, right on the join, a modern
sports centre and the largest tourist office you will come
across in the mountains. Between them, the villages provide for all the visitor's needs, with accommodation of
all standards, from hotel to Gastof to apartments.
Remember, you're almost in Austria now, and so 'zimmer
frei' ('rooms free') and 'ferienwohnungen' ('apartments
to let') notices will be commonplace. The nearest campsite is a couple of kilometres to the south-east, on the
road to Passo Montecroce Comelico (Kreuzberg Pass).
The good range of shops includes several selling sports
equipment, and there are numerous restaurants, bars
and hotels serving meals.

The villages are well served by public transport, with

a good bus service from the larger towns of Val Pusteria (Pustertal). Access into the mountains is also reasonably good, with a cable car to the north-west flank of the Croda Rossa (Sextener Rotwand), and access by car or bus to the Dolomitenhof Hotel in Val Fiscalina (Fischleintal). Passo Montecroce Comelico, another important jumping-off point for the mountains, is also accessible by both car and bus.

The Alpine Guides school, useful to obtain information on route conditions, can be found adjacent to the tourist information office; it is open daily in the summer from 1700 to 1900, tel. 0347 2341806, www.alpine.com.

This section includes two outings of only moderate difficulty (SESTO 1 and 2) and two challenging technical climbs (SESTO 3 and 4). All the routes, including the easier ones, require long days, which you will spend in wonderful mountain situations. Even a superficial glance at the map will show that the routes in this area lend themselves to being combined in various permutations to make outstanding traverses of this fine group of mountains. The descriptions below suggest just some of the permutations possible.

SESTO 1:
FERRATA NORD – CRODA ROSSA DI SESTO

Grade:	2, Seriousness: B
Departure point:	Prati di Croda Rossa (Rotwandwiesen)
Ascent:	1000m
Descent:	1000m
Via ferrata:	100m
Approximate time:	6 hours
Highest altitude:	2936m

You can be sure of a splendid mountain day, lots of airy positions and outstanding views from the summit, so it would be a hard-nosed purist who denied its legitimate inclusion in a book such as this.

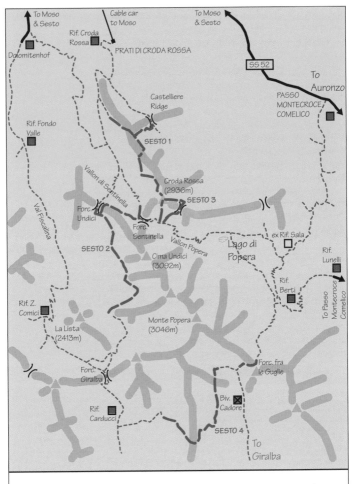

ROUTE Nos: SESTO 1-4

SESTO GROUP

2 Kilometres

The name Ferrata Nord has been used for this route, although it also referred to as a 'sentiero attrezzato' by some publications. However, its claim to being a fully-fledged via ferrata is tenuous, as it is certainly technically easy and has only a limited number of protected climbing pitches.

There is a choice of routes for the first part of the ascent. The original route, dating from the early 1970s, has now been largely eclipsed by the later variation which offers much more pleasant climbing. To make the most of your day, though, it is suggested that you descend by the original route, since this involves a very pleasant traverse from the Castelliere ridge back to the starting point.

An excellent modern gondola runs from the southern edge of the village of Moso from late June to early October (0800 to 1800). This takes you to the Prati Croda Rossa, which, with its various cafes and outdoor concerts, is a popular destination for holidaymakers. You follow the well-constructed path for about 400m across a grassy bowl and up to a junction, where you turn right (west) onto the path waymarked 100. Now you zigzag up through thin pines and small pine bushes, and between small rocky outcrops, to an easy-angled flight of wooden steps, shortly after which is a pleasant small col and a junction of paths. The via ferrata is signposted to the left (south-east) at this point.

The route now leads up over broken ground on the ridge of the Coston di Croda Rossa, another very attractive stretch of the route. The more difficult sections are protected with cables, with ladders surmounting the steeper rock steps. At the top of one of these steps you find yourself in a large and slightly oppressive rocky combe; it is into this combe, on the left, that the original route ascends, up a steep gully at the foot of which are splendid views of the Castelliere ridge. This gully is the suggested descent route, so make a note of its position as you continue up the combe. A little beyond the combe, the path drops slightly and passes the shattered remains of some First World War barracks buildings, and then on to an impressive war memorial on a large level area. Pass

VF Nord on Croda Rossa: this classic route can get very busy

yet more military remains and a stretch of slabby rock before arriving at the only significant challenge of the ascent, a rock wall of some 20m. This is well protected by cable, and is somewhat easier than its appearance suggests. The route now enters a rather shattered area with more rock steps, interspersed with scree slopes, which lead to the end of the route, with its large cross of modern design (allow about 3 hours from the gondola lift). At 2936m, you are a little below the actual summit of Croda Rossa, but the views are nonetheless stunning, and you will be reluctant to tear yourself away.

When the time does come to leave, however, do take care to retrace your steps during the initial part of the descent, or you might find yourself straying onto one of the two variations of the Zandonella route, which lead down to the south and the east. These are fine routes, but of a much harder standard (see SESTO 3). As already suggested, rather than merely reversing the ascent, it is worth making the detour by the Castelliere. The obvious gully leads down steeply to a col on the ridge, where you turn left (north-west) on a pleasant path (waymarked 15b) back to the gondola lift (allow about 2 hours for the descent).

SESTO 2:
STRADA DEGLI ALPINI

Grade:	2, Seriousness: B
Departure point:	Hotel Dolomitenhof
Ascent:	1400m
Descent:	1400m
Via ferrata:	2000m
Approximate time:	8 hours
Highest altitude:	2717m

This is one of a very few via ferratas which have a waymark number on the map (101). However, any walker unused to

Perhaps the route's most dramatic feature is the Cengia Salvezza or the Salvezza Ledge. This extraordinary piece of wartime construction – an artificial ledge cut by Italian troops into the sheer rock face – is all the more impressive for having been constructed entirely at night and in winter.

via ferratas, undertaking the section along the north flank of Cima Undici, would be in for quite a surprise! Even the experienced ferratist should be aware of the potential for this route to become iced up. It is, however, a route which must be included in your itinerary if you visit the Sesto group.

This route is described as an outing from Sesto, but it also lends itself to being included in a tour of rifugios from Misurina across the Sesto group, approaching from the south over Forcella Giralba. Even as a one-day outing, the Strada degli Alpini is quite a lengthy mountain itinerary, but it can be broken down into two parts if preferred. The logical break point is Forcella Undici, which also marks the transition from straightforward mountain walk to something rather more serious. The starting point is the roadhead at the Dolomitenhof Hotel (1460m), 3km south of the village of Moso. This is also the terminus for the rather infrequent bus services from San Candido (Innichen). A very pleasing path (waymarked 103) climbs steadily up Val Fiscalina, southwards, to Rif. Zsigmondy-Comici. Continue south-east from here to skirt round the back of La Lista, and turn east then north, still on path 101, but now signposted to Strada degli Alpini. The path now arrives, quite suddenly, at the Salvezza Ledge, the start of the via ferrata (allow 3 hours to here).

Whilst very airy, this first part of the route is well protected by cables and presents no difficulties, apart from putting away your camera and making progress. The highlight is perhaps where the ledge is cut right into the back of a deep, vertical chimney. Shortly beyond the end of the ledge the route crosses a major drainage line, at Busa di Fuori, where it is normal to encounter a small snow field, even in high summer. The popularity of the route, however, ensures that a well-trodden path makes for an easy crossing. A gentle rising traverse over scree slopes now leads to Forcella Undici (about 2600m), the point where you must decide whether to leave the remainder of the route for another day (allow about 1½ hours to here from start of the via ferrata). The exit route

is the 200m gully, straight ahead of you, which leads steeply down into the foot of a very large scree-filled basin, the Vallon di Sentinella (see below for directions from here back to the valley).

The continuation of the route, which is signposted, involves climbing up to the right (east) over easy rock protected by cables. After perhaps 50m of climbing, the route turns onto the north face of the Cima Undici and passes a crucifix and commemorative plaque. The rest of the route is an undulating traverse, mainly on good, broad ledges, with only limited exposure and no real difficulties, provided the numerous drainage lines you cross are not iced up. If you do encounter significant icing, you should consider seriously whether to proceed; water ice can frequently envelop the cables and coat the rock underfoot. On a north-facing slope, and at an altitude of some 2600m, such conditions can be encountered even in high summer during a cold spell. A programme of re-cabling and minor re-routing was underway in summer 2000, however, which should reduce some of these problems. Shortly after a rock step, surmounted with the

The traverse across the north face of Cima Undici, on Strada Degli Alpini, can ice up at any time

aid of a metal ladder, the route climbs a pronounced groove. At this point, a ledge off to the left leads to a (signposted) descent route. Note this for later reference. After a few more minutes of easy traversing, a final scramble up broken rock brings you to Passo della Sentinella (2717m; allow 1 hour from Forcella Undici). This is another fine situation, and it is easy to appreciate its importance as a wartime observation post, the remains of which are well preserved and covered with commemorative plaques.

A straightforward descent of the broad scree slope to the east is now possible should you wish to travel on to Rif. Berti or Passo Montecroce Comelico. A steep scree-filled gully to the north also looks like a suitable descent route, but a sign warns against this – it is raked with falling stones from the cliffs above. Consequently, it is suggested that you retrace your steps to the descent route referred to earlier. In addition to being safer, this provides about 150m of very pleasant, airy climbing down a gently sloping rib with numerous steep rock steps (allow about 45 minutes). The re-cabling programme will hopefully continue on this part of the route since there were quite a few loose bolts in summer 2000. In the meantime, do try not to swing around too energetically on the cables! The rib deposits you at the top of the scree-filled Vallon di Sentinella. A descent of some 300m now brings you to path 124, which skirts the foot of this scree-filled basin. Turn right (north) and drop gradually to the point where the path begins to climb gently again. Here a fork offers a choice of descent routes to the valley.

The left fork returns to Val Fiscalina and the Dolomitenhof Hotel, whilst continuing straight ahead takes you to the top station of the Prati di Croda Rossa cable car for the ride down to Moso (allow about 1 hour for each).

SESTO 3:

VF MARIO ZANDONELLA, INCLUDING SE VARIANTE – CRODA ROSSA DI SESTO

Grade:	4, Seriousness: B
Departure point:	Rif. Lunelli (1568m) or Passo Montecroce Comelico (1636m)
Ascent:	1500m
Descent:	1500m
Via ferrata:	1500m (for the circuit)
Approximate time:	8 hours
Highest altitude:	2936m
Note:	ice axe and crampons useful

These two routes can be incorporated, either together or separately, into a number of different traverses of the summit of Croda Rossa.

Quite how you tackle these two routes is entirely a matter of personal preference; whatever your choice, you will be guaranteed a splendid mountain day. It will be quite a long and tiring day, however, so the description combines the two routes in an outing from the south-east, since this is much the quieter side, and with less potential for traffic delays.

Departure point Rif. Lunelli

About 8km south-east of Passo Montecroce Comelico, a minor road leads up right (north-west) to Selvapiana, where you can park at Rif. Lunelli. Your day starts with a stiff climb up path 101 to Rif. Berti (1950m; allow 1 hour). Continue north-west up into the moonscape of the Vallon Popera, still on path 101, as far as Lago di Popera (2142m), where path 124 joins from the right (east). This is, in fact, the alternative approach described below.

Departure point Passo Montecroce Comelico

You should take this approach if you are dependent on public transport. Start from Passo Montecroce Comelico, and take path 15a-124, which leaves the road about 100m north-west of the hotel on the crest of the pass.

WWI structures on an easy traverse section of VF Zandonella

Climb pleasantly up through woodland (initially on 15a, then on 124), passing old fortifications from the early years of the cold war (Tito's Yugoslavia was seen as a real threat by Italy). About 30 minutes after setting out, pass a group of old farm buildings up to your right (about 1890m); the path is easily missed at this point, but climb through an area of boulders to join the old motor road (now impassable in places) coming up from Rif. Lunelli. After a short stretch on this dirt road, take path 124 off to the left, signposted to Rif. Berti. Your route now descends gently, through lovely mountain scenery, before climbing sharply up to the now abandoned Rif. Oliva Sala (about 2080m; allow about 1½ hours to here), still watertight and suitable as an emergency bivouac.

The path continues up to the side of the old rifugio. Within a few metres, take the left fork at a junction, signposted to the Belvedere and Forcella Popera. In about 5 minutes, at the Belvedere, the first views open up into the upper reaches of Vallon Popera with its vestigial glacier. From here on, several subsidiary paths occur, but your route is still waymarked 124 as it heads generally north-west to Lago di Popera.

The route

The two alternative approaches having now joined, the path, waymarked 101, heads up north-west into the area of moraine banks left by the retreating glacier. The next hour is hard going, although the path is initially well made. Once on the crest of the moraine bank, at about 2340m, an emergency helicopter landing site is passed before the route becomes less distinct as it climbs up towards Passo della Sentinella (see SESTO 2 above). Keep scanning the cliffs above to your right, and you will be able to pick out the start of the route at an old shelter built into the foot of a rock wall; the dark rectangle of the open doorway is easy to spot, a couple of hundred metres or so to the left (north-west) of the obvious gully which will be your descent route later in the day. You leave the main track to approach the route at a large and prominent boulder (about 2570m) with red and green waymarking pointing up the steep scree slope to the right. This waymarking now winds up the slope to the foot of the rock wall, past several large caves, and on to the shelter you spotted from below. A memorial plaque on the shelter wall, and the first length of cable, confirm that you are at last at the start of the via ferrata. You are now at about 2660m, and will have taken about 3 hours to reach this point, irrespective of your choice of approach.

The climbing starts easily enough, as far as a right-ward traverse on a broad ledge, where the protection ends briefly. The cable then resumes at a short ladder up a steep wall, which is followed by a band of broken, quite steep rock, uncomfortably friable in places. A second ladder (about 2750m) leads shortly to the remains of a group of old wartime buildings set into the rock wall; a plaque indicates that these date from 1917 and were constructed by the 30th Campagna Alpini Battaglioni Fenestrelle. The route continues along an intermittently protected ledge to the right, passing more wartime structures, before a short passage of very easily angled broken rock leads to a further rightward traverse on a broad scree-covered ledge, with very broken crags above and below. The cable resumes at the square corner at the end of the ledge, and leads up a fairly steep but broken chimney, which is climbed without real difficulty. Within a few more metres, at about 2910m, you arrive quite suddenly at a notch in a subsidiary ridge and are confronted with superb views of Sesto and Moso far below to the north-west.

To reach the summit of Croda Rossa, which is very close now, you must first descend about 10–15m into a shallow rift in the rock. The cable follows this rift in a traverse of some 100m until the summit cross comes into view up on the right. A couple of minutes' easy scrambling, past more wartime dugouts, and you are there, at an altitude of 2936m, about 1¼ hours after starting climbing. The view is quite stunning; not quite through 360 degrees because, sadly, the route visits a subsidiary summit, some 30m below the high point of Croda Rossa.

To descend via the **South-East Variante**, which is strongly recommended as a superb finale, walk 50m to the east to the red and green triangular waymarking, just beyond which is a large red arrow pointing to the left into an obvious gap between two large rocks. The cable begins here and leads airily down a steep rib, and more steeply down a broken rock wall, to the upper rim of a scree-filled cirque at about 2790m. It is likely that the bottom of the cirque will be filled with old snow, steep enough to make crampons useful, so proceed with caution if you don't have any with you! The cable now leads up the steep buttress straight ahead (although a red and green triangle in a small forcella to the left indicates an alternative scree descent into Vallon Popera, which would save 30 minutes or so if time was really pressing).

Some 40m of climbing leads to a pronounced shoulder, containing an old observation position (about 2740m). This provides access to a broad ledge, running generally south-west with intermittent protection. This ledge was clearly of some strategic importance during the Mountain War; the easy traverse takes you past a number of old dugouts, the remains of an aerial haulway and an old field kitchen, the stoves of which are still partly intact. After about 300m, the ledge ends at a small saddle, where cables lead down steeply to the scree slope which marks the end of the route (about 2720m), some 1¼ hours after leaving the summit.

The 200m descent of the scree to the main Vallon Popera track is steep, unpleasant and precarious; you would be well advised to keep your helmet on until safely down, and not to linger at the foot of the scree slope if other climbers are descending behind you! You now have a good couple of hours of steady walking during which you can savour the climb to return to your starting point.

SESTO 4:
VF ALDO ROGHEL AND
VF CENGIA GABRIELLA

Grade:	4 (Roghel) and 3 (Gabriella), Seriousness: C
Departure point:	Rif Lunelli (1568m)
Ascent:	1420m from Rif. Carducci or 1600m from Hotel Dolomitenhof
Descent:	685m to Rif. Carducci or 1670m to Hotel Dolomitenhof
Via ferrata:	Roghel 400m, Gabriella 1500m
Approximate time:	8 hours to Rif Carducci or 10½ hours to Hotel Dolomitenhof
Highest altitude:	2540m

Whilst it would, theoretically, be possible to tackle these routes separately, to do so would be somewhat perverse. In each case it would be necessary to reverse the entire route or face an extremely long walk out, ending up many miles from one's starting point.

The route described here combines the two in a splendid traverse of wild and rugged mountain terrain. Another option, which has considerable aesthetic appeal, is to build in an overnight stay at Rif. Carducci and then, on the second day, tackle the Strada degli Alpini (route SESTO 2) before returning to Rif. Lunelli, thus completing an outstanding circuit.

Whatever your choice, the starting point is Rif. Lunelli, access to which is described at SESTO 3. Once again your day starts with the climb up to Rif. Berti, from where path 109-152 leads off to the south, initially losing height to cross a small stream. About 300m beyond the stream, take path 109 off to the right, signposted Rif.Carducci and VF Roghel (about 1945m). The path, clearly waymarked, zigzags steeply up to the south-west up the scree slope to reach the start of the ferrata at an altitude of about 2370m, roughly 45 minutes after leaving Rif. Berti.

VF Aldo Roghel

Your first route consists of a steep climb up to Forcella fra le Guglie (2540m), followed by a steep descent into Ciadin de Stalata. The ascent faces generally north-east, and much of the route is in deep shade. Consequently, expect to find some icing at the start and end of the season (and don't discount the possibility at any time of the year when the weather is cold). Whilst the route is fully protected, many of the cable runs are unusually long and frequently quite loose, making for a fairly serious and committing route. The climb starts easily with an ascending traverse to the right followed by a rake to the left. The first steep wall follows, which is surmounted with the aid of several metal footholds. A broad scree-covered ledge leads rightwards to a steep crack (best climbed by bridging), which leads into a gloomy gully. This is climbed up the steep right wall before a rather thin traverse to the left, brings you back into the gully. Once more, the cable leads steeply up the right wall, again equipped with several metal footholds, before your third visit to the gully. The route finally escapes the gully, again by ascending the right wall. Whilst several easily angled passages follow, much of the climbing is up very steep rock, and consequently is quite strenuous in places. The greatest effort is required for an awkwardly bulging wall equipped with metal footholds and a disconcertingly loose cable (at about 2520m). Forcella fra le Guglie is reached quite suddenly, after about an hour's climbing.

You will be glad of the rest whilst you enjoy the view down into Ciadin de Stalata and to the attractively located Bivacco Battaglione Cadore. This, incidentally, offers the only possible escape route in a long and committing day; the bivouac provides good emergency accommodation, but the walk out to Giralba, to the south, is lengthy and initially not straightforward. From your vantage point in the forcella you can also see the track round the back of the great scree bowl, which you will be taking shortly, and the first part of the VF Gabriella. First, however, you face a 40 minute descent to the foot of the rocks below you. This starts with a gently descending traverse down an easy gravel-covered rake leading to the south. The cable then turns down the very broken rock wall below you, initially at an easy angle, but steepening appreciably as it continues. The rock wall ends in a gully, at about 2465m, where the cable continues to safeguard an easy scramble down into Ciadin dei Stalata. A sharp right turn now leads to the track you spotted from above, running around the scree bowl, roughly 45 minutes' walk to the start of VF Gabriella.

VF Cengia Gabriella

Your second route is in marked contrast to VF Roghel, with its vertiginous ascent and plunging descent. This is a long, undulating traverse round the south ridge of Monte Giralba de Sotto. The cable begins at about 2430m at the top of a short, rather dirty gully. Easily angled rock and a steep gravel rake lead to the start of the ledge ('cengia') which is the dominant feature of this route. Generally quite broad, sloping and scree covered, it requires only intermittent cable protection for the occasional airy passage as it undulates southwards. The views are, however, quite breathtaking, and since much of the route lacks any real technical difficulties, you are able to enjoy them to the full.

The ledge is not, however, continuous, and after about 30 minutes an airy 30m traverse across rock slabs provides an exciting interlude. About 20 minutes later, a series of rock steps leads down into a very broken jumble

On part of the exposed traverse of VF Gabriella above Val Stalata

of rocks with a large natural cave, beyond which the route continues with a tight squeeze under an overhanging roof. Shortly after, at about 2280m, and an hour after starting out, the route reaches its lowest point, and a long, generally ascending passage begins. An airy traverse across easily angled slabs leads towards an imposing-looking rock tower. A couple of hundred metres short of this feature, however, the route turns up a steep grassy slope, following a gravel path to an airy little ridge which looks down into a shallow, but-steep sided gully. The path leads right along the crest of the ridge and down into the gully, where the cable resumes for a leftward traverse of 100m or so before a series of rock steps leads upwards to a broken corner and a shallow gully. This is crossed to reach a further area of broken slabs, across which an occasionally airy traverse is made. A gently angled gully, cabled in its lower part, now leads up to a very broad grassy shoulder, the point where the route takes a sharp turn to the north-west. This is a splendid viewpoint, overlooking the point where Val Giralba divides: the western branch, Val Giralba Alta, running up to Rif. Carducci, now visible for the first time and on to Forcella Giralba. This also marks the high point of the route at about 2480m, and is about 45 minutes beyond the low point passed earlier.

The continuation of the route, once again on the prominent broad ledge, is clearly visible as it undulates gently north-west, following the curve of the rock wall rising up to Monte Giralba. About 30 minutes of easy walking brings you to the start of a series of plunging descents from the ledge down into Val Giralba Alta. Steep rock, followed by a gully and finally a broken wall, begins the descent. A short traverse then leads to a heart-stopping corner, where the cable plunges down steeply for about 80m into a dirty gully, which usually holds snow throughout the year. The route continues down the gully side, fortunately at an easy angle, since the protective cable is both intermittent and frequently damaged (at the time of writing). About 1¼ hours from the high point, the gully finally emerges into a large scree-covered bowl, which marks the end of the via ferrata (at about 2280m).

Depending on your plans (and your stamina), you now have a 45 minute walk to Rif. Carducci or 3½ hours to the roadhead at Hotel Dolomitenhof. From the foot of the gully, take path 110 round the scree bowl as far as path 103. This is the main route up Val Giralba, and leads easily to Rif. Carducci (2297m), which is a welcoming stop-over for those intent on completing the circuit by tackling Strada degli Alpini (SESTO 2) on the morrow. If you have energy to spare, and a comfortable bed in the valley, then continue on path 103 as it zigzags northwards to Forcella Giralba (2431m). The path now drops gently north-west to Rif. Zsigmondy-Comici (2224m), where the solitude you have almost certainly enjoyed thus far is likely to be shattered, since this is a very popular day's outing from Sesto and Moso. You now have a straightforward and most attractive walk down Val Fiscalina, still on path 103, to reach the road at Hotel Dolomitenhof (1454m), where you can pick up a bus, collect your car or start to hitch back to your base.

AURONZO

Maps:
Tabacco Carta Topographica 1:25,000 Sheet 01, 16 and 17 or Kompass Wanderkarte 1:25,000 Sheet 616

Tourist Information Office:
APT Auronzo, 32041 Auronzo di Cadore (BL) Via Roma 10. Telephone: (0435) 9359 or 400666, Fax: (0435) 400161
Internet: www.auronzo.com or www.auronzodicadore.it
E-mail: studio@auronzo.it or auronzo@sunrise.it

Auronzo di Cadore (850m) is quite a sizeable town along the banks of Lago Santa Caterina and the Ansiei river. It is well provided with all the facilities required by the visitor and, unlike some of the surrounding towns, where German is widely spoken, Auronzo has Italian as its first language. It enjoys a splendid position beneath the Marmarole group to the south and the Sesto group to the north, and with more dramatic views up the valley to the north-west towards the Tre Cime di Laverado.

Being very much on the edge of the main mountain groups it has a bustle about it which owes less to tourism than many of the other centres in this guidebook. However, the tourist office is very helpful, and each evening in the summer between 1730 and 1900 hours mountain guides are there to give advice, including information on route conditions.

Auronzo is quite easily accessible, being a fairly short bus ride from Calalzo di Cadore, which can be reached by train from Venice/Belluno or by bus from Cortina. Access to the five routes described in this section, however, really require the use of private transport.

The mountains in this area have a quiet, almost lonely feel to them, as they are frequently ignored in favour of their slightly higher or more dramatic neighbours. The via ferratas on offer to the visitor are not particularly technical, but two of them fit within quite long mountain days and offer options for through-trips with overnight stays.

AURO 1:
SENTIERO DEGLI ALPINI – MARMOROLE

Grade:	2, Seriousness: C
Departure point:	Val d'Oten above Calalzo
Ascent:	1500m
Descent:	1500m
Via ferrata:	450m
Approximate time:	8–9 hours, but see below for through-trip options
Highest altitude:	2650m

This is a high mountain route which has a number of options.

From Ponte Diassa (in Val d'Oten) a return route can be completed in a single day; this is the route described below. It is also possible to do a long through- route from Calalzo by continuing from Forcella Jau de la Tana down to Bivacco Tiziano (2264m) and continuing on path 260 down the remote Val d'Ansiei to Cap Alpina de Savio (11km from Auronzo on the Misurina road, SS48). To do this you would need to work out the transport logistics to get you to the start and from the finish; this would probably involve taking a taxi from Calalzo to Bar alla Pinetta, and checking the Dolomiti bus timetable for the other links. Another serious mountain route would be to go east from Forcella Jau de la Tana along the steep northern side of Punta Anita to Forcella Froppa, descending Vallon di Froppa. However, the high north-facing slopes are likely to hold snow early in the summer, so only consider these ideas later on in the season or after a winter with only minimal snow fall.

Approach is by driving 6km from Calalzo, following signs for Val D'Oten. The metalled road ends at Bar alla

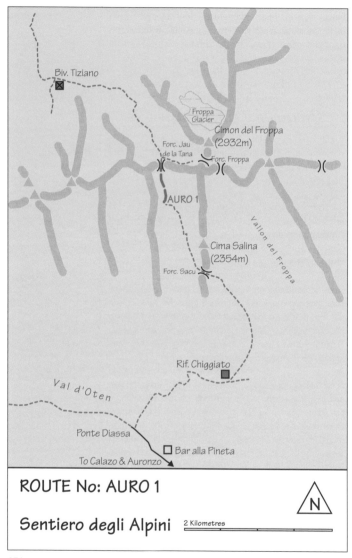

ROUTE No: AURO 1

Sentiero degli Alpini

2 Kilometres

Pineta (1044m), but it is possible to drive a further 800m on a jeep track, which is stony but passable with care, to a parking area at Ponte Diassa, 1133m (the walk up from Bar alla Pineta takes 15 minutes if you park there). Now climb path 260 up through the trees to Rif. Chiggiato (1911m), an ascent of 780m; allow 2 to 2½ hours. For early season information on the route, you might find it useful to ring the rifugio (which has 50 beds, and is open from late June until late September, tel. 0435 31452).

From Rif. Chiggiato continue on path 260 (also Alta Via 5) on fairly level ground until reaching Forcella Sacu. Path 260 then turns north-west towards the spur of Cima Salina, coming down from Monte Froppa. The waymarking is not particularly clear as the path rises up left through an area of small pine shrubs, then along ledges on the east side of Val di Tana. Between 2000m and 2100m, the path crosses the gully to a rock spur and then zigzags back climbing to the start of the ferrata protection (circa 2170m) in about 1½ hours from the rifugio. The ferrata works it way up with cables and steps to Forcella Jau de la Tana (2650m) in a further 1½ hours, making a total of 3 hours from the rifugio and 5½ hours from Ponte Diassa.

Return by descending the same route in approximately 3 hours.

AURO 2:
SENTIERO AMALIO DA PRA – MARMOROLE

Grade:	2, Seriousness: B
Departure point:	Pian dei Buoi above Lozzo di Cadore
Ascent:	550m
Descent:	550m
Via ferrata:	200m
Approximate time:	4 hours (3–3½ hour circuit from Rif. Ciareido)
Highest altitude:	2298m

The ferrata involves an undulating traverse of a series of ledges. Since it crosses a number of steep north-facing gullies it is not recommended at the beginning of the summer or after new snow.

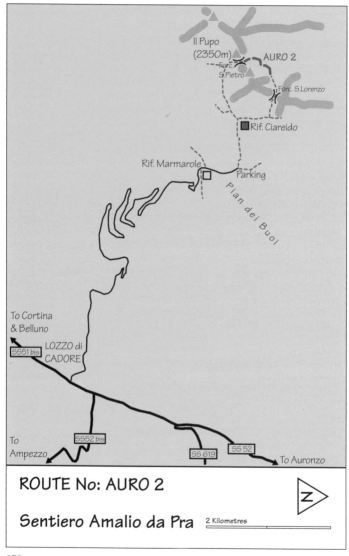

Il Pupo
(2350m)

AURO 2

Forc.
S.Pietro

Forc. S.Lorenzo

Rif. Ciareido

Rif. Marmarole

Parking

P i a n   d e i   B u o i

To Cortina
& Belluno

SS51 bis

LOZZO di
CADORE

To
Ampezzo

SS52 bis

SS 619

SS 52

To Auronzo

ROUTE No: AURO 2

Sentiero Amalio da Pra

2 Kilometres

N

This route enables a circuit of Monte Ciareido (2504m) to be achieved. The ferrata is on the north-west side of the mountain and is approached from Rif. Ciareido (1969m) on its south side. Conditions should be confirmed with the warden at Rif. Ciareido (tel. 0435 76276).

Drive from Lozzo di Cadore, which is on the SS51 bis, about 8km south of Auronzo, following brown signs to Pian dei Buoi (total distance 12km). Above Le Spesse (863m) the road has controlled access from 1 July to 31 August, with uphill traffic having access between 0900 and 1300, and downhill traffic 1400 to 1700. Between the hours of 1700 to 0900 access is uncontrolled, but meeting something coming the other way would be an interesting experience! The road is narrow, steep, and has numerous 180 degree turns and very limited passing places, but it is metalled for most of the way. However, the road does enable a height gain of over 1000m to be achieved; so whilst it is a testing drive, its benefits do not need further explanation! At the end of the tarmac, 500m of rough track leads to a parking place by Rif. Marmarole 1786m (closed in 2001), but improves again to more parking in a further 700m at Pian dei Buoi (1810m). From here you can walk up to Rif. Ciadeido in around 30 minutes.

Although the ferrata can be completed in either direction, it is recommended as an anti-clockwise circuit. So, from the rifugio head north for 10 minutes on Alta Via 5 (path 272) before turning left (west) uphill to climb to Forcella San Lorenzo (2223m), about 45–60 minutes from the rifugio. From the forcella descend briefly to the west following a large ledge under Torre Pian dei Buoi, but beware of loose rock underfoot and falling stones from above. From here there is a wonderful panorama of the Sesto Dolomites to the north and Monte Ciareido rising above on the south. In about 20 minutes the route descends easily at first, then quite steeply, on cables for 25m. After crossing a gully you climb back up for about 80m to a rock spur, then continue to traverse through two small cols towards Forcella

*'Il Pupo' above
Forcella di San Pietro
on the Sentiero
Amalio da Pra*

San Pietro, which is dominated by the striking view of a large rock pillar, Il Pupo (2350m). The route from Forcella San Lorenzo to Forcella San Pietro takes around 1¾ hours. Now descend, steeply at first, and then follow the waymarked path back to Rif. Ciadeido in 40–45 minutes. From the rifugio return to the parking area at Pian dei Buoi.

AURO 3:
VF MAZZETTA – PADOLA

Grade:	2, Seriousness: C
Departure point:	Car park above Padola (1350m)
Ascent:	1200m
Descent:	1200m
Via ferrata:	150m
Approximate time:	7–8 hours
Highest altitude:	2347m

This ferrata is not particularly difficult, but it is in a remote and not much frequented area. This, coupled with the long ascent, makes this excursion a serious mountain undertaking best completed in stable weather.

As the high north-facing gullies of Croda di Tacco and Cima Padola can hold snow early in the season, it is worth checking conditions with the mountain guides in Auronzo. For a serious mountain trip various options can be worked out, including a long ascent from Auronzo and, perhaps, a night in Bivacco Carlo Gera. However, a simple ascent from Padola is recommended (and described below), with a return route descending the same way.

Padola is 15km (under 30 minutes) from Auronzo on the SS532, over Passo di San Antonio. In Padola, follow signs to Malga Aiarmola, up Via Ajarmola and continuing up Via Al Castella to the end of the metalled road (about 750m) and a large parking area at Acque Rosse (1350m). From the car park, walk unrelentingly uphill (path 152), first on a jeep track, which soon becomes a path and continues climbing. Eventually the path meets a forestry road, which then arrives in a few more minutes at Casera Aiarmola (1600m), where there are some old stables and a welcoming (especially on a hot day!) trough with running water. Time taken from car park to here is 45–55 minutes.

Now continue heading uphill (path 152) signposted Biv Gera (Col dei Bagni 164 on the other side of the signpost). In 250m path 164 continues right at the fork as the

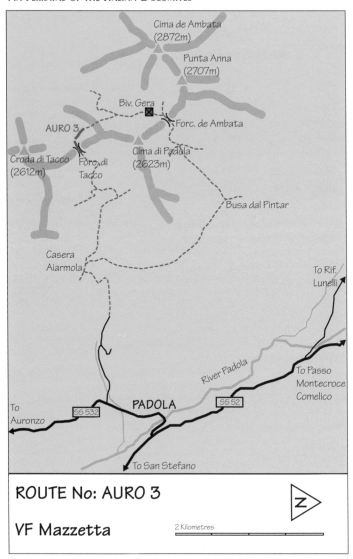

Cima de Ambata
(2872m)

Punta Anna
(2707m)

Biv. Gera

Forc. de Ambata

AURO 3

Croda di Tacco
(2612m)

Forc. di
Tacco

Cima di Padola
(2623m)

Busa dal Pintar

Casera
Aiarmola

To Rif.
Lunelli

River Padola

To Passo
Montecroce
Comelico

PADOLA

SS 532

SS 52

To
Auronzo

To San Stefano

ROUTE No: AURO 3

VF Mazzetta

2 Kilometres

N

main track and presents an option for a longer circuit (see below). However, you follow the left fork uphill on path 152 to climb directly to Forcella di Tacco (with Sentiero F. Mazzetta also signposted at this point, 'Sopra Casera Aiarmola, 1650m'). The path continues first in trees, then out onto the scree of Giao Glauzei, and back into the trees, where the junction with path 153 is signed. Pass the first boulder, and the path junction is reached in a couple of minutes. Path 152 continues (yes, uphill again!), but as the path runs out on the side of the old glacial moraine, it crosses over to the left side (orographically right) to pick up good waymarks, which climb the steep slopes on grass and rock to reach Forcella di Tacco (2347m). Allow 3–3½ hours from the car park.

The ferrata starts just below the forcella on your approach (east) side, and after a few metres of climbing leads to the forcella, with tremendous views into the bowl below Croda di Tacco, a distant panorama of Marmorole and Sorapiss, and the now spectacular view back down to Padola 1150m below. From the forcella, descend on good cables for about 150m. You pass a small gully, make a slightly exposed move round a corner, and continue down to arrive in the scree bowl below Croda di Tacco, losing height to just below 2200m. This descent takes you into Val di Ambata (approximately 40 minutes from Forcella di Tacco), and with a further 10 minutes' climbing on gravely ledges and intermittent protection you arrive at Bivacco Carlo Gera (2240m). Return by the same route, arriving in 1¼ hours back at Forcella di Tacco, and in a total of 2–2½ hours down path 152 back at the car park. The total length of day is 7–8 hours.

Circuit option

An optional route, which makes a circuit for the day, is to follow path 164 from Casera Aiarmola to Busa dal Pintar (1743m), and then follow path 126, initially easily but becoming steep, to Forcella di Ambata. From Forcella di Ambata descend to Bivacco Gera and continue to the ferrata from there, ascending to Forcella di Tacco and returning to Padola. This circuit route cannot be wholly recommended,

Please note, however, that this circuit involves unprotected grade I/II climbing on the east side of Forcella de Ambata which is best tackled in ascent. Consequently, an anti-clockwise circuit is recommended.

however, as path 164 has been badly damaged by forestry work; it may recover in some years' time.

AURO 4:

Ferrata Sartor – Monte Peralba, Sappada

This straightforward but pleasant route can be easily climbed on its own, or combined with route AURO 5 to make either a long single day or a two-day excursion with an overnight stay at a refuge.

Grade:	2, Seriousness: B
Departure point:	Rif. Sorgenti
Ascent:	880m
Descent:	880m
Via ferrata:	250m
Approximate time:	4½ hours; about 8 hours with route AURO 5 (see below)
Highest altitude:	2694m

Whilst Sappada is in the north of Belluno province, almost 40km from Auronzo, it is less than an hour's drive away, since it is connected by good valley roads rather than the usual Dolomitic mountain passes. Follow the SS52 to St Stefano di Cadore, then SS355 to Cima Sappada, where Rif. Sorgenti is signposted. Even if you decide to stay in Sappada a car is essential for this route, as the minor road up to Rif. Sorgenti is 8km in length. Whilst it is narrow and windy, it is metalled the whole way to a large and obvious parking place (marked on the Tabacco map) about 750m before the rifugio. A jeep track (path 132, and with no public vehicle access) leads up to Rif. Calvi. Either follow the track (recommended) or, after 20 to 30 minutes, Sentiero delle Marmotte, arriving at Rif. Calvi in less than an hour.

To the right (south-east) of Rif. Calvi is Monte Chiadenis. One of its ferratas (AURO 5) can be reached in less than 10 minutes. Monte Peralba is to the left (north) of the rifugio. Both routes can be climbed separately (with

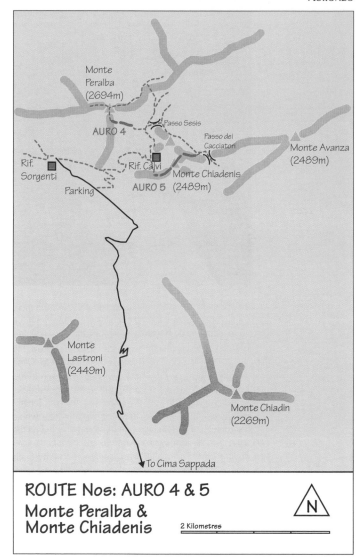

ROUTE Nos: AURO 4 & 5
Monte Peralba &
Monte Chiadenis

2 Kilometres

Left-over snow early in the season at the start of Ferrata Sartor, Monte Peralba

an overnight stay in either Rif. Sorgenti or the smaller Rif. Calvi), but if you are feeling energetic and the weather is good, climbing both routes in one long but satisfying day is highly recommended.

For the Monte Peralba ferrata, follow path 131 and ascend fairly steeply for about 15 minutes until reaching a sign for 'Ferrata Sartor', where the path now traverses left and zigzags up to the start of the route at around 2350m (allow 30 minutes from the rifugio to the start of the route). The ferrata takes about 30 minutes in total; it is on good rock, with nice positions and excellent views down to Rif. Calvi. After 15–20 minutes on the ferrata there is a Y-branch. The right branch is steeper and slightly harder, but both branches lead to the same place, where the red waymarks are then followed to Monte Peralba summit (take care not to displace loose stones at first) in a further 30 minutes. It is an interesting summit, with a Madonna statuette, a cross and even (beware!) a bell.

You descend to the east, following waymarks until an arrow points (north) down a steep gully. There are some cables in the upper part of the gully, but they can be covered by snow early in the season. As the gully opens up, zigzag down following red waymarks until a traverse path leads roughly east to Passo Sesis (2312m), 1–1¼ hours from the summit. If you are only climbing Monte Peralba, descend on path 132 to Rif. Calvi in around 20 minutes and continue down to the car park in a further 30–40 minutes. However if you have decided to extend your day by combining this route with AURO 5, continue from path 173 towards Passo del Cacciatori and pick up the route description below. Climbing both Monte Peralba and Monte Chiadenis in this way will extend your day to a round-trip of about 8 hours.

AURO 5:
VF NORD AND VF SUD-OVEST –
MONTE CHIADENIS, SAPPADA

VF Nord:	Grade: 3, Seriousness: B
VF Sud-Ovest:	Grade: 2, Seriousness: B
Departure point:	Rif. Sorgenti
Ascent:	650m
Descent:	650m
Via ferrata:	300m and 400m
Approximate time:	5 hours; about 8 hours with AURO 4 (see AURO 4)
Highest altitude:	2489m

Monte Chiadenis is easily reached from Rifs. Sorgenti and Calvi (see route AURO 4 for a full description of the approach and a suggested combination of the two routes in one day). In fact there are two ferratas on Monte Chiadenis, both of them good routes. The easier of the two is on its south-west ridge, accessed quickly from Rif. Calvi, whilst the harder route on its northern side is accessed from Passo del Cacciatori. The recommended route, described below, comprises an ascent by the harder (grade 3B) route first and a descent by the easier (grade 2B) route. However, as the mountain can be climbed in either direction, it is likely that whichever way you choose you will have to pass people coming from the opposite direction. Needless to say, should you wish to visit the summit, but are deterred by the prospect of the harder route, you could simply ascend and descend the easier route of Monte Chiadenis. The timings for ascent/descent would be about the same.

Monte Chiadennis, the start of Ferrata Nord

From Rif. Calvi follow path 131/132/140, ascending fairly steeply for 15 minutes, taking the right fork at the sign for Ferrata Sartor. The gradient now eases, and the path bears north-east towards Passo Sesis (2312m), taking less than 30 minutes in total from the rifugio. Now follow path 173 towards Passo del Cacciatori, and in 15 minutes a right turn uphill is signposted to the start of Via Ferrata Chiadenis. Climbing Monte Chiadenis from this direction involves some quite steep ascents in places. Furthermore, the cables are of the loose rather than tensioned variety, and you must watch out for parties above (descending perhaps), as there is some loose rock around. Follow the first long run-out of cable to a wedged boulder. Then climb down to the left and ascend a gully by means of a number of quite testing moves up a series of short walls and chimneys. After about an hour of climbing, the route traverses (occasionally unprotected) along ledges, avoiding Pic Chiadenis. You pass a number of wartime caves, and arrive at the summit of Monte Chiadenis 10 minutes from the start of the traverse.

The descent (south-west from the summit) from Monte Chiadenis to a col south of Rif. Calvi takes roughly 1½ hours, depending on the amount of traffic. Generally the cable protection is sound, but there are some short unprotected sections of free climbing. The last 30m of down-climbing is quite steep compared to the rest of the descent, but protection on this section is good. The ferrata ends at a strategically located col with a number of wartime fortifications. Return to the car park in 30–40 minutes, either by following the jeep track or, more directly, down a waymarked path, the Sentiero delle Marmotte.

AURO 6: VF DEI 50 –
VAL PESARINA

The Clap (meaning stone in Carnian) occupies a central part of the chain of mountains in the extreme north-western part of Friuli Venezia Giulia. The VF dei 50, a long, remote and spectacular route taking in the summit ridge of the Creton di Culzéi, is the result of the hard labour of a group of enthusiasts named the Gruppo dei Cinquante del Clap.

The information for this route has kindly been provided by Anne Brearley, BAEML Trieste, Italy and Les Ainsworth, Cumbria U.K. The authors have not yet had the chance to check this out for themselves, but are looking forward to it!

Grade and Seriousness:	Grade: 4, Seriousness: C
Departure point:	Pian di Casa SS465 (1236m), then Rif. De Gasperi
Ascent:	1400m
Descent:	1400m
Via ferrata:	about 1600m
Approximate time:	allow 9–10 hours from Pian di Casa
Highest altitude:	Creton di Culzéi, 2458m

Park at Pian di Casa (Val Pesarina), and take path 201 (Alta Via 6) to Rif. De Gasperi 1767m in about 1½ hours. An anti-clockwise circuit of the ferrata is recommended going north-east from the rifugio on path 316 (Sentiero Corbellini) for about 30 minutes to the point where the path is eroded due to one of the stream gullies of Rio Bianco (1693m). Although not signed there are traces of a path climbing upwards to red paint marks and the start of the ferrata in about 10 minutes (altitude 1800m).

The climb is on good rock, always well protected and waymarked by red spots and arrows. The upper gully leads to a series of ledges and crests, with spectacular views opening to the south and east, to reach the Forca Alta di Culzéi (2170m), about 2–2½ hours from the start of the ferrata. (There is an escape route from the Forca Alta. It is apparently possible to descend northwards via a steep scree slope to the Cadin delle Vette Nere, which later meets the path 317 for Passo Siera. From Passo Siera you can then return to Rifugio De Gasperi on Sentiero Corbellini in about 3 hours.)

Here begins the long and exposed ridge which connects the peaks of the Riobianco to the Creton di Culzei. From Forca Alta di Culzei you climb by way of pinnacles and ledges to the summit of Cima alta di Riobianco (2400m) before traversing towards the Creton di Culzéi on the northern side of the ridge. From the high point of

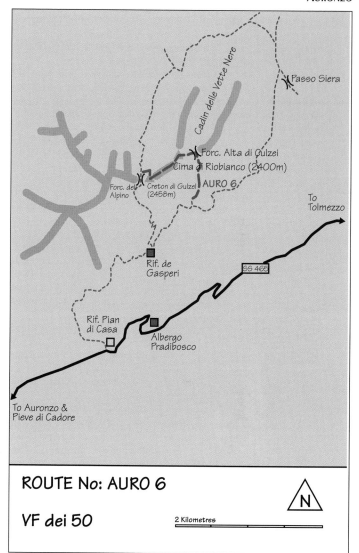

ROUTE No: AURO 6

VF dei 50

2 Kilometres

The fairly circuitous trip into Val Pesarina might seem too much for just this one route. However, if you want to explore this lovely, quiet corner, the area offers a good many other possibilities for rugged mountain walking with a range of route options including some short protected sections (note '+++++' crosses on the Tabacco map) and the Alta Via 6.

Cima alta di Riobianco follow well-marked red signs in a northwards descent of about 70m. In case of poor visibility or snow this summit zone is a serious place to be and merits careful route finding.

The route subsequently climbs up to a point just beneath the gap separating the two Riobianco peaks, alta and bassa. From here a series of descending ledges lead to the more dramatic gap between the Cima Bassa and the Lastron di Culzéi, 2450m (not shown on Tabacco map). Ascend a short chimney to the wide flat sloping summit crest of the Lastron, and soon the summit cross of Creton di Culzéi (2458m) is gained, about 2 to 2–2½ hours from Forca Alta di Culzei and 4–5 hours from the start of the ferrata.

The descent path begins northwards with some down climbing; it is always signed and protected leading down to the Forca dell'Alpino (2302m). The route is now waymarked 232 and returns south to Rif. De Gasperi at first by a steep gully filled with loose debris and scree, later becoming the zigzag Sentiero Malavoglia. Allow about 1½ hours from the summit of Creton di Culzéi to Rif. De Gasperi, and retrace your steps on path 201 to Pian di Casa in a further hour.

APPENDIX 1:
GLOSSARY OF MOUNTAIN TERMS

Here is a simple glossary of words or expressions that you may find on maps, in Italian guidebooks, directional signs, weather forecasts, etc.

ITALIAN	GERMAN	ENGLISH
Ago	nadel	needle, pinnacle
Alpe, malga	alp	alp, upland meadow
alta via	hohenweg	high level path
alto	hoch	high
attrezzato	klettersteig	protected
baita	berghutte	mountain hut
bianco	weiss	white
biglietto	fahrkarte	ticket
bivacco	biwak	bivouac hut
bocca	sattel	pass, saddle
bocchetta	kleine scharte	small pass, gap
bosco	wald	forest
cabinovia, telecabina	gondellift	gondola lift
caduta di sassi	steinschlag	stone-fall
camere libre	zimmer frei	rooms to let
canale	rinne	gully
canalone	schlucht	gorge
carta	karte	map
cengia	band	ledge
chiuso	geschlossen	closed
cima	spitze	summit
col, colle	hugel	hill
corda	seil, kabel	rope
cresta	grat	ridge
croce	kreuz	cross
croda	felswand	wall, cliff
curve di livello	hohenlinien	contour lines
destra	rechts	right
difficile	schwierig	difficult
diritto	geradeaus	straight ahead

VIA FERRATAS OF THE ITALIAN DOLOMITES

ITALIAN	GERMAN	ENGLISH
discesa, giu	absteig	descent, down
dislivello	hohenunterscheid	altitude difference
esposto	exponiert	exposed
est	osten	east
estate	sommer	summer
fiume	fluss, strom	river
forcella	scharte	gap, small pass
funivia	seilbahn	cable car
ghiaio	schutt, geroll	scree
ghiacciao	gletscher	glacier
ghiaccio	eis	ice
gradini	klammern	stemples, iron rungs
grande	gross	large
gruppo	gruppe	massif, group
impianti	aufsteigsanlagen	lift system
lago	see	lake
lontano	weit	far
marcia	tritt	foot-hold
montagna	berg	mountain
mugo	latschen	small pine bushes
nebbia	nebel	fog
nord	norden	north
noleggio	verleithen	to hire
occidentale	westlich	western
orientale	orientalisch, ostlich	eastern
ovest	westen	west
parco naturale	naturpark	natural park
parete	wand	wall, cliff
parcheggio	parkplatz	parking
passo	joch	pass
pensione	gasthof	guest house
percorso	wanderweg	path
pericolo	gefahr	danger
pericoloso	gefahrlich	dangerous
piano	ebene, hochflache	level ground, plateau
piccolo	kleine	small
piz, punta	gipfel, spitze	summit
ponte	brucke	bridge

ITALIAN	GERMAN	ENGLISH
rallentare	langsam	slow down
rifugio	hutte	mountain hut
rio	bach	stream, brook
ripido	steil	steep
rosso	rot	red
salita	aufsteigen	ascent
sasso	fels, stein	stone
scala	leiter	ladder
scendere	abstammen	descend
segnalazione	bezeichnung	waymarks
seggiovia	sessellift	chairlift
sella	sattel	saddle
sentiero	fussweg	footpath
sinsistra	links	left
soccorso	bergrettung	rescue
strada	strasse	road
sud	sudden, sud	south
tempo	wetter, zeit	weather or time
torrente	sturzbach	mountain stream
traversata	durchqueren	crossing
ultima	letzte	last
valanga	lawine	avalanche
val, valle	tal	valley
vento	wind	wind
via	weg	way, route
vietato	verboten	not permitted

APPENDIX 2:
INDEX OF ROUTES IN GRADE ORDER

This index of routes is arranged in order of difficulty, based on the grading system used in the guide (1 being the easiest grade and 5 the hardest). The commitment of each route is indicated by the 'Seriousness 'grade (also detailed at the start of each walk). The route name indicates the section of the book in which each route is found (PEDRA = Pedraces, etc). Each section centres on the geographical location that provides the best point of access to the routes in that section.

ROUTE	ROUTE NAME	SERIOUSNESS	PAGE
Grade 3			
SELVA 3	VF Oscar Schuster – Sasso Piatto (Plattkofel)	B	73
CORV 4	Via Ferrata Brigata Tridentina	B	89
CORV 5	Piz da Lech (Boeseekofel)	B	94
FASSA 10	VF Paolin-Piccolin -Cima dell'Auta Orientale	B	151
FASSA 11	VF dei Finanzieri – Colac	C	155
FALZ 1a	Ascent of Punta Sud by		
	Tomaselli descent route	C	178
CORT 2	VF Ettore Bovero – Col Rosa	B	191
CORT 3	VF Michielli Strobel – Punta Fiames	B	193
CORT 13	VF Francesco Berti	C	226
CORT 15	VF Alfonso Vandelli	B	233
MISUR 2	VF Delle Scalette – Torre Toblino	B	239
MISUR 7	VF Merlone – Cima del Cadin de NE	B	250
SESTO 4	VF Cengia Gabriella	C	269
AURO 5	VF Nord – Monte Chiadenis, Sappada	B	287
Grade 4			
SELVA 4	VF Delle Mesules (Possnecker path) –		
	Piz Selva	C	75
ARAB 2	Via delle Trincee – La Mesola	B	107
FASSA 1	VF Laurenzi – Molignon	C	119
FASSA 13	Marmolada West Ridge to		
	Punta Penia summit	C	162
CORT 8	VF Giovanni Lipella – Tofana di Rozes	C	208
SESTO 3	VF Zandonella inc. SE Variante	B	265
SESTO 4	VF Aldo Roghel	C	269
AURO 6	VF Dei 50 – Val Pesarina	C	289
Grade 5			
ARAB 1	VF Cesare Piazzetta – Piz Boe	C	102
FASSA 14	VF Eterna Brigata Cadore – Punta Serauta	C	166
FALZ 1	VF Tomaselli – Punta Sud	C	172
CORT 11	VF Punta Anna & VF Gianni Aglio –		
	Tofana di Mezzo	C	214

APPENDIX 3:
INDEX OF ROUTES BY MOUNTAIN GROUP

This index of routes is arranged by mountain group. The route name indicates the section of the book in which each route is found (PEDRA = Pedraces, etc). Each section centres on the geographical location that provides the best point of access to the routes in that section.

APPENDIX 4:
MOUNTAIN RESCUE

Hopefully, you never have any cause to call out the rescue services. However, if you do, this checklist, with translations in Italian and German (in italics) may be of help in a crisis as an aide memoire to help you to provide the rescue services with the appropriate details of your situation.

Call-out for Mountain Rescue in the Dolomites:
Telephone Soccorso Alpino 118

- Time of Accident/L'Ora (Zeit)

- Accident Location/Luogo (Platz)

- Type of Incident/Incidente (Vorfall):
  Fall/Caduta (Fall)
  Heart Attack/Infarto (Herzanfall)
  Illness/malattia (Krankheit)
  Any Other/Altro (Andere)

- Number of Party at Accident Location/Numero di personne chi rimangono (Zuruckbleibende Personen)

- Number of Casulaties/Numero di personne chi Vittima (Verletzte Personen)

- Details of Casualty/Vittima (Verletzte):
  Name/Nome (Name)
  Age/Eta (Alter)
  Sex/Sesso (Geschlecht): Male/Uomo (Mann) or Female/Donna (Frau)

- Level of Consciousness/Livello di Conscinza (Bewusstsein):
  Alert/Conscienza Normale (Wachsam)
  Confused/Conscienza ridotta (Konfus)
  Unconscious/Niente (Nichts)

- Symptoms/Sintomi (Symptome):
  Fracture/Frattura (Bruch)
  Sprain/Distorsione (Verrenkung)
  Wound/Ferita (Wunde)

- Part of Body/Parte Di Corpo (Korper Teil):
  Arm/Bracchio (Arm)
  Back/Schiena (Rucken)
  Chest/Petto (Brust)
  Leg/Gamba (Bein)
  Hand/Mano (Hand)
  Head/Testa (Kopf)
  Shoulder/Spalla (Schulter)

APPENDIX 5:
Useful Addresses

Holidays/Accommodation
Collett's Mountain Holidays
Harvest Mead
Great Hormead
Buntingford
Herts
☎ 01763 289660/289680
admin@colletts.co.uk
www.colletts.co.uk
Provides accommodation and organises via ferrata and walking holidays.
Based in Arabba.

ENIT London office: Italian State Tourist Board
1 Princes Street
London W1B 2AY
☎ 020 7355 1439
enitlond@globalnet.co.uk
www.enit.it

Trentino Information Service
39 Compton Road
Wimbledon
London SW19 7QA
☎ 020 8879 1405
trentino.infoservice@virgin.net
www.trentino.to

Waymark Holidays Ltd.
44 Windsor Road
Slough SL1 2EJ
☎ 01753 516 477, Fax: 01753 517 016
enquiries@waymarkholidays.co.uk
www.waymarkholidays.co.uk

Map Suppliers
Edward Stanford Ltd
12 Long Acre
London WC2E 9LP
☎ 020 7240 3611
sales@stanfords.co.uk

The Map Shop
15 High Street
Upton on Severn
Worcs WR8 0HJ
www.themapshop.co.uk

Cordee
3a De Montfort Street
Leicester LE1 7HD
☎ 0116 254 3579
www.cordee.co.uk

Special Interest
The Alpine Garden Society
AGS Centre
Avon Bank
Pershore
Worcs WR10 3JP
Tel: 01386 554 790
www.alpinegardensociety.org

APPENDIX 6
ROUTE LISTING

CORTINA – TOFANA

CORT 8	VF Giovanni Lipella – Tofana di Rozes	4 C	208
CORT 9	Sentiero Astaldi	1 A	210
CORT 10	Sentiero Giuseppe Olivieri	1B	212
CORT 11	VF Punta Anna and VF Gianni Aglio – Tofana di Mezzo	5 C	214
CORT 12	VF Lamon and VF Formenton – Tofana di Dentro	2 B	219

CORTINA – SORAPISS: THE SORAPISS CIRCUIT

CORT 13	VF Francesco Berti	3 C	226
CORT 14	Sentiero Carlo Minazio	1 C	230
CORT 15	VF Alfonso Vandelli	3 B	233

MISURINA

MISUR 1	Monte Piana	1 A	237
MISUR 2	VF Delle Scalette – Torre Toblino	3 B	239
MISUR 3	Sentiero del Curato Militare Hosp – Torre Toblino	2 A	243
MISUR 4	Sentiero De Luca/Innerkofler – Monte Paterno	2 B	244
MISUR 5	Sentiero delle Forcella – Monte Paterno	1 B	246
MISUR 6	Sentiero Bonacossa	1 A	247
MISUR 7	VF Merlone – Cima del Cadin de NE	3 B	250
MISUR 8	Cengia del Doge – Marmarole	1 C	253

SESTO

SESTO 1	Ferrata Nord – Croda Rossa di Sesto	2 B	257
SESTO 2	Strada degli Alpini	2 B	261
SESTO 3	VF Mario Zandonella, including SE Variante – Croda Rossa di Sesto	4 B	265
SESTO 4	VF Aldo Roghel and VF Cengia Gabriella	4C/3C	269

AURONZO

AURO 1	Sentiero Degli Alpini – Marmarole	2 C	275
AURO 2	Sentiero Amalio da Pra – Marmarole	2 B	277
AURO 3	VF Mazzetta – Padola	2 C	281
AURO 4	Ferrata Sartor – Monte Peralba, Sappada	2 B	284
AURO 5	VF Nord and VF Sud-Ovest – Monte Chiadenis, Sappada	3B/2B	287
AURO 6	VF dei 50 – Val Pesarina	4 C	289

APPENDIX 7
BIBLIOGRAPHY

Via Ferratas in the Italian Dolomites, volume 2, Graham Fletcher and John Smith, Cicerone Press, 2003

Treks in the Dolomites: Alta Via 1 and 2, Martin Collins and Gillian Price, Cicerone Press, 2002

Rifugios: Guide to Refuges in Trentino, published by (and available free from) APT Del Trentino

Museums: Guide to the Museums and Collections in Trentino, published by (and available free from) APT Del Trentino

The Italian Alps, D.W. Freshfield, 1875

The Dolomites, C. Douglas Milner, 1951

Dolomites, Selected Climbs, Ron James, Alpine Club

The First World War, John Keegan, Pimlico, 1999

The Great War on the Little Lagazuoi, Committee Cengia Martini,1998 (www.dolomiti.org/lagazuoi)

Battleground Europe (Italy) Asiago, F. MacKay, Leo Cooper, 2001

Gebirgskrieg 1915–1918, 3 volumes, Heinz von Lichem (only available in German or Italian)

Contemporary Italy: Politics, Economy and Society since 1945, Donald Sassoon, Longmans, 1986

Concise History of Italy, Peter Gunn, Thames & Hudson, 1971

NOTES

LISTING OF CICERONE GUIDES

MOUNTAIN SAFETY

Every mountain walk has its dangers, and those described in this guide-book are no exception. All who walk or climb in the mountains should recognise this and take responsibility for themselves and their companions along the way. The author and publisher have made every effort to ensure that the information contained herein was correct when the guide went to press, but they cannot accept responsibility for any loss, injury or inconvenience sustained by any person using this book.

International Distress Signal
(To be used in emergency only)
Six blasts on a whistle (and flashes with a torch after dark) spaced evenly for one minute, followed by a minute's pause. Repeat until an answer is received. The response is three signals per minute followed by a minute's pause.

The following signals are used to communicate with a helicopter:

Help needed:
raise both arms
above head to
form a 'V'

**Help not
required:**
raise one arm
above head,
extend other arm
downward

Note: *mountain rescue can be very expensive – be adequately insured*

MOUNTAIN SAFETY

Emergency telephone numbers:
Police: 113
Fire: 115
Car breakdown: 116
Mountain rescue: 118

Note: mountain rescue can be very expensive – be adequately insured

Weather reports:
www.arpa.Veneto.it
☎ ++39 0436 780007
Fax: ++39 0436 780008

www.provincia.tn.it/meteo
☎ ++39 0461 238939
Fax: ++39 0461 237089

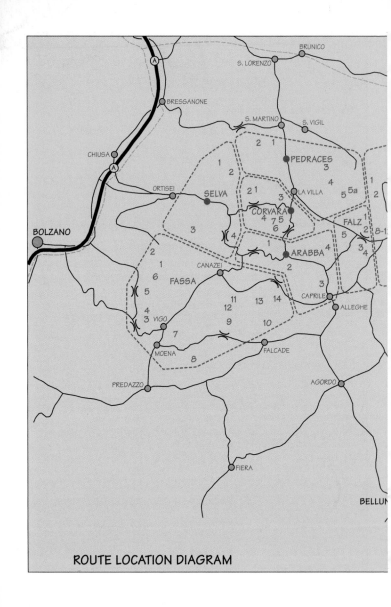

ROUTE LOCATION DIAGRAM

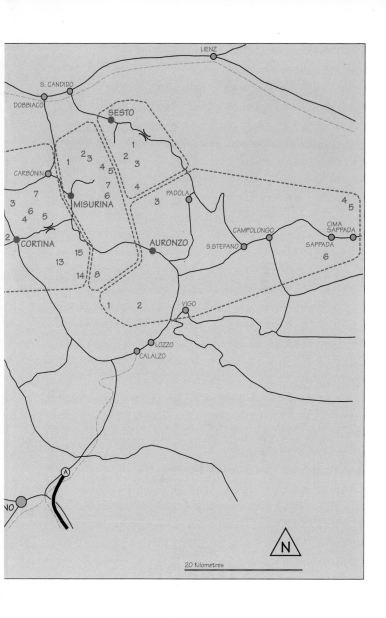

LIENZ

S. CANDIDO

DOBBIACO

SESTO

1
2 3
4
5
7
6

1
2
3

4

PADOLA

CARBONIN

7

3

3
4 6
5
2

MISURINA

3

4 5

CIMA
SAPPADA

CAMPOLONGO

CORTINA

AURONZO

S.STEFANO

SAPPADA

6

15

13

14 8

1
2

VIGO

LOZZO

CALALZO

A

NO

20 Kilometres

N

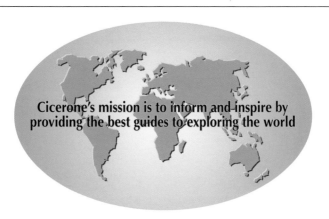

Cicerone's mission is to inform and inspire by
providing the best guides to exploring the world

Since its foundation over 30 years ago, Cicerone has specialised in publishing guidebooks and has built a reputation for quality and reliability. It now publishes nearly 300 guides to the major destinations for outdoor enthusiasts, including Europe, UK and the rest of the world.

Written by leading and committed specialists, Cicerone guides are recognised as the most authoritative. They are full of information, maps and illustrations so that the user can plan and complete a successful and safe trip or expedition – be it a long face climb, a walk over Lakeland fells, an alpine traverse, a Himalayan trek or a ramble in the countryside.

With a thorough introduction to assist planning, clear diagrams, maps and colour photographs to illustrate the terrain and route, and accurate and detailed text, Cicerone guides are designed for ease of use and access to the information.

If the facts on the ground change, or there is any aspect of a guide that you think we can improve, we are always delighted to hear from you.

Cicerone Press
2 Police Square Milnthorpe Cumbria LA7 7PY
Tel:01539 562 069   Fax:01539 563 417
e-mail:info@cicerone.co.uk   web:www.cicerone.co.uk